T5-AVN-123

THE EPISTLE TO THE ROMANS

by

HOWARD RHYS

New York
THE MACMILLAN COMPANY
1961

First Printing

The Macmillan Company, New York
Brett-Macmillan Ltd., Galt, Ontario

PRINTED IN THE UNITED STATES OF AMERICA

Library of Congress catalog card number: 61-13522

To

DONALD FRASER FORRESTER, S.T.D.

Former Professor of New Testament
at The General Theological Seminary in New York City,
whose scholarship and guidance created the foundation
for any knowledge of the Bible that I may have;

and to

FREDERIC MAGEE ADAMS, D.D.

Dean Emeritus of Trinity Cathedral
in Trenton, New Jersey, whose pastoral understanding
and human sympathy have influenced all my relationships
since I was his curate,

this volume is dedicated by the author
with respect and affection.

In this book I wish publicly to express my gratitude to the Reverend Julien Gunn, of the Order of the Holy Cross, for invaluable assistance in correcting the proof, to colleagues at the University of the South, especially to its Seminary Librarian, Mr. Camp, and its Secretary, Mrs. John Hodges, for aid in technical details, and to my wife whose patient helpfulness extended to correcting page proof but cannot be measured by any standard.

TABLE OF CONTENTS

Appendix

GENERAL INTRODUCTION

Literature

No other book of the New Testament, apart from the Fourth Gospel, has inspired so much study as has been devoted to this epistle. Romans has been a focus of attention both for exegetes and for theologians. The recent German commentary by Otto Michel, for example, offers five full pages containing nothing except the names of books, and of their authors, along with the dates of writing. Here attention is directed only to works that have appeared in English; publications in other languages will be listed in the Bibliography.

For the first quarter of the present century, the standard work in English was that of Sanday and Headlam, and in many ways its value is very great even today. As a textbook it was displaced by C. H. Dodd's commentary in the Moffatt Series, which is easy to read, inexpensive, and of proved excellence. In 1958 there appeared the study by C. K. Barrett, which adds much to what has previously been done; the outline of the epistle found in that book has been adopted here although there are alternative schemes worthy of consideration. Theological treatments of Romans are equally numerous. That which has been most influential in the past four centuries was produced by Martin Luther. In our own time there have been added studies of comparable scope by Karl Barth and Anders Nygren, which have been available in English for several years, and in 1959 appeared the translation of the theological commentary of Emil Brunner. In this present work the objective is to set forth what Paul himself intended, with only an occasional glance at his message for the modern world; for that reason no direct reference will be made to any of the theological analyses of the epistle, however useful they may be to the general reader. There will, however, be frequent discussion of exegetical works in foreign languages as well as of those in English.

Some background in what is called Biblical theology will be necessary for the complete understanding of the apostle, and a few books from which it may be derived should be mentioned. A convenient point of departure might be *Paul and Rabbinic Judaism* by W. D. Davies. This might be followed by Alan Richardson's *Introduction to New Testament Theology*, by Fernand Prat's *Theology of St. Paul* or by Rudolf Bultmann's *Theology of the New Testament*. Perhaps the two most important works from which the thought of the epistle may be understood are *The Atonement in New Testament Teaching* and *Forgiveness and Reconciliation*, both by Vincent Taylor.

Since this epistle is the most complete exposition of theology ever attempted by Paul, each student who approaches it will expect to find his own understanding of Christian truth reflected within it. Thus it is difficult for anyone to approach it with an entirely open mind, to avoid imposing his own ideas upon the text. H. Lietzmann has come closer to doing so than the other critics. But there is no universal agreement among scholars on what is the primary theme of Romans. Those who place the chief stress upon the concept of *justification* have a strong case, but this concept itself has engendered so much controversy among Christians that it seems wiser to say that the theme is *God's scheme of salvation*, however clumsy that phrase may be. None the less, what is said in Romans of *justification* must be considered seriously, for it has been of enormous significance in the history of theological controversy.

Date

There is general agreement about the place Romans occupies in Paul's career. It was written during his second visit to Corinth, at the time when he was collecting the offering for the relief of the "poor brethren" in Judea. The date is variously estimated from 56 to 59, and probability favors the early spring of 58. It is clear that the controversy that gave rise to the Corinthian Epistles is past. Paul feels that his work in the Eastern half of the Roman Empire is complete. He has established the Church in the important cities of five provinces, and has touched on two other localities. From the centers which he has developed, the Gospel can be extended to other areas, and he has sufficient confidence in his converts to leave that task to them. One thing remains for him to do in this territory. He must bring the offering of his own local churches to Jerusalem. His object is to strengthen the unity between them and the original congregations of Palestine. The interest of Paul's converts will go with their contributions, and it should be repaid with the gratitude of those who receive their aid.

Yet there is danger for Paul himself in returning to Jerusalem. He is distrusted by the more extreme of the Jewish Christians, who accuse him of perverting the Gospel, and he is regarded as chief of traitors by the Jewish authorities. The former may betray him to the latter, and he does not care to contemplate the consequences if this should happen. So he calls upon everyone he can, asking them to pray for his safety in this endeavor. The journey to Jerusalem entailed a stop in Thessalonica or Philippi, perhaps in both places, to add the contributions of the Province of Macedonia to those of Achaea. Acts also mentions a brief meeting with the elders from Ephesus at Miletus. Some time would be required to confer with the leaders of the church in Jerusalem. Then, if all went well, Paul would be free to seek new worlds to conquer for Christ.

Paul's Later Plans

In accord with Paul's former practice, these new worlds should be areas in which no previous missionary work had been done. It would be strange indeed if no one had yet brought the Gospel to Alexandria. Apollos, who hailed from that city, would have been an obvious person to serve as its evangelist. It is evident that work had been begun in Rome long before this, and Rome could serve as the center for most of Italy. Cyrene, with its large Jewish population, presumably also had been the scene of missionary activity, perhaps initiated by Simon who carried the Lord's Cross. Three areas remained apparently untouched, Gaul, Spain, and western Africa. Among these, Paul chose Spain as his next field of labor.

At least one reason for his choice can be found. Secular records of the period show that there were many colonies of Jews in Spain. As he had done in Galatia and Achaea and elsewhere, so in Spain could Paul approach such Jews in his capacity as a well-trained rabbi, and expect a hearing. As had happened in other places, he might expect some measure of response from the synagogue, particularly from the "God-fearers" who were informally attached to it. Perhaps there was less hope from Spain than from Greece, but it could be well worth the effort. Such was Paul's hope. Arrest in Jerusalem frustrated it, but the plan itself was sound, and when this epistle was written there was a fair prospect for its realization.

Purpose of Writing

If Spain was Paul's objective, as he said, what was the purpose of taking time to write to Rome? Here, too, his previous career gives the answer. Paul felt that a base of operations was necessary for any major missionary work. Antioch, although it had not been a Pauline foundation, had served for Cyprus, Galatia, and Pisidia and even for work farther west. Later the local church of Ephesus developed sufficient strength to support other missions. There was no reason why the apostle could not begin again in Rome. Yet if he were to do so, he would need the good will of the Roman Christians, and he could not be assured of having it because of the controversial character of his own ministry. This epistle was written in order to secure such good will. It is an exposition of the Gospel as Paul understands it, and it was given because it was only fair that the church in Rome should be informed of what it was being asked to support. One must not think of this as a polemic. Galatians is polemic because it is addressed to a group of Christians over whom Paul held special authority, and whom he saw to be in danger of abandoning the substance of the Gospel for a shadow. In Rome, Paul held no special position, and he had no reason to suppose that the dangers against which he had contended in Galatia were a serious threat there. Indeed, antiquity bears witness to an extraordinary faculty shown by the Roman church for avoiding commitment to dangerous concepts of theology.

Therefore we must dismiss from our minds the thought that Romans is in essence an expansion of Galatians. Human nature being what it is, Paul feels it necessary to discuss the religious problems of Galatians; they could become problems in Rome also. Religious issues from I Corinthians are equally in evidence, as a study of the text will show. Both of these letters had been written only a few years earlier, and it is not surprising that the issues dealt with in them still occupied the apostle's mind. Here we have a mature expression of Paul's religion, comprehensive because it is addressed to people who knew little of him personally, systematic as far as it was possible for a man of such intense character to follow a system, calm because he has no direct pastoral responsibility for Rome and has no immediate knowledge of anything there in need of correction. Philippians is equally mature but less complete. For an understanding of Paul at his best it is to this epistle that one must turn, but one must examine it without preconceptions if one is to find in it the religion of Paul rather than a set of proof texts for one's personal opinions.

The Church in Rome

Something ought to be said about the church in Rome to which the epistle is addressed. No one knows how early it was founded, nor by whom, but almost certainly the first work was not done by apostles. While the tradition that Peter labored in Rome seems well founded, there is no suggestion either here or in Acts that he arrived prior to the time when Paul was brought there as a prisoner. Under the circumstances it is not possible to say how this local church was organized or how it designated its clergy; nor is it possible to answer a number of other questions. A fair guess is that the first missionaries were Roman Jews converted while on pilgrimage to Jerusalem, who had returned to the imperial city. Two Jewish Christians of Rome, Aquila and his wife Priscilla, were later associated with Paul, and greetings are sent to them in the final chapter of this epistle.

But if the Roman church was founded by Jewish Christians, it soon had to live without its first leaders, for the Emperor Claudius banished all the Jews from Rome in 49. Suetonius, the historian, says that the emperor's reason for doing this was because of certain riots among the Jewish population *impulsare Chresto,* and some people take this to mean "stirred up by Christ"; the error of a letter in the name would not be a cause for surprise. On the other hand, Acts indicates that at the time of Paul's arrival in Rome the Jews there knew little or nothing about Christianity, and its author is at least as likely to be informed on such a matter as Suetonius; thus one must assume that the riots had arisen from other causes. The emperor was not anti-Semitic, and he made no effort to molest Jews in other places. Aquila and Priscilla withdrew to Corinth where they met with Paul, and later they accompanied him to Ephesus. After Nero's accession in 54, the edict of banishment seems to have lapsed. Nero chose as a favorite an attractive Jewess who later became his fourth wife, Poppaea. Those Jews who had any good reason for returning to Rome did so. Among them were Aquila and Priscilla, whose house became a place of assembly for Christians.

Yet for five years the leadership of the Roman church had devolved perforce upon its Gentile members. Thereafter, the church in Rome was dominantly Gentile, although it included a Jewish minority at the time when Paul wrote. But this Gentile dominance would not guarantee that submission to the Torah had no appeal in Rome. The observance of Israel's ordinances was one practical expression of religion that gave to those who attempted it the assurance that they were doing something in the service of Almighty God. Aware of this fact, Paul felt it necessary to warn that Torah could not be regarded as an appropriation of righteousness or salvation or anything else. Yet the problem at Rome was quite different from that of Galatia, and even Paul's distinction between the *strong* and the *weak* among the brethren was not identical with that between those who held to Jewish Torah and those who disregarded it. Paul here is explaining the general principles of his religion; he is not dealing with particular pastoral problems. The size of the Roman church cannot be determined with accuracy. It was probably larger than that of Corinth, but not so large as those of Ephesus and Antioch at the time.

Authorship, Integrity, and Style

In regard to the authorship of this epistle there is no serious debate. If Paul wrote anything, he wrote Romans, together with Galatians and the two Corinthian epistles. There may be a few interpolations; 16:24 is generally recognized to be one, and many have ascribed the doxology of 16:25–27 to Marcion. But all the significant matter of the epistle is from Paul. The integrity of Romans, the question of whether it was originally written as a unit or was a combination of two letters intended for diverse destinations, is much more doubtful.

For one thing, there is textual support for the theory that chapters 15–16 do not belong with the rest. One manuscript omits these chapters, except for appending the final doxology at the end of Chapter 14, and Origen had knowledge of this form of the text. Other manuscripts use the doxology at both places. With this much support, several critics have suggested that the two final chapters were a brief note to Ephesus, and that the long list of greetings in Chapter 16 consists of people known to Paul there.

Yet there is more against this theory than in its favor. To compare Romans with other Pauline epistles, the only other example in which we find a long list of greetings is Colossians, and Colossae was the one place apart from Rome to which a letter was addressed which the apostle had not himself visited. In Corinth and Philippi, where he was as well known as in Ephesus, he did not find it necessary to mention everyone he knew by name. We may conclude that it was Paul's custom to fill out such a list when writing to a church that he had not visited. So we may assume that the greetings of Chapter 16 are intended for Rome and that Paul's desire is to mention everyone he has ever met who is now resident in the capital. Moreover, Dodd and others find very close connections between Chapter 14 and 15:1–13, and the consensus of scholars favors the integrity of the epistle.

One other question is whether the work is really addressed to Rome, for the city is mentioned in two places only, and in some manuscripts it is omitted even from these texts. It has been proposed that we have here a general epistle. Reasons why Paul might have wished to write to Rome have already been considered, and it is clear enough that the apostle's missive to a church he did not know at firsthand would have to be phrased in general terms. Thus we have no reason to deny the traditional claim that this systematic exposition of Paul's religion was intended for Rome. The objections urged against it are far from convincing. The few questions of text can be left to the study of the epistle itself. They are not significant enough to be considered in the introduction.

Most critics give some thought to the style of the work. It is roughly what might be expected from Paul. The few peculiarities are explained in diverse ways by people who do, or do not, desire to stress the apostle's knowledge of Greek culture. Paul was certainly a man who learned quickly, and he had traveled much in the Greco-Roman world. So it is not surprising that he shows knowledge of the literary device known as the *diatribe,* which was used by the Stoic philosophers. This stands midway between the *dialogue,* used by Plato and Justin Martyr, and the *treatise.* It consists in stating and answering possible objections to the main argument. In its Pauline dress the diatribe takes the form, "*You* (the hypothetical opponent) *will say.*" In terms of style Paul's use of the form is quite correct.

On the other hand, there are examples of Semitism within the epistle. Paul had something more important to do with his time than to overcome the background of his own life. It is futile to try to explain away either feature of his style. Paul assumes a fair knowledge of the Old Testament, and certainly recognition of its authority, on the part of all Roman Christians, Gentiles just as much as Jews. Barrett's commentary, estimable as it is, assumes a much more precise knowledge of good Greek usage on Paul's part than an impartial study of the epistles would support. In some degree the same fault is present with Dodd, and perhaps even more with the French scholar Lagrange. This is not vulgar Greek, but neither is it literary. The language is invariably dignified, and has some pretensions to grace, but Paul is writing in a tongue that is not quite his own, and to people who will be less than critical of his use of it. Moreover, even Demosthenes could not have been expected to handle such themes as Paul presents with complete facility, for they are beyond the capacity of human speech. The apostle is more concerned with content and significance than with the manner in which his message is expressed. What the style lacks in elegance is made up in vitality, but the consequence is a certain ambiguity, particularly when translation is attempted. This is at least partly responsible for the number of diverse interpretations that have been drawn from the epistle. It is also the source of some of the theological dissent that has persisted into our own generation.

The Translation

The English rendering of St. Paul's epistle that is here offered is awkward, and on occasion ungrammatical. It is so by design. The apostle's Greek was neither easy nor grammatical. He wrestled with his themes as he wrote, and he intended his readers to wrestle with the concepts in their turn, for he would not allow them to accept any easy generalities as substitutes for the Gospel as he understood its meaning.

In reality the work of translation in itself requires uncommon talent in which sympathy with the original author's convictions is quite as important as the capacity to perceive his meaning. It is extremely rare for a translator to avoid placing his own stamp upon the work, and it is very easy to alter the sense of the original in significant ways. None of the existing translations appear to the present writer to have been true to the apostle's meaning without lapse through the whole sixteen chapters, and most of them frequently have erred in making Paul too easy for the English reader.

Accordingly, the aim here has been accuracy rather than elegance, and while the accuracy may well be questioned it is certain that the lack of elegance has been achieved. Whenever there has been serious doubt regarding the true Greek text, the matter has been discussed in the commentary, and reasons have been given for the choice that was made. In most texts where varying interpretations are possible, these have been discussed in the same manner, and although it is possible that theological preconceptions are reflected here as they are in other English versions of the Scripture, efforts have been made to guard against misrepresentation as far as a fallible human being may do so.

Conventions Followed in the Commentary

While many Greek words are discussed in detail, a transliteration into our alphabet has been given together with the English translation. Had Greek type been used, the problems of publication would have been increased, and those to whom it would have meaning will find no difficulty in recognizing the words in their present form. The conventional Latin transliteration has been followed without variation, *c* or *k* for *kappa*, *y* for *upsilon*, *ch* for *chi*; both *epsilon* and *eta* appear as *e*, both *omicron* and *omega* as *o*. There is no wish to impose an arbitrary translation of theological key words upon the reader.

In the translation itself certain parentheses appear. These are in every case alternatives to the word or phrase they follow. When a single word is so treated it is introduced by "or," as in 1:1: "Paul, a slave (or, servant) of Christ Jesus." When a phrase is considered, it is introduced by "alternatively," as in 1:12: "by means of the mutual faith we have (alternatively, the trust we have in one another)." When Paul's idiom is incomprehensible in English, it has been paraphrased and the literal statement introduced in parentheses by "literally," as in 2:9: "to every human being (literally, soul of man)."

The reader may profit by considering the concepts discussed in the appendixes in connection with those chapters to which they are related. The same is true with the brief definitions contained in the "Glossary of Terms." The "Table of Contents" will show which of these ideas is being considered in each section of the epistle.

No footnotes have been employed in this study. There are many references, and a few direct quotations or translations included in the text. In every case the author believes that these have been introduced by the name of the author from whom they have been taken. The vast majority are from the commentaries by C. K. Barrett, C. H. Dodd, M. J. Lagrange, H. Lietzmann, and O. Michel which are listed in the Bibliography. Those who wish to refer to such works directly will find the comments cited in connection with their treatments of the same portions of the epistle.

Plan of the Epistle

1:1–7	Address
1:8–15	Occasion for the Epistle
1:16–17	Theme to Be Developed
1:18–32	Sin and Retribution in the Pagan World
2:1–11	The Impartiality of God's Judgment
2:12–16	Conscience
2:17–29	Judgment on the Jew Who Violates His God-Given Law
3:1–8	The Advantage Possessed by the Jew
3:9–20	God's Indictment of All Mankind
3:21–31	God's Righteousness
4:1–12	Abraham's Faith
4:13–25	Faith and Promise
5:1–11	Justification and Salvation

5:12–21	The New Man and the New Humanity
6:1–14	Newness of Life
6:15–23	The New Life as Freedom and Obedience
7:1–6	Christ's Death Has Ended the Bondage to Law
7:7–25	Sin and Salvation in Experience
8:1–11	The Life in the Spirit
8:12–30	Adoption, Redemption, and Glory
8:31–39	The Christian's Assurance
9:1–5	Israel's Tragedy of Unbelief
9:6–13	God's Elective Purpose
9:14–29	Freedom and Election Under God's Sovereignty
9:30–33	Why Israel Stumbled
10:1–13	Human and Divine Righteousness
10:14–21	The Innocence of Israel Apart from the Witness of the Law
11:1–10	The Holy Remnant
11:11–24	The Rejection of Israel Is Not Final
11:25–32	God's Goal Is to Have Mercy upon All
11:33–36	Hymn of Praise for God's Goodness
12:1–2	Basis of Christian Service
12:3–21	Social Duty as a Christian's Offering to God
13:1–7	The Christian and the State
13:8–10	The Law of Love
13:11–14	The Urgency of the Present Situation
14:1–12	Weak and Strong Conscience
14:13–23	Love for Others the Basis of Unity
15:1–13	Abnegation as the Expression of Unity
15:14–33	Paul's Plans and God's Purpose
16:1–23	Personal Instructions and Greetings
16:24	An Interpolation
16:25–27	Concluding Doxology

CHAPTER 1

Righteousness

1:1–7 Paul, a slave (or, servant) of Christ Jesus, called to be an apostle, appointed for the Gospel of God, which He promised beforehand by means of His prophets in the Holy Scriptures, with reference to His Son, who, in human terms, was from the seed of David; and who, in terms of a spirit of sanctification, was constituted as Son of God in Power after a Resurrection from the dead, Jesus Christ our Lord, through whom we received grace and apostolate for an obedience of faith among all the Gentiles for His Name's sake, among whom you also were called by Jesus Christ; to all those who are in Rome, beloved of God, called to be saints. Grace to you, and peace from God our Father and the Lord Jesus Christ.

* * *

For a discussion of this superscription all subsequent scholars must feel a debt to Lietzmann. In letters between Jewish sanhedrins at this period, the opening formula was: "To our brethren in ———, may your peace be multiplied." An example of the classical Greek pattern of correspondence may be taken from Demosthenes: "Philip, to the Athenian people, greeting." The Greek word for *greeting* is derived from the same root as Paul's term *grace*. Surprisingly, the Greek formula rather than that of the synagogue is employed in the Jewish Christian Epistle of James. Paul's usage is taken from the sanhedrin model, and in all his genuine epistles it includes at least the following elements: "Paul, to those who are at ———, grace to you, and peace." Any of these Pauline terms may be expanded in a variety of ways, but the essential formula never varies. The new feature Paul adds to the synagogue formula is *grace*. While the *grace* always means the gift of God, and *peace* always means the good of man, the combination of these terms may represent an effort to incorporate the main feature of the Greek address into the Jewish scheme. In the Pastoral Epistles and II John *mercy* is inserted between *grace* and *peace*, and in Jude *mercy* displaces *grace*; these later developments may reflect the formula used in Syriac Baruch: "Mercy and peace be with you." Paul's form is followed exactly in I and II Peter, and in I Clement.

The phrase *slave of Christ Jesus* (or *Jesus Christ* if one is to depart from the text of the B manuscript) is Semitic, not Greek. Slaves of Greek shrines were legal property, but in the Septuagint the Greek word for *slave* translates the Hebrew EBED which is closer to the idea of a servant, and among the Jews *to serve* had the same sense as *to worship*. The call as an apostle stands for Paul's experience on Damascus Road. As Paul emphasizes in Galatians, this was a call from God and not from man. Its absolute demand makes the term *slave* a more accurate representation of it than *servant* could be. The terms of this call are then defined. In the first place it is an appointment in the Gospel of God, or in other words a vocation to ministry. Here *Gospel* means the whole Christian message, as it does frequently in the New Testament. But while that message is referred to as the Gospel of God, in the sense that God is its author and has initiated the saving act in which it is founded, Christ is here placed on the same level with God when Paul describes himself as *slave of Christ* in precisely the sense in which the Old Testament prophets had called themselves *servants of Yahweh*. This fact must be remembered for the interpretation of verses 3–4. But first Verse 2 takes up the early Christian theme of the work of Christ as predicted or promised by the prophets and in the Scriptures. Paul was among the strongest advocates of this explanation of the Old Covenant. The Gospel of God is then shown to be a message about God's Son; it is a Gospel concerned with that which the Son of God accomplished.

This reference to *God's Son* appears before there is any mention of the Incarnation. This fact implies that the apostle holds Jesus to be eternally Son of God in this epistle, as in Philippians 2:5–11, and he returns to the same point in Chapter 8 of Romans. Once the eternal position of Christ is declared, Paul at once asserts that in His incarnate life Jesus was the heir of David. There is no historical objection to this claim, but in itself it would not have been significant because there must have been as many members of the House of David in Palestine then as there are Mayflower descendants in Massachusetts now, so that only those who were able to win distinction in their own right would have reason to refer to such ancestry. Here the chief reason for making such a claim is to show Jesus as the legitimate Messiah of Israel. Yet it is only in His *humanity* (according to the flesh) that Jesus is an heir of David as Messiah; in His *essential nature* (according to the spirit of sanctification) He was appointed or constituted *Son of God in Power*. This title has been the subject of much discussion, as have the words that go before it. First of all, Paul does not here refer to the Holy Spirit, for he does not write the neuter accusative of the adjective *holy* but the genitive of the noun *sanctification*. The *holiness* which means *being set apart for God* and separated from the rest of humanity may be predicated of Christ in a preeminent sense because He is eternally the Son of God. Thus Paul is not saying that Christ has been appointed Son of God, for He was such prior to His Incarnation; instead the apostle declares that He was appointed *Son of God in Power*, and the *Power* means His Exaltation, His eschatological victory, the fact that after living a human life as Son of David He is now an object of worship. This interpretation resolves the difficulty of the text without resorting to the dubious expedient of translating the participle *declared* when it cannot properly bear such a meaning. At the same time it escapes the temptation of the adoptionist writers to translate the preposition *from* (EX) as if Paul had written *by means of* (DIA). It is not by means of His Resurrection but simply after it that Christ has been appointed or established as *Son of God in Power*. The Death and Resurrection formed a necessary prelude to the Exaltation of the Lord's Humanity, but the cause of that Exaltation must be sought in the divine will and in the essential nature of Christ. One hardly needs to add that in this context the apostle is discussing the personal Resurrection of Christ and not the general resurrection expected in the Last Day.

The plural of Verse 5 is an editorial *we* that could be replaced by a singular. Paul is not saying that the readers have received *grace* from Christ while he himself has obtained *apostolic office*; he is interpreting his own office of ministry as a spiritual gift or charisma that he has received from Christ. He goes on to state the purpose for which that commission was given. Both Jews and Christians at this time used the plural of the Greek word *nation* for *Gentiles* as distinguished from Israel rather than for *nations* as including Israel. Paul is simply saying that he is the Apostle to the Gentiles, that he has received his commission or spiritual gift for the purpose of promoting *obedience to the faith* among all the Gentiles for the sake or Name of Christ. The opening words of the verse make it clear that he regards the commission as received from Christ Himself. Some scholars have argued that *faith* for Paul never has an objective sense such as is given in this interpretation, that we must interpret the genitive of the word for *faith* as a genitive of source, and translate "the obedience that comes from faith." Paul's use of language, however, even of his key words, is not so precise. While it is certainly true that the overwhelming majority of Pauline texts that employ the word *faith* give it the sense of subjective trust in God, there are exceptions to this rule, and the superscription of an epistle is one of the places where the objective use of *faith* would be perfectly natural. Verse 6, then, refers back to the Gentiles, and asserts that the people addressed in this epistle are included among them. It has already been noted that after the banishment of Jews from Rome in A.D. 49, it was inevitable that the Church there should be dominantly Gentile. The readers are persons called by Jesus Christ, and Paul draws no distinction between those who are *called* and the *elect* because he always considers God's calling as effectual.

In Verse 7 the G manuscript omits the reference to Rome, and Origen shows knowledge of this omission in some of the texts of his time. Yet while the addition of a place name is more probable than its deliberate omission, the weight of evidence is against G, and the reading is probably to be explained as follows: A scribe who was writing what he heard missed the word *Rome* after taking down the preposition *in;* he then dropped the final syllable of the adjective *beloved*, and took what was left as the dative of the noun *love*. Since he then had an intelligible phrase, "to all those who are in the love of God," he did not attempt to correct it. This was a perfectly human mistake.

In apposition to "all those who are in Rome, beloved by God," Paul added, "called as saints (or, called to be saints)," using the last word in its Jewish sense as *God's chosen*. In his judgment Christians were called to be set apart for God, even when their present performance was far from ideal. After saying this, Paul simply completes his formula of grace and peace from God our Father and from the Lord Jesus Christ. Once more Christ is set beside God. So in this longest among the superscriptions of his epistles, Paul has attempted to assure this church where he is personally unknown but in which he can claim some authority in his capacity as Apostle to the Gentiles, to make clear to the Romans that the Gospel he preaches and for which he asks support is the same Gospel that they have received from other Christian teachers. The heart of this assurance is in verses 3–4, where Paul makes use of what was probably a credal formula. Yet whatever formula lies behind these verses, it is one that can readily be interpreted in the Pauline sense as a witness to the preexistent Christ who has entered into time and has accomplished a saving act, thereby inaugurating a New Age for all who respond to Him in faith.

* * *

1:8–15 First of all I thank God through Jesus Christ with regard to all of you, because of your faith which is reported (or, proclaimed) in the whole world. For God is my witness, whom I worship in my spirit by the Gospel of His Son, how I make mention of you without ceasing, requesting continually in my prayers if somehow now at last I may prosper in my journey by the will of God to come to you. For I long to see you, in order that I may impart to you some spiritual gift for your strengthening, that is, to find encouragement among you by means of the mutual faith we have (alternatively, the trust we have in one another) both on your part and on mine. For I do not wish you to be ignorant, my brethren, that often I have had it in mind to come to you, and that I have been prevented up to now, in order that I may get some fruit among you also, as among the rest of the Gentiles. For to Greeks and to barbarians, to civilized men and to uncultured I am obligated. Thus for my part I am eager also to preach the Gospel to you who are in Rome.

* * *

Thanksgiving for the faith or Christianity of his readers is a standard feature of the Pauline epistles, absent only from Galatians, which was called forth by an occasion that gave no cause for thanksgiving. Dodd gives an exhaustive list of examples from secular literature of some sort of prayer by the sender for the recipient. In the Christian epistles this prayer for the readers became a liturgical form, and it is most fully developed in Ephesians. Here the heart of the liturgical prayer is Verse 9, but this is carried forward in Verse 10 to include Paul's personal appeal to God that he may be enabled to visit the church in Rome. However formal the language here, it expresses a sincere desire. In early Christian writings generally, liturgical forms were capable of embodying personal longings, particularly as used by Paul. A reason is given for the thanksgiving over the Romans, and it may also carry over to the apostle's desire to visit them. Their faith is a matter of common knowledge among all Christians, for its sincerity and apparently also for its correctness. Among the formal phrases of Verse 9, "God is my witness" is a favorite Pauline term.

Verse 11 carries the liturgical prayer over into Paul's own plans. Not only does the apostle pray that he may visit Rome; he also explains his purpose in desiring to do so. He hopes to impart some spiritual gift to the Romans for their benefit, presumably something related to his own understanding of the Gospel rather than to such gifts as prophecy with which they were already well supplied. Then, lest he may have said too much in writing to a mission that he had not himself founded, he suggests that there may also be benefit to be derived from the Romans, a result of the mutual exchange of faith and understanding. Paul feels that he must be careful not to provoke resentment by the appearance of arrogance. Then Verse 13, with another Pauline formula that is found again in Romans 11:25 and twice in I Corinthians and once each in II Corinthians and I Thessalonians, he tells that his desire to visit Rome is of long standing. It is useless to speculate whether Paul had been prevented from fulfilling this wish by the command of God, by the opposition of Satan, by the edict of Claudius, or by the pressure of his missionary work in the Eastern part of the empire; perhaps the last is the most likely reason, but any of the others would serve to explain the fact, and Paul does not specify the hindrance. In any case, he desires to set forth the Gospel among the Romans as he has done among the other Gentiles. *Fruit* here probably means conversions, but it may stand for an increase in the Roman comprehension of the truth of God. Verses 14–15 add that Rome is in some sense Paul's responsibility simply because he is the Apostle to the Gentiles. Dodd says all that needs to be said about the antitheses of Greeks and barbarians, wise and ignorant. *Greeks* were the cultured people of the empire, those who spoke Greek; the *barbarians* were those who lacked such culture. Paul clearly includes both himself and the Roman Christians among the *Greeks* and the *wise*, but he acknowledges an obligation also to those who lack culture or education.

* * *

1:16–17 I take pride in the Gospel, for it is God's power for salvation to everyone who believes, to the Jew in the first place and also to the Greek. For in it God's righteousness is revealed from faith unto faith, as it is written, "he who is righteous by faith shall live."

* * *

While these verses state the theme of the epistle, the text of the sermon, as one might call it, they ought not to be separated so sharply from verses 8–15 as some scholars would have us believe. The first clause of Verse 16 looks back directly to what Paul has just been saying about his eagerness to preach the Gospel in Rome as in other places. As is common in Greek usage, the apostle says that he is not ashamed when he means that he is proud; in this, Moffatt's translation is excellent. Paul is proud of the Gospel because it is a power (perhaps the meaning is really "a mighty act") of God that makes for salvation. There is little dispute regarding these words; argument arises over the balance of the verse. We may assume here that Paul is thinking of the content of the Gospel, the saving work of Christ that is proclaimed therein. This is the power or mighty act of God, and it must be remembered that for Paul, God initiates the total work of Christ.

At this point the exegetical problems appear. Is the emphasis on *everyone* or on the participle *who believes*, on the universality of God's offer or on the necessity of faith? Those who stress the theology of the section would favor the latter view, but the following words that seek to define the universality of God's call demand that we prefer the former. Faith assuredly is necessary, but it is the scope of God's action that Paul is describing. Christ's work makes salvation available to everyone, first of all to the Jew and afterward to the Greek. When *Greek* is contrasted with *barbarian*, the distinction is between cultured and uncultured, as in Verse 14; when it is contrasted with *Jew*, as in this verse, it stands for *Gentile*. This is the rabbinic usage of the period. Marcion, who rejected the Old Testament as the groundwork of Christian revelation, expurgated the word from his text. Paul, however, intended to say that the Jew had priority in God's offer.

Christ had appeared in Israel, and He could not have exercised His incarnate ministry in any other nation because Israel alone had received the preparation of God's earlier revelation. Moreover, Paul's own practice was to proclaim the Gospel to the Jews first, and afterward to Gentiles, as is shown in Acts. Thanks to God's choice of Israel, a more satisfactory initial response could be hoped for among Jews than among Gentiles, but it is the apostle's purpose to demonstrate that in the last resort all humanity stands on the same footing before God.

Verse 17 introduces a key theological concept of the Pauline system, the *righteousness* (DIKAIOSUNE) of God. In the Gospel the *righteousness of God* is being revealed. Greek thought tended to define righteousness in abstract terms as a quality or attribute, in this case predicated of God. Study of the Hebrew language, however, shows that the thought behind Paul's words is not abstract at all. In Jewish usage the *righteousness of God* is not a divine attribute but a divine activity, and it is virtually certain that by this phrase Paul means to say that in the Gospel there is revealed the fact that God is *doing right.*

This does not force us to believe that those who first received the epistle would have understood it in the way the apostle intended. In order to do so they would have had to understand the Hebrew interpretation of divine activity. For this, Dodd and Barrett are especially helpful in showing that the Hebrew verb was generally employed in a forensic sense as describing God's action in vindicating those whom He ought to vindicate, in pronouncing them righteous. In this we find the genesis of all the controversies over *imputed* and *infused* righteousness. In Jewish thought, if God pronounced a man righteous it was because He found some proper ground on which He could do so. In rabbinic treatments this was usually taken to mean that the man was actually righteous in the sense of having fulfilled the Torah. But as Paul saw it, no one kept the Torah in full; his own best efforts had not enabled him to do so. Thus if Paul had been vindicated, this was not because of any attainment of his own. Starting from this point, Luther asserted that the vindication was entirely an act of God's mercy and that the person who received it did not merit it in any way, and he alleged that the majority of the early Church Fathers had maintained this position. In the eyes of Catholic legalists, an act of divine mercy entirely unrelated to merit was immoral and unworthy of God, and they found no difficulty in showing that most of the early Church Fathers actually supported their position. Lagrange has it that the *righteousness of God* is that which makes a man actually righteous rather than the pronouncing of an undeserved acquittal.

Today we cannot afford to say either that Luther rescued the Gospel from centuries of neglect or that divine inspiration inevitably prevented the Church Fathers from misunderstanding Paul. Luther's Catholic critics are right in saying that an *imputation* of righteousness which is entirely fictitious is arbitrary and indefensible. On the other hand, the statement that God effects an *infusion* of righteousness on the basis of which He can award salvation is equally far from the fact, for salvation is inevitably a gift that no man can earn. The *faith* that Paul connects here and elsewhere with *righteousness* is the other necessary term in the transaction. It must be understood as a response of man to God's active *righteousness.* It is not an accomplishment, for it is a subjective commitment of the self, and it is inspired by God, yet somehow it is related to merit. Confronted by God's active *righteousness,* man is left with the choice of rejecting it or of committing himself to it, of loving or of disregarding it. To have *faith* is to respond to God with love, and the love of God which initiates the *faith* is then free to express itself by the *gift of salvation.* After this there may come an *infusion* of actual *righteousness* in the continuance of the redeeming interchange, but man enters upon the *way of salvation* before he is actually made righteous. This position is not far removed from Melanchthon's revision of Luther's theological interpretation of the text, and it is no more likely to win universal assent, but it does have the merit of safeguarding the moral order of God's dealing with man while making clear that *salvation* is a *gift* from God in mercy to those who are willing to accept it rather than a credit balance that man may secure with God by the value of what he does.

The difficult phrase *from faith unto faith* remains to be considered. It should be recognized as a Semitic idiom. Barrett's rendition of it, "on the basis of nothing but faith," helps to make it clear to the average Christian reader, but one must probe its meaning more deeply. The words *from faith* may be referred to the *righteousness of God;* if so, they will mean that God's righteousness that depends on faith is revealed in the Gospel. Following this theory, *unto faith* will probably mean that the reason why it has been revealed is to prompt those who received it to greater faith. This would lend emphasis to Luther's teaching that man's appropriation of the *righteousness* is by *faith.* Yet if Paul had intended to say this precisely, he would have achieved his aim more readily by making the words *from faith* follow immediately after *righteousness* rather than leaving them to the end of the sentence. Alternatively, the words *unto faith* may be seen as a statement that faith is not only the source but also the goal of man's entire relationship with God. The best explanation of *unto faith,* however, holds that the phrase is concerned strictly with the human response to the *righteousness of God* that is revealed in the Gospel. It is revealed only to the man who responds with faith; no one else will be able to perceive it at all. When a man comes to *faith,* then he finds that the *righteousness of God* is indeed revealed in the Gospel. In this way the words *from faith* may be explained. Then, if *unto faith* is anything more than Semitic intensification, it shows that the salvation that results from the active *righteousness of God* is given only in response to faith; that is to say, it is given only to the man who has faith. This seems to be in close accord with the interpretation of the scheme of salvation given above.

Such is the Gospel that Paul preaches and that he proposes to expound in full in the course of this epistle. Finally, Paul attempts to support this teaching by a citation of Scripture, Habakkuk 2:4, from which he omits the pronouns both as written in the Hebrew Bible and in the Septuagint. The righteous man shall live in consequence of faith. Here the preposition EX, which normally means *from,* is not precisely equivalent to DIA (*by means of*). The man whose righteousness is from faith shall live, but it is not said that he shall live by means of his faith. As usual, Paul pays little attention to the context of his citation. The future verb for him probably means that *life* is to be understood eschatologically. The faith of the righteous man shall enable him to enter into the life of the New Age. This is perfectly in accord with Paul's teaching, both here and elsewhere. It sets forth at once the goal of Christian living and the manner of reaching it, while avoiding any suggestion that the newness of life depends upon human accomplishment.

* * *

1:18–32 For from Heaven the wrath of God is revealing itself upon all impiety and unrighteousness of men who suppress the truth by unrighteousness, because that which can be known of God is revealed among them; for God made revelation to them. For since the creation of the world His invisible nature was perceptible, observed in His works, both His eternal power and His deity, to the end that they might be without excuse, because recognizing God they did not honor Him as God or give Him thanks, but they were deceived (or, made foolish) by their reasonings, and their heart which had no understanding was darkened. Saying that they were wise, they were made fools, and they exchanged the glory (or, appearance; or, honor) of the incorruptible God for (or, into) a likeness of an image of corruptible man and of birds and of beasts and of serpents; wherefore God gave them up in the lusts of their hearts to the uncleanness of dishonoring their bodies among themselves. These changed the truth of God into falsehood, and they gave worship and devotion to what was created instead of to the Creator who is blessed unto the ages. Amen. Because of this God gave them up to passions of dishonor. For both their females changed the natural intercourse (or, use) into that which is contrary to nature, and likewise also the males, abandoning the natural intercourse with the female, were inflamed in their lust for one another, males with males accomplishing what was contrary to order (or, God's design) and receiving the recompense which was due their perversion (or, error) in their own persons. And just as they deliberately (alternatively, having in full knowledge) rejected (or, did not honor) God, so did God give them up to a base intention (alternatively, reprobate mind), to do the things which are indecent, to be filled with all unrighteousness, wickedness, avarice, baseness; full of envy, murder, faction, deceit, malice; gossips, slanderers, hateful to God (alternatively, men who hate God), arrogant braggarts, impostors, inventors of evils, disobedient to parents, insensate, treacherous, heartless, without pity. They are aware of God's decree that those who do such things are deserving of death, and they not only do them, but also give approval to those who do them.

* * *

For the balance of this chapter, Dodd's treatment is easily the best in any language. His analysis of the concept of the *wrath* is clear and complete, both from the point of view of history and of philosophy, and he does not hesitate to show the misleading character of the Moffatt translation. God is not angry with anyone. The passion of anger is unworthy of the perfection of the divine nature. But neither is God moved by maudlin sentiment. There is a moral order created by God Himself, and it can no more be disregarded with impunity than can the laws of physical nature. Whoever violates the moral order brings down upon himself the *wrath,* which is the due retribution. It is not *God's wrath* in the sense of personal resentment against those who disobey divine commands, and Paul much more often mentions *wrath* without adding the genitive *of God* than with this addition; this fact will be seen in later portions of the epistle. Yet one can describe the *wrath* as *God's* in the sense that God is responsible for and gives assent to the moral order of His universe. So the *wrath* in one way is impersonal, the working out of the natural consequences of human sin, the effect upon human nature of turning away from God and so depriving itself of His guidance or inspiration.

Verse 18 is clearly designed as a careful balance of the statements in Verse 17. *God's wrath* is the execution of judgment as *God's righteousness* is the instrument of salvation. Both are being revealed, the *righteousness* in the Gospel, the *wrath* from Heaven. The *righteousness* is revealed to everyone who believes for the purpose of salvation, the *wrath* against all impiety or irreligion and against all unrighteousness or immorality of the men who put away from themselves the truth by means of unrighteousness. Obviously the Greek verb KATECHO here cannot bear its alternative meaning of *hold fast.* Irreligion and immorality, as has already been made clear, bring upon themselves judgment in the nature of God's moral government of the universe.

Verses 19–20 are, as Dodd has shown, the clearest statement of what might be called *natural religion* to be found in Paul's writings. The source of this teaching is to be sought in the Old Testament; one need look no further than Psalm 19 for its inspiration, although a number of other texts could be offered which make the same point. There were Stoic parallels, and other possible sources, but we can be sure that Paul was acquainted with the Hebrew Scriptures. God's essential nature as Creator is evident in His creation itself; anyone who gives heed to what is there manifest ought to be able to appropriate its teaching. This is not comparable to the rabbinic claim that the Torah was offered to all nations and that Israel alone accepted it. Paul is saying that enough of God's nature is revealed in His works for men to recognize His power and deity apart from any supernatural revelation, so that they are without excuse if they fail to do so. St. Thomas Aquinas made precisely the same point some centuries later. Not all interpreters agree to this understanding of the verses, but it is the obvious manner in which Paul's words should be taken.

Verses 21–23 go on to show how mankind has misused the opportunities God has presented to the human race. The first participle would normally be translated "although they knew," but in reality men failed to recognize what they ought to have perceived. Instead of accepting the truth, they sought a substitute of their own devising; but as Verse 23 indicates, this effort of human reasoning was evidence not of wisdom but of folly. Instead of attaining its goal, the human accomplishment has been unworthy of God, unworthy even of man. The Gentile world has substituted for the DOXA (glory, appearance, honor, but here probably *revelation*) of God the likeness of an image. Paul's language here is temperate; he is not sure how far he should go in describing idols to the Romans with whom he is not personally acquainted. Yet he makes his point without equivocation. Images, whether of men, birds, beasts, or reptiles, can never represent the reality of God. There is no need to say that Paul here is thinking of those religions that practiced worship of sacred animals, or contrasting them with the human images of the Greco-Roman pantheon. To a Jew idolatry was idolatry, no matter how the divine was misrepresented. Nor is Paul giving any special attention to those pagans who had advanced philosophical reasons against the worship of such images. So far from finding God through their reasonings, men have been deceived to the point that they pay divine honor to objects that are not worthy even of themselves.

Paul goes on in the next two verses to show that the fundamental religious error has vitiated everything else that man has undertaken. In this he takes his stand within the tradition of Israel. Idolatry is the source of all other evils because it destroys man's fellowship with God and so cuts him off from the only power capable of protecting him from depravity. Since man has not worshiped God, God has allowed man to follow his own inclinations. Punishment is not the direct act of God but the inevitable consequence of the withdrawal of His protection. So it does not take the form of suffering, but of continued regress into self-chosen evil. Without true religion man's heart becomes subject to lust and uncleanness. From false worship he goes on to the defilement of the body that God gave him, a body that is in some sense stamped with God's image. Men have exchanged the truth of God for what is false, and since they have done so they can accomplish nothing that is good. Paul adds, in characteristic Jewish fashion, a brief expression of praise when he mentions the Creator. He is still thinking strictly of the faults of the Gentiles.

Verses 26–27 then sketch the extent of pagan depravity. While not all of the pagan world was given over to homosexuality, Aristophanes had found it sufficiently widespread in Athens to say in one of his comedies that the audience contained a clear majority of sodomites. Other cities were no better. Of course, homosexuality was not unknown in Israel, but there the attitude was different; it did not receive the easy tolerance that appears in Greek literature and in the Latin of Vergil and Catullus. Paul felt strongly about all types of sexual sin, but regarded this as infinitely worse than simple fornication. He was, perhaps, inclined to exaggerate its debilitating effects, as in the final clause of Verse 27.

The remaining five verses consist in a list of vices. The last word on such ethical lists has probably been said by B. S. Easton in the article "New Testament Ethical Lists" which appeared in the *Journal of Biblical Literature* of 1932. Such lists had first been devised by the Stoics, and later had been adopted by Greek-speaking Jews; from the latter the Christians learned to use them. Catalogues of vices are more common than those of virtues. Verse 28 introduces the present list. After the earlier castigation of sexual misbehavior, Paul here concentrates on antisocial qualities: injustice, malevolence (for which one manuscript mistakenly substitutes the similar Greek word for fornication), greedy self-assertion (brilliantly treated in Dodd's commentary), meanness (or cowardice). These four terms form one group, of which the terms are in the dative case. A second group, in which the nouns are in the genitive and depend upon the adjective phrase *filled with*, contains the words envy, murder, faction, deceit, ill will. Next come faults denoted by adjectives in the accusative plural and applying to people generally: talebearers, slanderers, people who are hateful to God (or less probably who themselves hate God), who are arrogant, self-important, braggarts, inventive in evil, disobedient to parents (and to other proper authority), irresponsible, perjurors, callous, cruel. It is not an optimistic estimate of the human race. Verse

32 sums it all up, saying that these people knew better, or at least could have known better. Yet they did something even worse than failing themselves in the face of temptation; they applauded or condoned such actions in others, thus converting vice into a principle of action. Such was the condition into which the Gentiles had contrived to get themselves by their loss of God through bad religion. From them Paul turns next to the Jews to show that their condition is in fact no better. Even with the help of revelation people give no cause for easy optimism. To Paul's mind no group of people had proved this more clearly than those who refused the culmination of God's revelation to them by the rejection of Christ.

CHAPTER 2

Judgment

2:1–11 Wherefore, man, you are without excuse in passing judgment (literally, whoever is passing judgment); for in the fact that you are passing judgment on someone else you are condemning yourself, for you who are passing judgment are doing the same things yourself. Now we know that God's judgment is in accord with the truth upon those who do such things. But consider this, man, you who are passing judgment on those who do such things and are doing them yourself; are you going to avoid God's judgment? (Alternatively: Do you consider that you are going to be acquitted by God's judgment?) Or do you despise the extent (or, wealth) of His kindness and forbearance and patience, not knowing that God's kindness is leading you to repentance? In terms of your severity and impenitence of heart (literally, impenitent heart) you are storing up wrath for yourself in a day of wrath and of revelation of God's righteous judgment, who shall repay each man in accord with his works, to those who seek with perseverance in well-doing for glory and honor and incorruptibility, life eternal; to those who from ambition and disregard of the truth obey unrighteousness (alternatively, and obedience to unrighteousness disregard the truth), wrath and fury, tribulation and anguish to every human being (literally, soul of man) who does what is evil, to the Jew in the first place and also to the Greek (or, Gentile); but glory and honor and peace to everyone who does what is good, to the Jew in the first place and also to the Greek (or, Gentile). For there is no partiality with God.

* * *

Although it has been argued that Gentile critics may be included in this paragraph, there is every indication that a sharp contrast is being drawn between these words and the attack upon Gentiles of the previous chapter, and that these censures are addressed strictly to the Jews as the people most prone to pass religious judgment upon others. The style is that of diatribe; hypothetical objection is put into the mouth of an opponent and is then answered. Jews were prone to pass harsh judgment upon Gentiles for their failure to meet the demands of righteousness, but in so doing they expose themselves to the same condemnation. Paul may have been acquainted with the words ascribed to Jesus, "Judge not and you shall not be judged." As Barrett has shown, all men share in the fundamental sin of seeking to displace God from His rightful primacy. The Jewish form of doing this is the assertion that man can put God under obligation to himself by performance of Torah; yet this would be as much a declaration that man does not stand in need of God as is anything that the Gentiles have done. Verse 2 is probably a conventional Jewish claim that those who indulge in the sins already ascribed to the Gentiles will fall under a divine judgment administered in accord with truth. Of this, Jews feel that they possess the certainty of revelation. Then Verse 3 asks whether the Jew who manifests in his own life the faults he has condemned in another form with reference to Gentiles can expect to escape the condemnation he has called down upon those Gentiles.

Verses 4–6 then explain to the Jew the present situation which he has so grossly misunderstood. This is the time of God's forbearance, and by his attitude the Jew (who believes that he is storing up merit for himself by his devotion to the Torah) is in fact storing up wrath. The ideas of the goodness and forbearance of God here seem to be related to the Wisdom of Solomon, particularly in chapters 11–15 of that book. The judgment is, of course, eschatological; it is to be visited in the Day of Wrath. Verse 6 quotes Psalm 62:12 or Proverbs 24:12 (which in the Septuagint are identical). From this one would gather that the judgment itself will be related to performance, and this may serve as a warning against the effort to eliminate actual *righteousness* from the Pauline scheme of salvation. While it is true that Paul taught constantly that *faith* will suffice for a man *to be put in the right* by God's grace, no man can say with honesty that the apostle did not believe that good works had a part to play in the life of a Christian.

Verses 7–10 go on to show what the alternatives in God's judgment are. Barrett defines the *works* which form the basis of judgment in terms of that *patient endurance* which looks beyond human activity to its divine complement. The reverse of this *patient endurance* is *ambition*. Barrett relates the Greek word for this latter quality to a verb that means *to act as a hireling*, and on this interpretation it would refer to the Jewish aim of earning salvation. If the word is more properly related to the noun that means *jealousy*, as many linguists contend, his point would be weakened but not demolished, for then the term would mean self-aggrandizement. Actually, the content of verses 7–8 resembles that of II Corinthians 1:6. At Romans 1:16 salvation had been promised to everyone who believes, first of all to the Jew and then to the Gentile. Now, in 2:9, tribulation is promised to everyone who does evil, first of all to the Jew and then to the Gentile. Verse 10 then repeats the promise of favor from 1:16, substituting *to him who does what is good* for *to everyone who believes*. Then Verse 11 repeats what was already suggested in Verse 2, that there is no partiality with God; this warns the Jews against trusting in ancestral privilege. Those who find the teaching of justification by faith difficult to comprehend are tempted to employ this section as an argument for righteousness by good works. Some Catholic scholars have done so. But one cannot afford to separate this paragraph from the verses that follow. Man still depends upon the *patient endurance* of Verse 7, and the following words explain this in further detail.

* * *

2:12–16 For as many as sinned apart from Torah also perish apart from Torah; and as many as sinned under (or, in) Torah shall be judged by means of Torah. For those who are pupils of Torah are not in the right with God, but those who are doers of Torah shall be put in the right. For when the Gentiles who do not possess Torah naturally perform the provisions of the Torah, not possessing Torah they are a law for themselves;

they are showing that the reality (literally, work) of the Torah is written in their hearts, while their conscience bears witness and their thoughts condemn or perhaps excuse them to (or, between) one another, in the day when God through Christ Jesus shall judge the secret things of men, according to my Gospel.

* * *

The purpose of this section is to make clear the reasons why Jew and Gentile stand in the same position before God and in regard to salvation. The first chapter has already established something that may be called *natural law*, to which all men by their own nature are answerable. This combination of the Stoic thought of natural law and the revealed Torah of Israel was available for Paul in Hellenistic Judaism; an example is found in Philo. Dodd assumes that verses 14–15 are a parenthesis, and that 16 logically follows upon 13, but Lietzmann, who is the most convincing commentator on this section, is able to defend the existing order of the verses. The Gentile who sinned apart from Torah will be judged in equity. In essence the argument is Stoic. God has implanted a *natural law* in all men, and Gentiles who do not possess written Torah can perform its functions. This they may do because, as Verse 15 shows, they possess the threefold witness of (1) natural law in their hearts, (2) the internal witness of personal conscience, (3) the external witness of collective conscience. With these three forms of guidance at their disposal, Gentiles are without excuse for sin. This had already been said in 1:20. On the other hand, if Gentiles follow this guidance that is available to them, their opportunity for salvation is in no sense inferior to that of the Jews. Turning back to the Jewish side of the issue, one must remember that in Paul's reasoning the possession of Torah is not in any sense a guarantee of salvation, but rather an instrument of judgment that replaces the *natural law* as the measure of responsibility for the Chosen Nation.

One must remember that the verb in Verse 13, commonly translated they *shall be justified*, does not mean that those who perform the demands of Torah attain a moral status. Paul regularly uses this word to describe what Barrett calls "a relation of gracious favor and peace between God and man." Hypothetically this could be achieved by the perfect performance of Torah, but in fact Paul denied that anyone did fulfill the Torah perfectly, and so he thought rather of God's sentence of acquittal than of an infusion of virtue. A man is made righteous in God's eyes when he freely accepts his created status because he has learned to trust or to have faith in God. Verse 16 then relates this teaching to Paul's eschatology, speaking of a day when God shall judge. The Latin translators were right in taking the verb as a future; the difference between present and future in the Greek is shown only by the accent. The Aleph and D manuscripts add *when* after *day*, and this improves the grammar without changing the meaning. Lietzmann holds that *through Jesus Christ* refers to the Lord as Judge in the eschatological order. Although this is far from clear as the words stand, it does agree with general Pauline teaching. The judgment is to be based upon *attitude* (the secret things of men), rather than upon *performance* either of the Torah or of natural law. This is what gives importance to the witness of conscience. God's sentence of *being in the right* will not be pronounced because of deeds done, but upon people who believe.

* * *

2:17–29 But if you, who call yourself a Jew and rely upon Torah and make your boast in God, and shall recognize His will and are giving approval to the things which are excellent as you are taught from the Torah, and are convinced that you are yourself both a guide for the blind and a light for those who are in darkness, a guide for the indifferent (or, ignorant), a teacher for the uninstructed, possessing the form of the knowledge and of the truth of God which is in the Torah—you, therefore, who are teaching another, do you not teach yourself? You, who are preaching not to steal, do you steal? You, who are saying not to commit adultery, do you commit adultery? You, who despise idols, do you rob temples? You, who make your boast in Torah, are you dishonoring God through the transgression of the Torah? For because of you the Name of God is ill spoken of by the Gentiles, as it is written. For circumcision indeed is of benefit if you shall perform the Torah. But if you shall be a transgressor of Torah, your circumcision has become uncircumcision. On the other hand, if the uncircumcision shall maintain the statutes of the Torah, will not his uncircumcision be accounted for circumcision? And that which is uncircumcision by nature which fulfills the Torah shall judge (or, condemn) you the transgressor of Torah in spite of the fact that you have it written and have circumcision. For it is not he who is so externally that is a Jew, nor is that circumcision which is so externally in the flesh: but he who is so in attitude (literally, in secret; alternatively, internally) is a Jew, and circumcision is of the heart by spirit, not by letter, whose praise comes not from men but from God.

* * *

Some scholars subdivide this section after Verse 24. Verses 17–20 form a single sentence, and one that is not clear enough in meaning to be translated with ease. The Jews of the period regarded their national designation as a title of pride, and as a guarantee of all the privileges of knowledge of God and performance of His will as revealed in the Torah, and of the capacity to distinguish between good and evil by means of the Torah. In the world at large Jews believed themselves called to instruct the heathen, both by word and by example. The term *guides of the blind* seems also to be reflected in Matthew 15:14. Verse 19 probably is influenced by Isaiah 42:6–7 and 49:6. The word for *pride* or *boast* is frequent in Paul's vocabulary.

After this opening sentence, Paul moves to his argument that the Jew is exposed to judgment. In Verse 21 Michel makes a careful distinction between *teaching,* or formal instruction, *proclaiming* or preaching and *saying* or exegetical citation of the Scriptures. More significant in its theological bearing is Barrett's declaration that Israel as a whole had robbed God of His due honor and by a subtle arrogance had appropriated it to the Nation. This concept had a long history. Hosea had portrayed Israel as God's bride who had proved guilty of adultery. In a day when the temptation to worship other gods had passed, the prophet's message might well be recast to say that when the Jew exalts himself as judge and lord of others he has claimed for himself the devotion that should be offered only to God.

The questions in verses 21–22 are clearly rhetorical. Jewish teaching forbade the robbing of heathen temples, although such robbery may sometimes have been committed on the pretext of contempt for false gods. In Verse 23 Paul declares that Jewish failure to perform the whole Torah, and to fulfill it in the radical and inward sense Jesus had put forward as the way of exceeding the righteousness of the scribes and Pharisees, brings dishonor upon the Name of Israel's God. There can be no question that Verse 24 reflects Isaiah 52:5, and in spite of

Lietzmann's doubts a relation between Verse 24 and Ezekiel 36:20–21 also seems to be well established.

Verses 25–29 then form a summary of the whole argument by comparing *circumcision* and *uncircumcision.* These terms may be understood either as the fact of circumcision or its absence, as a relationship to God contrasted with estrangement from Him, or they may stand respectively for the Jewish and the pagan worlds. Of these possibilities the second will give the greatest value to the text. If circumcision is a spiritual relationship to God, then performing Torah will mean the fulfillment of that relationship. Thus the man who transgresses Torah by disregarding his total dependence upon God annuls his own circumcision, whereas an uncircumcised Gentile who fulfills this relationship with God that Torah is intended to express is included within God's Covenant, and outward circumcision becomes irrelevant for him. Such inclusion within the Covenant is a creative act of God. It confers upon the Gentile the spiritual state of a man who is truly circumcised. This teaching is not conventional Judaism, for many rabbis argued that the fact of circumcision would itself save a man from Gehenna, but it must also be remembered that Rabbi Meir adopted something very like Paul's position. Paul here is presenting Torah as the instrument of judgment that every privilege must be. The Jew who is endowed with the Torah, if his performance is not better than that of the pagan, inevitably will be in a worse spiritual condition than if he had not been so endowed; this is the principle that Jesus Himself enunciated in the saying that much shall be required of the man to whom much is given. On the other hand, the spiritual condition of the Gentile who has fulfilled the right relation to God does not differ fundamentally from that of the Jew who has done the same.

Lagrange sees Verse 27 as a reflection of Matthew 12:41, and it is certain that the picture of the uncircumcised who had done right acting as judge of the circumcised who had not done right is a parallel to the saying of Jesus that the men of Ninevah would judge the Jews of His own generation. The mention of circumcision of the heart in Verse 29 is supported by many Old Testament texts, notably Deuteronomy 10:16 and 30:6, Jeremiah 4:4 and 9:26, Ezekiel 44:7; it is mentioned also in Philo and the Odes of Solomon. Barrett interprets Verse 28 by Calvin's teaching of an *invisible church*, and while this is an exaggeration the verse can be used in support of that concept because it does emphasize that outward or physical Judaism and circumcision count for nothing and that only the inward or spiritual reality has value in God's sight. The contrast here is strictly between human flesh and spirit, and the Holy Spirit of God is not considered directly. The Jew whose circumcision is spiritual, a circumcision of the heart, receives praise from God, and this praise is not related to human opinion or to the attainment of the person who receives it. It depends entirely on divine favor or election, and the only qualification man can offer is a trusting humility, that which Paul elsewhere describes as *faith*.

CHAPTER 3

Man's Failure

3:1–8 So what is the advantage of the Jew, or what the benefit of the circumcision? Much from every point of view. First of all, they were entrusted with the words of God. So what if some of them lacked faith? Surely their lack of faith will not cancel God's trustworthiness? God forbid! Let God be true and every man false, as it is written: "That thou mayest be acquitted in thy words and thou shalt be victorious when thou art brought to trial." But if our immorality sets forth the righteousness of God, what shall we say? Not that God who imposes the wrath is unjust? I speak in human terms. God forbid! In that case, how is God to judge the world? But if the truth of God by my falsehood has expanded to His glory, why am I for my part still condemned as a sinner? And why not, as we are slandered and as some people assert that we say, let us do evil that good things may result? Their condemnation is just!

* * *

These verses might be subdivided either after Verse 2 or Verse 4, but they can well be taken all together. The treatment of Lagrange here is more convincing than that of anyone else. The style is that of the diatribe. Possible objections to Paul's teaching are put into the mouth of some hypothetical questioner. Dodd holds that Paul has allowed his personal pride in Judaism to overrule his judgment. Lagrange goes to the opposite extreme and says that the questioner here need not be thought of as Jewish rather than as Gentile. Both of these positions are to be avoided.

The first of the questions grows out of the previous chapter in which it had been shown that the Jew stands under God's judgment quite as much as does the Gentile. This assertion leads naturally to the question of whether there is any good in being a Jew or in being circumcised. Many Paulinists today would answer that there was no benefit whatever. Paul himself does otherwise. He states that there is great advantage in every way, or from every point of view, as Goodspeed has translated the words. He proposes to give a list of the benefits. His method of argument, however, is not systematic in its development. After stating the first point of advantage, he fails to go on to a second because of the value he ascribes to the fact that Israel has been entrusted with the *words* of God. There are several interpretations for *words* here. The most popular in Christian history has been to consider them as the messianic promises. Again the term may be taken as referring to God's moral law in distinction from the ceremonial provisions of the Torah. The most convincing explanation, however, will be to understand the *words* as the total content of Holy Scripture, certainly including the messianic promises and the moral law, but not restricted to these items. The whole revelation of God has been entrusted to Israel, and while salvation is possible for Gentiles the Jews have an advantage that can never be canceled.

The second question, in Verse 3, states the claim of the Jews perhaps more clearly than does the answer already given in Verse 2, but this time presses it to an extreme Paul will not accept. Even the failure of Israel has carried forward God's revelation. Certainly some, indeed most, of the Jews have been unfaithful to God's Covenant. So they have brought upon themselves the judgment God has declared and must inflict by the terms of His own Covenant. In this judgment God's reliability may be proved, and so the unfaithfulness of Israel serves for God's glory. Can that unfaithfulness then be considered meritorious, so that God's judgment should not actually be inflicted?

To this suggestion Paul replies with one of his favorite phrases, one he uses in Romans ten times and also in several of the other epistles. In classical usage the words were no more than a strong negative, and the rendering *certainly not* has been adopted by several modern translators. In many instances where he uses it, however, it is clear that Paul intends something much more stringent, and the King James translation *God forbid* seems the most satisfactory. This answer is expanded by citations from Psalm 116:11 and Psalm 51:4, both as in the Septuagint. Actually, Paul is in difficulty here because of his desire to assert Jewish privilege, a desire that is in conflict with his determination not to allow such a privilege to be maintained without regard to man's response to God. On God's side Paul declares that there are faithfulness, truth, and righteousness (doing right); on man's (or, Israel's) are infidelity to the Covenant, falsehood, and immorality. Thus God's judgment is just and necessary to maintain His own nature.

The questions of verses 5 and 7 attempt to probe more deeply into the claims of Israel, although their terms could be extended to serve as an excuse for any type of wrongdoing. Paul has already made the point that human unrighteousness or immorality has served to call forth or to reveal the active *righteousness of God*. Assuming that his theme is still the disobedience of Israel, Paul ranges himself with his compatriots; he speaks of "our unrighteousness." Since it has had such beneficial results, is not God unfair in visiting it with the *wrath?* The Greek is so expressed as to expect assent to this proposition. Paul first of all declares that this reasoning is simply *in human terms*, which obviously are less than satisfactory when referred to God. Then he dismisses the argument with the declaration *God forbid!* If God had to consider that He often overrules evil intentions and brings from them good results, a moral judgment of the world would be impossible. The verb for *judge* in Verse 6 is in the future tense; Paul is still thinking chiefly of a future eschatology.

Verse 7 repeats the question in more philosophical terms, substituting *truth* on God's side for *righteousness*, and *falsehood* on man's for *immorality*. Here there is more stress upon the manner in which human failure calls forth corrective action from God and so serves to set forward His glory. In logic the position is at least tenable. If my wrongdoing has prompted God to greater acts of grace in order to compensate for it, why should I be condemned when I have proved an instrument for good? The fallacy here is the uncritical assumption of a false premise, of a claim that the outpouring of God's grace is inevitably to be desired. From this it is but a short step to the most drastic of the misrepresentations of Paul's teaching, a misrepresentation that has recurred many times throughout history. If grace is the sole means to salvation, one might say that sin is good because it calls forth redeeming grace. Whenever he was faced with the accusation that his teaching meant approval of evil on the ground that good might result from it, Paul always reacted in the same way. This was not a proposition to be discussed. It was to be rejected out of hand with a simple appeal to authority or to the moral constitution of God's creation. Here what he says is that people who show such perversity deserve to perish eternally. He could have worked out an argument in logic, but he did not take the time. On this point Dodd fails to do justice to Paul, for his commentary assumes that there is no real advantage in Judaism and therefore that the entire argument is weak or unworthy. Such is not the case. The Jew had a real advantage over the Gentile in Paul's day, not so much in circumcision as in the one point that Paul develops. The Jew enjoyed a much more effective preparation for the Gospel than did anyone else. He began with some valid knowledge of God, and a useful religious system. If he came to *faith*, he could carry his response to its proper goal more readily than could the Gentile who did not know the Covenant or the Promise. Because of the intensity of his own feeling, Paul fails to establish this argument as well as might be done, but the case itself is not lacking in merit.

* * *

3:9–20 Then what? Do we have an advantage? Not absolutely. For we have already made the charge against both Jews and Greeks that all are subject to (literally, under) sin, just as it is written, "There is no righteous man, not even one, there is no man who understands, there is no one who is seeking God. All have turned aside; together they have been perverted, there is no man who does what is virtuous; there is not so much as one. Their throat is an opened grave, they deceive with their tongues, venom of asps is under their lips; their mouth is filled with cursing and bitterness, their feet swift to shed blood; destruction and affliction attend their ways, and they did not know the way of peace. There is no reverence for

God before their eyes." We know that whatever the Torah says, it is speaking to those within the Torah, so that every mouth may be shut and all the world may be accountable to God. Wherefore from works of Torah no flesh shall be put in the right before God; for through Torah comes knowledge of sin.

* * *

Paul now attempts to show the consequences of what he has been saying, and he begins with the question, "Then what?" The next three words have caused as much debate as any other triad within the New Testament. The verb is in the middle, or passive, voice, which in the present tense are identical in form. If middle in meaning it should imply, *Are we Jews engaging in self-defense?* This is open to the complaint that no object is stated, and in strict grammar an object ought to be stated if the verb is to be used in this way. If it is a true passive, it would mean, *Are we Jews surpassed by the Gentiles?* This, however, is impossible; no Jewish objector to Paul's arguments would suggest that Israel was inferior to the Gentiles in any aspect of relationship to God. Accordingly, most scholars, including Lietzmann and Lagrange and Barrett, take the verb as a deponent, which gives the meaning, *Do we Jews excel others?* This is the only way in which the word can be used to set forward the argument.

The problem of interpreting the negative and the adverb is no less difficult. Do these words mean *not absolutely* or *absolutely not?* Moffatt translated them with the latter sense, and several scholars have accepted this judgment; Barrett supports this claim with a text from Paul's Stoic contemporary Epictetus in which these words can mean only *absolutely not*. Yet in much ancient writing, including Paul's I Corinthians 5:10, the words have to be understood as *not absolutely*. Moreover, unless we are to suppose that Paul has forgotten entirely what he said in Verse 2, the apostle must be prepared to allow at least a relative superiority to the Jews. This fact would seem decisive. The entire chapter is intended to develop a consistent argument to the effect that all men without exception stand in need of God's grace, and whatever Paul's inconsistencies elsewhere he cannot be considered as at cross-purposes with himself here. Those who contend that the words are to be taken as a strong negative, base their claim not upon the text of this epistle but upon theological convictions reached independently of it. The advantage of the Jew in the scheme of salvation, already asserted in Verse 2, is now declared to be no more than a relative one. Both Jews and Greeks or Gentiles are subject to sin. Here *sin* is virtually personified. In similar texts later in the epistle it will be represented as a sort of cosmic demon that has gained dominion over all mankind.

In verses 10–18 Paul supports this statement with a collection of Old Testament citations. These are quoted loosely from memory. Some of them, but not all, are in agreement with the Septuagint. There is no reason to suppose that they are derived from an early Christian collection of *testimonies*; they set forth a strict Pauline emphasis, and it is not likely that anyone other than the apostle would have selected them. The texts used are Psalm 14:1–3 (or Psalm 53:1–3 which is almost identical with it), Psalm 5:9, Psalm 140:3, Psalm 10:7, Isaiah 59:7–8, Psalm 36:1. Michel believes that the citations are arranged in poetic form as three Semitic couplets, but this is probably the ingenious calculation of a modern scholar rather than the true analysis of Paul's own work.

Verse 19 then provides a summary, saying that the Torah, by which Paul in rabbinic fashion means the entire Old Testament, applies only to those within its discipline, therefore to the Jews. As Barrett expresses it, Paul is saying that the Old Testament proves the Jews, and a fortiori all other men, to be guilty before God. The world is brought to trial, and no man can answer the charge. From this situation there can be no human escape, and Paul supports his assertion with some words from Psalm 143:2, adding his own thought that no one can be put in the right before God *by works of Torah.* Again Barrett's words are worthy of quotation: "In dealing with the supreme representative of those who presume to judge, (the Jew), Paul indicates that a Jew's death-warrant is written into his own birth certificate, because the religion in which he glories accuses him in order that the whole world may be found guilty. When rightly understood, the Old Testament declares justification to be a universal impossibility even while it offers it. The Torah or *practice of religion* brings to light not righteousness but sin. As long as God's *righteousness* is manifested and understood in terms of *Law* it must spell *wrath,* and man's only hope is that God may find some other means beyond *Law* and *religion* of manifesting His righteousness." While it might be impossible for a person to compose these lines unless he shared Barrett's religious convictions, and while these words undoubtedly exaggerate Paul's own position, we have here the sort of exaggeration that can contribute to a clearer awareness of the apostle's meaning.

* * *

3:21–31 But as it is (or, now), God's righteousness has been made manifest apart from Torah, receiving testimony from the Torah and the Prophets, God's righteousness through faith in Christ, for all those who believe. For there is no distinction; for all sinned and deprived themselves of the glory of God, but they are put in the right as a gift by His favor (or, goodness) by means of the redemption which is in Christ Jesus, whom God set forth as a reconciliation (or, expiation; or, propitiation) by means of faith in His Blood, with a view to a demonstration of His righteousness because of the passing over of the sins that had formerly occurred, by God's forbearance (alternatively, in the time of God's forbearance), for the purpose of the demonstration of His righteousness in the present time, to the end that He might be in the right Himself and might put a man in the right by faith in (or, of) Jesus. So where is presumption (or, boasting)? It was excluded! By what sort of law (or, principle)? Of works (or, performance)? Not so, but by means of a law (or, principle) of faith. For we consider that a man is put in the right by faith apart from works (or, performance) of Torah (or, law). Or is God only for the Jews? Is He not also for the Gentiles? Yes, also for the Gentiles, if it is true that God is One, who shall put circumcision in the right from faith, and uncircumcision by means of faith. Then are we abolishing Torah by means of faith? God forbid! Indeed, we are establishing (alternatively, truly interpreting) Torah.

* * *

This section is the culmination of much that Paul has already said. In 2:1–11, with an illustration from the law of retribution, Paul had shown that Gentile philosophy with its thought of natural law had failed to make a godly world. From 2:12 to 3:20, with reference to the Jews, he worked round to the assertion that none of the Jews actually observed their Torah in all its fullness. If one thinks about relations with God in terms of *law*, which Barrett would extend to embrace all the efforts of morality and religion, then both Jew and Gentile must be judged by their performance, and on that basis both must be condemned. So the point of this section is that salvation is to be found in Christ and that it cannot be found apart from Him.

No single commentary will be accounted satisfactory to every reader here, and the choice among them will be determined largely by one's decision regarding the meaning of the word HILASTERION. If one stresses the normal sense of the word in Greek, *propitiation*, and so understands by it that Christ is a sin offering (which is what Luther did), then Otto Michel gives the most convincing statement of the teaching. Yet even Michel's art cannot overcome the problems of this explanation. The function of the sin offering in Israel was in no sense comparable to that which Paul ascribed to Christ, for it did not take away sin any more than the psalm or prayer that may be said as a penance is held by modern Catholics to remove sin; any suggestion that the Jews thought that it did is based upon a misconception. In addition, the Septuagint uses a verb cognate with this word to translate the Hebrew KAPHAR, which means to *cover* or *conceal*, and of this verb God is sometimes the subject; obviously God cannot make a sin offering or propitiation of any sort for Himself.

A second interpretation of HILASTERION is that of *expiation*. Here the difficulties are not so great. God can expiate man's sin by His own saving act in Christ, and Paul does stress an expiatory value in Christ's Death. Most modern English-speaking scholars seem to favor this interpretation, including both Dodd and Barrett.

Lietzmann's explanation, however, seems yet more satisfactory. He takes the word as a noun, and equates it with KATALLAGE of II Corinthians 5:19; the latter word certainly means *reconciliation*. This is truly Pauline. God has appointed Christ Crucified as the Mediator of Atonement for humanity. Christ's Death is a *ransom* from the fate with which man was threatened because of sin. The content of that Atonement, which may certainly be seen as an expiation, is in essence man's *reconciliation* with God. With this may be compared Colossians 1:20–22. While it is true that Paul's language here gives some excuse for the historic Latin theory of the Atonement (which culminated in Anselm's concept of satisfaction), and while much of what is said here is certainly forensic in tone, that Latin theory is far from Paul's intention. For Paul, man secured the benefit of what Christ had done *through faith*, and for this process ideas of the propitiation of an angry God, or speculations of the object to whom Christ's ransom was paid, are in fact irrelevant.

This is also an appropriate point at which to discuss Paul's use of the term DIKAIOSUNE. One may assume that Paul derived it from the Septuagint rather than from secular writing, and in Jewish understanding it did not describe a quality of character but a position granted to men in their relationship with God. As applied to God, the word meant *God in His action,* God making a demand upon pain of judgment or giving help to perform this same demand through mercy. In this the conventional Judaism of Paul's day placed the main emphasis upon judgment, while Paul and the Christians generally placed the greater emphasis upon mercy. When referred to God, this term should be translated *righteousness,* for it describes God as acting in accord with His own Nature, but when referred to man it should be translated *justification* because it describes a position of acquittal or forgiveness or fellowship rather than a quality of character. Here Paul is discussing the *righteousness* (understood as a position) that comes *from God,* in contrast to anything that may have its origin in man. It is a *gift,* not an *achievement.* The background of Verse 21 is eschatological, and the *righteousness* here discussed has nothing to do with any moral code. The present time is contrasted with the period of striving that has preceded Christ's inauguration of the *New Age.* In the same way the Christian life is being contrasted with the false approach of that striving. This is indicated by the Greek words used. Paul's full formula for salvation may be expressed by the phrase *faith in God mediated by Christ and called forth by the Gospel.* Paul looks upon Jesus as standing with God rather than with man, and he looks upon the Gospel as the expression of the purpose of Jesus. Thus when he speaks of *faith in Christ* or *faith in the Gospel,* he means *faith in God.* So one may paraphrase the opening clauses here as "But now God's being in the right is made manifest, a being in the right which is entirely apart from moral code." Paul has little interest in abstract divine attributes; like other Jews he prefers to speak of the manner in which God acts, and of the results of God's action for mankind.

The rest of Verse 21 may be dealt with simply. The testimony that the righteousness that comes from God receives from the law and the prophets is actual only for those who commit themselves to Jesus. Law and prophets between them stand for the totality of Scripture. Those who fail to commit themselves to Jesus can read the Scripture without perceiving its true meaning. So in Verse 22 the position of being in the right that God confers upon men comes only to those who believe, and it comes through a faith that has for its object Jesus Christ. Lietzmann holds that the concept is equivalent to that of *mystical union with Christ* which the apostle expresses elsewhere. The late Byzantine texts complicate the thought of the verse by rendering it *for all and unto all who believe,* but there is no advantage in this addition. When Paul says that there is no distinction he is referring to the issue of Jew and Gentile; in God's sight all have shown the same rebellious self-assertion, although in varying ways, and this self-assertion is the fundamental sin of pride. So all have deprived themselves, or perhaps simply fallen short, of the *glory of God.* Lietzmann would equate this with *praise from God,* but a better case may be made for saying that all men have failed of God's purpose for them. It is, however, excessively ingenious to find in this statement a reference to rabbinic beliefs about the glorious primal physical characteristics of Adam. What Paul is saying is that all men have disqualified themselves for heavenly existence.

Verse 24 shows one of Paul's characteristic ambiguities in the use of Greek, and one which is virtually impossible to set forth in English. After writing that *all sinned,* he adds a passive participle, *they are put in the right.* The participle is written in the nominative case, which implies that it refers to those who sinned, whereas it probably should be in the accusative to agree with *all those who believe* in Verse 22. Only the believers can be thought of as put in the right in relation to God, not the sinners who have not come to belief. The word translated above *as a gift* is rendered by Goodspeed as *for nothing,* but this would not change the meaning. The position which the believers have received is a free gift of God's grace. Whatever Paul's doctrine of *justification,* it always includes this idea of *free gift* and it is always related to the *redemption* that is effected by Jesus Christ. Such is his teaching here. Since Paul never offered a clear definition of what he meant by APOLYTROSIS, there can be no certainty about its exact translation; *ransom* will do as well as *redemption.* The New Testament never states a price in connection with this *ransom,* and it does not refer the word directly to the Death of Jesus or to His Blood. Since sin is being considered here as a legal matter with a definite penalty of judgment, it may be argued that Paul includes the thought of *price* at least by implication, but the evidence is not strong enough to constitute proof, and there are also contrary factors. In the Old Testament ransom is not essentially related to propitiatory sacrifice, and the two are not tied together here.

In Verse 25 Paul goes on to say that God has set Christ before us *in His Blood* (by which he means Christ's Death) as a reconciliation by means of the faith that is related to His Blood or Death. This is a direct statement of the Pauline teaching. Commit yourself with complete trust in the saving act of God in Christ, and your reconciliation with God will be effected. This saving act itself serves for a demonstration that God was in the right (that God acted rightly and in accord with His own nature) in the passing over of the sins of former ages. It was a perfectly moral transaction. God was giving opportunity for repentance, and indeed was preparing for the demonstration that would enable men truly to repent. God is also acting rightly in the eschatological period inaugurated by Christ when He demands the response of repentance to what He has done in Christ, and when He gives the status of acquittal (justification) to those who make the response of faith. Of course, in giving to his teaching on salvation this eschatological framework, Paul was bound to run into theological difficulties. This fact is seen in the many diverse interpretations that have been given to his teachings. All Christians were forced to seek a theory capable of explaining their experience in Christ. The experience itself they saw as a new reality in the world, a reality no one could understand in full. All Christians were sure that Christ had accomplished *redemption* by His Death, but they were not at all sure of *how* He had done so. Paul, the most vocal among them, tried to give a number of explanations of *how* Christ had achieved the result, but he did not presume to set any of them forward as final or authoritative.

Here Paul is insisting that *God's righteousness* means more than its human counterpart; it is united with God's *mercy* and it depends upon His *gracious will*. It is desirable here, and perhaps even necessary, to make a distinction between the passing over of sins in a particular situation and the complete forgiveness of all sin. Separate words are used in the Greek.

Verse 27 takes up the thought of Verse 9 regarding the boasting of the Jews. Since one cannot earn salvation by the performance of Torah but can only receive it as a free gift in response to faith, boasting or pride in human achievement becomes impossible. Barrett holds that Paul uses the Greek word for *law* to stand for any conceivable religious system in which man might seek personal merit and that the apostle does not limit its scope to that of Judaism. This may be accepted providing that one does not place too much emphasis on the idea. The thought of a *law of faith* in verses 27–28 is also found in Galatians 2:16. Because God is *One*, as He is by definition, He must be God of the Gentiles as truly as He is God of the Jews, and since Torah belongs to Israel alone *faith* must be the justifying principle for both Jew and Gentile. So if they both have faith, Jew and Gentile are truly equal before God. The differing Greek prepositions here used are simply variants of style, and their use without distinction of meaning continues through the two following chapters. In Verse 31 Paul concludes that his insistence upon faith in no sense abolishes *law*, which here stands for the Old Testament as a whole; instead the authority of Scripture is established by Paul's interpretation, for the Old Testament itself declares the value of faith. As in IV Maccabees 5:25, so here *to establish the Torah* is *to maintain that the Torah is right*. It is the apostle's conviction that the religious system based upon God's revelation to Israel, when it is rightly understood, leads directly to the religious point of view he maintains as a Christian. In the following chapter he attempts to prove his point from the "salvation history" of Israel itself.

CHAPTER 4

God's Promise

4:1–12 So what shall we say that Abraham, our physical ancestor, has found? For if Abraham was put in the right from performance (or, works) he has a cause for pride (alternatively, has a boast); but not in relation to God. For what does the Scripture say? "Abraham trusted in God, and it was accounted to him for being in the right." Now to a man who works pay is not accounted as a favor but as an obligation;

while to a man who does not work, but who trusts in Him who puts the impious in the right, his faith is accounted for being in the right, just as David also says of the blessedness of the man to whom God accounts being in the right apart from performance (or, works): "Blessed are those whose lawless acts were forgiven and whose sins were atoned (or, covered); blessed is the man whose sin the Lord will assuredly not take into account." Then is this man blessed in a state of circumcision or also in a state of uncircumcision? For we say, "Faith was accounted to Abraham for being in the right." So how was it accounted? While he was in circumcision or in uncircumcision? Not in circumcision but in uncircumcision; and he received a token of circumcision as a seal of the being in the right that belongs to the faith which existed in the uncircumcision, that he might be a father of all those who have faith through uncircumcision so that being in the right might be accounted to them, and a father of circumcision to those who not from circumcision alone but also from following (literally, walking in) the example (literally, the footsteps) of the faith of our father Abraham which existed in uncircumcision.

* * *

The construction of this entire paragraph is difficult, and for a literary translation it probably should be paraphrased.

Here Lagrange provides a more complete treatment than anyone else. Yet before one attempts the exegesis, it is necessary to discuss the textual problem of Verse 1, and on this, Lietzmann's arguments should carry conviction. Following the B manuscript and Origen, both Moffatt and the Revised Standard Version have omitted the word *found* that appears before *Abraham* in the Aleph and D manuscripts and after *our* in several others. The Aleph and D reading is to be accepted here because it is much more likely to have given rise to the alternative texts than they to it or to one another. So for this verse the King James Version is to be preferred to the Revised Standard and other modern translations. In its position in Aleph and D, however, this perfect tense infinitive *to have found* is difficult to understand. It would be much easier to ask with the B manuscript, "What shall we say about our father Abraham?" or with the Byzantine texts, "What shall we say that Abraham our father has found in physical terms?" The real question must be understood as, "What shall we say that Abraham our physical ancestor has discovered in relation to God?" This question might be asked by a Jew or a Jewish Christian, but scarcely by a Gentile. To such a questioner Paul's reply is a Midrash or commentary upon his previous explanation of the status of Jew and Gentile within the Church. From the story of the patriarch, who seems to have been thought of in Israel as the prime example of a man who was justified before God, Paul proposes to show that even Abraham's acquittal and receiving of God's promises depended upon his faith and not upon what he did. Verse 2 states the logical consequence of the orthodox Jewish position. If Abraham had obtained his standing as *righteous* in consequence of his own accomplishment, he might have something in which to take pride, but it would be a pride in man's achievement and would have no particular connection with God. In contrast to this, the Scripture declares that Abraham *trusted* God and that this was accounted to him as *being in the right in relation to God.*

This citation of Scripture is the Septuagint of Genesis 15:6. Much of the debate to which this verse has given rise turns upon the possible Latin translations of the Greek word ELOGISTHE—*reputatum, imputatum,* and *deputatum.* Of these, the first two imply a legal fiction, the thought that faith was estimated in God's sight as equivalent to an actual righteousness that Abraham in fact did not possess. But there is no need to give such a sense either to the Greek verb or to the Hebrew it translates. Indeed, we must not assume that Paul is discussing *actual righteousness* at all. Because Abraham demonstrated trust in God, God accepted this attitude as a satisfactory response. Thereafter Abraham had a right relationship with God, and this did not depend in any way on what he had done but simply upon the commitment he had made in faith. If the Jews wished to say so, Abraham had performed righteous acts even before this time, but these had not secured for him a right relationship with God, for such a relationship is possible only as the gift of God Himself. By faith Abraham had become able to receive God's gift, and his works (however good they might have been) had nothing whatever to do with this. Thus if we are to express this in Latin we should use the participle *deputatum.* Abraham was not *made righteous* at this point, either in fact or in fiction. Yet although he did not necessarily possess any objective righteousness, faith had brought him to a right attitude, and this was the beginning for him as an individual of that salvation which God offers only as a gift. So Abraham is the positive illustration of the process of salvation; the negative illustration that follows may be easier to understand. The sinner whose performance has been discreditable, who has no actual righteousness in which to boast, can come into a right relationship with God. He can do this if he is willing by faith to accept forgiveness. Without faith on the sinner's part even God cannot forgive, for the sinner who does not respond in faith will refuse the gift of pardon, and probably will refuse to acknowledge any need to be forgiven.

Verses 4–5 then lay a groundwork for the further assertion that Abraham is accounted to be in the right in relation to God by means of faith, and this without regard to works or performance, by showing the difference between what we may obtain by effort and what we may obtain by trust. In Verse 6 Paul employs the rabbinic principle that one text of Scripture may be used to explain another. So he quotes Psalm 32:1–2 in the Septuagint. David is spoken of here not as an individual but as the psalmist who speaks for God. The actual citation of these verses then completes the negative explanation of Paul's meaning. Forgiven sinners, those whose faults are not to be punished by God because they have come to stand through *faith* in a right relationship to Him, are truly blessed. This may be compared with the statement Jesus is supposed to have made to the Pharisees, that publicans and harlots were entering the Kingdom of God before them. This was true because the publicans and harlots were more ready to accept forgiveness; they had no actual righteousness, but their knowledge that they had none predisposed them to trust in God rather than in themselves.

With verses 9–12 Paul returns to the value of circumcision. In Jewish belief circumcision was a prerequisite for all the rest of the Torah, but Paul asserts that it had had nothing whatever to do with Abraham's attaining a right relationship to God. Indeed, in the rabbinic explanation of history some twenty-nine years had intervened between Abraham's acceptance of God's promise in Genesis 15 and the occasion of his circumcision in Genesis 17. Therefore Abraham was *justified* (he fell heir to the promise) through *faith* without reference to circumcision or Torah, although Paul does not mean to say that Abraham had been a flagrant sinner before this time. Yet even if he had been a flagrant sinner, and was now penitent and ready to trust in God, Paul would maintain that the right relationship with

God would have been possible. Circumcision he describes as a *seal* or *token* of the right relationship with God that is acquired by *faith.* Later Jewish literature describes circumcision as a *seal,* and it may be that the usage was popular as early as Paul. Christian patristic writers assuredly describe Baptism, their equivalent to circumcision, as a *seal,* and there are those who contend that the same usage appears in Revelation. From this, one might deduce that the Christian form of this idea was even pre-Pauline. But the apostle is not discussing Baptism here. He is saying that Abraham's history placed the patriarch's *justification* before his *circumcision* for a purpose, namely, that he might be the spiritual ancestor of all the faithful, whether circumcised or uncircumcised. Moreover, at least in the logical sense, Abraham is the father of the believing Gentiles even before he can be said to be the father of Israel. His *faith* is the pattern of Gentile *faith.* Indeed, he is the father of Israel only inasmuch as Israelites possess *faith.* Elsewhere Paul declares that physical relationship does not constitute a valid claim to descent from Abraham in a religious sense; the same point is made in the Fourth Gospel. In Barrett's words, "the privilege of descent from Abraham is accorded to Jews only in virtue of their *faith,* because Abraham *believed* and was *justified* before he was circumcised."

* * *

4:13–25 For the promise to Abraham or to his seed that he should be the heir of the world is not by means of Torah but by means of righteousness which comes from faith. For if they were heirs by Torah, faith has been canceled and the promise is abolished. For the Torah accomplishes wrath, and where Torah does not exist neither does transgression. For this reason it depends upon (or, is of) faith, that it may be a gift (or, favor; or, grace), to the end that the promise may be guaranteed (or, confirmed) to every descendant, not to him who is so from the Torah alone but also to him who is so from the faith of Abraham, who is father of us all, just as it is written, "I have appointed thee father of many nations," in relation to Him whom he believed, God who causes the dead to live and calls into existence the things which do not exist; who (pronoun refers to Abraham) trusted in a hope beyond expectation (literally, against hope) that he would be "father of many nations" in accord with what was spoken, "so shall be thy seed." And he was not weak in faith when he recognized that his own body was moribund (literally, already dead), since he was about a hundred years old, and when he recognized (these four words are not in the text but are repeated from above) the deadness of Sarah's womb; in regard to the promise of God, he did not deny (literally, decide against) it by unbelief, but by faith he was given potency, and he gave praise to God and was fully assured that what He promised He is also able to fulfill. Wherefore it was accounted to him for being in the right. It was not written for his sake alone that it was accounted to him, but also for our sakes, to whom it is to be accounted, to those who trust in Him who raised up Jesus our Lord from the dead, who was handed over because of our transgressions and was raised up for the sake of our justification.

* * *

Paul is attempting to prove that his concept of the right relationship with God as depending upon *faith* and not upon performance is the true consequence of the Old Testament and the Jewish religion when these are properly interpreted. But because this is clearly contrary to conventional Judaism ever since the Exile, he is obliged to proceed by careful steps. After establishing that Abraham's righteousness did not depend on circumcision, and hence not in any sense upon Torah, he must now show that the reward for Abraham's righteousness likewise had no relation to Torah. This is comparatively easy, because Genesis expresses that reward in terms of *promise*, and by definition a promise cannot be the same thing as a contract. For verses 13–17 Michel is probably the most helpful writer. A contract is a matter of *law*; if one party fulfills his part, the other must reciprocate. As this works out in Verse 16, if man fails to fulfill Torah God's offer becomes void in legal terms, and is replaced by penalty or *wrath*. This is the response proper to *transgression*, which is the breach of a known positive law. But if there is to be any real salvation, God's relation to man must be understood in terms of a promise that is a *free gift*, something not to be connected with performance but with the response of *God's grace* to *man's faith*. So Paul sets forth a threefold contrast: *promise, faith, grace* over against *law, transgression, wrath*.

In Genesis the actual promise to Abraham had been that he and his descendants should inherit the land of Canaan. Later Jewish speculation had expanded this to the thought that Israel should inherit the world, and from his Christian presuppositions Paul is drawn to this concept. Since the apostle regards God's *promise* as intended for the spiritual rather than the physical descendants of Abraham, including what he hopes will be vast numbers of Gentiles, the world as a whole seems an appropriate heritage. Again this heritage is shown to be dependent on *the righteousness that comes from* (or is related to) *faith.* If the heritage were to depend on Torah, there would be no part left for *faith* to play, and the legal idea of contract would destroy the meaning of *promise.* Actually, what Torah or any legal principle brings to reality is not *promise* but *wrath,* for it imposes upon man a greater responsibility, so that actual misdeeds are by Torah converted into guilty transgressions. So in Paul's argument the principle of *justification by faith* becomes a logical necessity without which human salvation could not be a matter of God's gift or favor but rather of legal contract. Beyond this, the principle is essential if a Gentile mission is to be considered proper; only if the *promise* depends on *faith* instead of on *performance of Torah* will it be possible to include Gentiles within its terms, and only through the spiritual relation of *faith* can Abraham be regarded as the father of many nations in addition to Israel, Ishmael, and Edom.

In Verse 17 Paul declares that the faith of the patriarch Abraham was directed toward "the God who causes the dead to live and calls what does not exist into existence." In this there is more involved than appears on the surface. The *promise* that he should be father of many nations, to a man who by reason of age was sexually impotent, can find no fulfillment in human terms. In Abraham's case capacities already dead must be restored by divine power. A few scholars note that Paul has passed over Abraham's initial doubt, which is recorded in Genesis, but the fact that the patriarch could come to faith at all under the circumstances is against all expectation, and therefore such faith may be considered as putting him in the right. Perhaps the "leap of faith" derives much of its value from the difficulty encountered in taking it. In any case, if God's promise to Abraham is to be fulfilled, a use of God's power analogous to that required for creation itself will be needed, just as a use of God's power analogous to that required for creation is needed to raise Jesus from the dead or to raise those who are united with Jesus. This point also is important in the development of Paul's thought. The primitive Christian conviction, expressed in I Corinthians 10 and in many of the Greek hymns of the patristic age that have been translated into English, is that the spiritual condition of those who have accepted the *revelation* in Jesus does not differ essentially from the spiritual condition of those who accepted God's *revelation* prior to Jesus. The point is soon to be made that those who believe in the Resurrection of Jesus have put their faith in *the God who causes the dead to live*. Here and now Paul is preparing for this declaration.

The phrase of Verse 18, "in hope against hope he put his trust," is less of a problem than at first appears. In English we sometimes use the phrase *against hope*, and by it we mean *contrary to any reasonable human expectation*. Such is the sense of *against hope* here. Despite all evidence to the contrary, Abraham put his trust in a hope that he would be a father of many nations. As was noted above, Paul ignores Genesis 17:17, and says only that Abraham was not weak in faith for consideration of his own or his wife's physical debility. Indeed, *faith* is shown as giving the strength to fulfill what the *promise* offers. By faith Abraham is made strong, and because he is made strong he gives praise to God who made him so. The statement of Verse 21 that what God promises He is able to perform is general in its reference; it may be compared with the other Pauline assertion from the apostle's own life, "my grace is sufficient for thee"; other examples of the same thought can be found in the New Testament. In Verse 22 it is the conviction of this truth concerning God, demonstrated by the patriarch's self-commitment to it, that is accounted as *justifying faith*, as the reality of being in the right.

Verses 23–25 form an appendix, as far as the story of Abraham himself is concerned, but for Paul's argument, and for Christians generally, they are the culmination of the whole. The Old Testament has been written for the sake of the followers of Jesus rather than for the people of whom it tells. As Abraham put his faith in *the God who causes the dead to live*, so Christians are putting their faith in *the God who raised Jesus from the dead*. These two statements are equivalent; indeed, all the faith of the saints of the New Covenant is equivalent to that of the saints of the Old. As the *faith* of Abraham was accounted to him for *being in the right*, so the *faith* of the Christians will be accounted to them for *being in the right*. There is no fundamental difference; both are equally *justified*. But there is a difference in the dispensation of God's grace. Abraham was put in the right apart from any mention of specific transgressions. With us it is not so, and cannot be so. Our transgressions must be dealt with by God, and they are dealt with in the saving act of God in Christ. Because of our transgressions it was necessary that Christ should be delivered up to death, that He should endure the *wrath* that transgressions brought into being. Because He overcame *death* (the ultimate penalty the *wrath* could inflict), we are set free from the *wrath*, from the power of *sin*, from *death* itself. Jesus was raised up for our *justification*. While DIKAIOSUNE can be translated in a variety of ways, DIKAIOSIS in Paul must always be taken simply as *justification*. In this saving act of God in Christ we find the heart of Paul's Gospel.

CHAPTER 5

Justification and Original Sin

5:1–11 So since we were put in the right from faith, let us accept peace in relation to God through the agency of our Lord Jesus Christ, through whom we have also obtained the access to this position of favor (literally, this grace) in which we have taken our stand, and let us make our boast in a hope of the glory of God. And not only this, but let us also make our boast in our (or, the) afflictions, since we know that affliction effects (or, gives rise to) perseverance, and perseverance character (or, proof), and character hope. Now hope does not put one to shame, because the love of God has been poured out in our hearts by means of the Holy Spirit which was given to us. Now if Christ, while we were still without strength, at a favorable time died on behalf of impieties (or, impious persons), for a person will scarcely die on behalf of a righteous man, although (literally, for) on behalf of a good man (or, a good cause) a person perhaps would dare to die; but God establishes His own love toward us because while we were still sinners Christ died on our behalf. So how much more, now that we were put in the right by His Blood (alternatively, His Death) shall we be saved from the wrath through His agency! For if, from being enemies, we were reconciled to

God by means of the Death of His Son, how much more now that we are reconciled shall we be saved by His life (one must understand the exalted Life)! Not only so, but we also make our boast in God through our Lord Jesus Christ, through whom we now received the reconciliation.

* * *

As in the previous uses of the same verb, the aorist passive participle refers to status rather than to quality. Christians are those who formerly were sinners, and through the saving act of God in Christ they were *put in the right in relation to God*. One must not extend this idea to suggest that Christians now are formally virtuous; Paul says only that we were put in the right as a result of our faith. Whether the verb *have* should be read as indicative or subjunctive is a major textual problem. All the good manuscripts with the exception of G originally read the present subjunctive. Correctors of B and Aleph have adopted the present indicative. Representative scholars attempt to solve the problem as follows. Barrett contends that the subjunctive must be rejected because the context is not hortatory. Moffatt accepts the subjunctive and translates it *let us enjoy peace*; Dodd agrees with this and holds that no one has peace with God in an absolute sense. Bardenhewer considers that the context is hortatory and that the subjunctive is appropriate. Lietzmann and Michel prefer the indicative on the ground that the results of *justification*, like the initial reality itself, are not in Paul's thought the fruits of human striving. Sanday and Headlam, followed by Lagrange, suggest that simple exhortation would be better expressed by an aorist than by a present subjunctive and that the meaning of the more strongly supported reading is *let us accept the reconciliation* (or peace with God) which is offered to us. In essence this is the sense of Moffatt's translation as well. Since the consensus of the better manuscripts offers an objective basis of judgment, while decision regarding what conforms to Paul's thought is inevitably subjective, the Sanday and Headlam conclusion has been accepted here, but in view of the diversity of competent opinions one cannot insist upon it. *Peace*, therefore, can be defined as *reconciliation*, a relationship between God and the believer that is brought into being by Jesus Christ.

Another textual issue appears in Verse 2, where the manuscripts

B and D and W agree in omitting the dative *by faith.* Here the scholars appear to be almost unanimous in support of the omission, and even if the words were included they would add nothing that Paul has not already made clear. Through Christ we have obtained an access. The imagery is that of temple worship, and might be derived either from Jewish or from Gentile sources. Paul might be thinking either of access to *God,* whose Name he would be inclined by his Jewish training to avoid, or to the *favor* understood as a status in which the Christians are placed by Christ. The following verb, which is properly translated *we have taken our stand,* would support the thought of a status which the Christians had obtained. The latter part of Verse 2 is certainly an appeal to the believers to take pride in their hope of the *glory* or of the *approbation* of God. Both these ideas could have a place in Paul's teaching. *Glory* would look to the restoration of man's proper spiritual state, and so would set forth the meaning of redemption. *Approbation* would be concerned with relationship to God. In view of Paul's convictions about eschatology, the thought of a recovery of *glory* may seem to be the more probable.

Verse 3 then turns from the future hope to the conditions of the present. Not only do Christians have cause for pride in the future glory they may expect, but equally in the present trial which they must endure. In Colossians it will be made clear that Paul thinks of uniting his own sufferings with those of Christ. While the thought is less clearly enunciated here, it is evident that he regards such union with the sufferings of Christ as a possibility for all Christians. The reason for Paul's failure to stress this idea here is found in the shift of his interest to a different thought, to the salutary effect of trial, well endured, upon *character.* Trial well endured creates perseverance or "patient endurance," while such perseverance is the foundation of reliability. Reliability may be more satisfactory than the more inclusive word *character.* Reliability or character then leads to assurance. It may be debated whether the assurance rests in God alone or whether the endurance of trial contributes to it; the latter seems to be in Paul's mind here, although this must not be pressed as a point of theology. In addition, the trials are eschatological, and so they contribute to the Christian's assurance concerning the future.

The love mentioned in Verse 5 certainly proceeds from God to us, and there is no consideration here for love moving from man to God despite the interpretation of Augustine. The imparting of God's love is an aspect of that *new life* that Christ has already inaugurated, for it is received and is made known to us by the gift of God's Spirit. Only those who have so responded to God by *faith* that they have received the Spirit are able to know how completely God loves them. Lacking this eschatological gift, man can only attempt the self-assertion of legal religion or yield to the despair that accepts damnation. The Christian can be aware of God's love even as he recognizes his own unworthiness. Verses 6–8 expand upon the theme of God's love. This is an example of Paul's method of argument on the subject.

If Christ gave His life for us *while we were weak* (or, undeserving), and did so in accord with the divine plan and at the time God had appointed, now that our relationship with God has been converted into one of reconciliation, Verse 9 makes it clear that we have every reason to expect that we shall be delivered from the operation of the *wrath*. Verse 7 must be regarded as an aside. God's love goes beyond all human analogy. Few will give their lives even for the deserving, but Paul will not make his statement too strong, for some people have been known to do so. There is no merit in trying to distinguish between the *righteous* and the *good* here, although it has been suggested that *good* here may be neuter and that the apostle is thinking of a good cause or of the public good rather than of a good man. In fact, people have been known to sacrifice themselves both for causes they valued and for persons. The point is the contrast between human hesitation in sacrificing self for that which one values and the attitude of God in making His self-offering in Christ for that which He knew to be utterly unworthy. Verse 8 then sets forth the prime demonstration of God's love, something to be received with amazement, the offering of Christ for the undeserving. In comparison with this, nothing more that God can do for us will have great significance. The mention of *Blood* in Verse 9 is to be taken merely as a synonym for Christ's *Death on the Cross*. Verse 10 is then a repetition of the substance of verses 6–9, with the emphasis placed upon our changed relationship to God, which can now be defined as *reconciliation*. The *life* by which we shall be saved is the *exalted Life* of Christ rather than His earthly ministry. Thus it means His victory over the power of death, and it includes all the results of that victory, especially the imparting of the life of Christ to the believer. The fact of reconciliation, so far beyond any human understanding, is the abiding reason for the Christian's pride or confidence in God, and it comes through Christ. All through this section Christ is clearly represented as standing with God rather than with man. No one can think of this portion of Scripture as justifying the belief that Paul regards Christ as less than fully divine.

* * *

5:12–21 Wherefore, just as through one man's agency sin entered into the world, and through the agency of sin death, and so death came upon all men because all sinned: for until the advent of Torah sin was in the world, but sin is not taken into account in the absence of law (alternatively, where there is no law): but death exercised power from Adam until Moses, and even upon those who did not sin in the likeness of Adam's transgression, who is a type (or, pattern) of Him who was to come. But the free gift was in no way like the transgression. For if by the transgression of the one the many died, much more did the favor of God and the gift by favor which is from the one man Jesus Christ prevail (or, abound) for the many. And the gift has no likeness to that which was effected by the one man's having sinned. For while the judgment from the one was for condemnation, the free gift resulting from many transgressions was for acquittal. For if by the transgression of the one death exercised power by means of the one, much more shall those who receive the abundance of the favor and of the gift which belongs to being in the right reign in life through the agency of the one Jesus Christ. So whereas by means of a single offense (alternatively, one man's offense) the result for all men was for condemnation, so also through a single act of righteousness (alternatively, one man's act of righteousness) the result for all men was for justification which belongs to life (alternatively, for a life of justification). For just as by means of the disobedience of the one man the many were put in the position of sinners, so also by means of the obedience of the one the many shall be put in the position of being righteous. Then Torah came in in addition in order that the transgression might increase; but where sin (as a cosmic power) increased, the favor (or, grace) overwhelmed it (or, abounded the more), in order that just as sin (as a cosmic power) reigned by death (also as a cosmic power), so also favor (or, grace) might reign by means of righteousness (understood as God's doing right) with the goal of (or, for) eternal life through Jesus Christ our Lord.

* * *

Before attempting the exegesis of these ten verses, which in itself is no light task, one must first give consideration to the meaning of *original sin*, for a great deal of error has arisen in regard to this concept, and some of that error has found its way into classical formulations of theology. Prior to Paul, Judaism had no concept of *original sin* as such. In the canonical Scriptures, Job 14:4 does no more than declare that no one can derive the pure from the impure; any connection between this and physical inheritance is simply the result of bad Latin translation. Psalm 51:5 comes somewhat closer to the idea, but the fact is that the psalmist is thinking of himself as a part of a sinful generation and is discussing his solidarity with the rest of the Nation in sin rather than any tainted physical heritage. Turning to Ecclesiasticus and the Wisdom of Solomon, one comes no closer to the thought of *original sin*, and indeed the latter book is emphatic in maintaining individual responsibility for all wrongdoing. While Philo declares that all are sinners without exception, he does not go so far as to ascribe this condition to heredity. Such Pseudepigrapha as Enoch, Jubilees, and Psalms of Solomon give no hint of such a doctrine. Only those apocalypses written after the destruction of Jerusalem, such as IV Esdras, make any attempt to relate the sin of Adam to that of mankind generally, and even there the discussion turns only on the point that Adam's free will showed a propensity to evil as well as to good, and that this evil propensity was followed; this is also said, of course, of Adam's descendants.

Since Paul could not have derived a doctrine of *original sin*, as understood by Augustine and the later Latin Fathers and the Continental Reformers, from any form of Judaism before his own time, the question naturally arises as to whether he held it himself. In truth he did not. Like other Jews of his time, he recognized a universal human inclination to evil, which was balanced but not always rendered ineffective by a corresponding human inclination to good. Adam, in Paul's teaching as in that of other Jews, had possessed this inclination even before the "Fall," and when he sinned he had followed his evil impulse for the first time. So this "Fall" did not confer a propensity to sin upon Adam's heirs such as they would not have had if Adam had avoided sin. The evil inclination is inseparable from a *will* that is truly *free*, and a *free* will is a necessary component of human nature.

Yet the sin of Adam did have results. Because of it *the sin* (conceived as a personal demonic power) was able to find entrance into a world that God had created *very good.* What formerly had been a *possibility* because man had a *free will* now became an *actuality.* While Adam had given an entrance to "Demon Sin," he was henceforth quite unable to exclude this cosmic power from the universe in which he lived. Moreover, Adam's sin was the transgression of a specific command to which a defined penalty had been attached. Adam had defied God and had known that he was doing so. His act had been a form of self-assertion, of a desire to be God. He had been told that if he should eat from this tree he would die. In Jewish thought, if he had not eaten the fruit of this tree he would have possessed immortality. So death is the punishment for sin, and the instrument by which *sin* (the cosmic power) demonstrates its control over man. In Paul's mind *death* also seems to be a personal demon. All men die, not because of Adam in particular but because all men sin. If Adam had preserved his innocence and his heirs had sinned, death would have come upon them while he would have retained his immortality. Such is the real meaning of what Paul has to say.

Thus if one is to discuss *original sin* in the Augustinian sense, in Paul's epistles there is no such thing. The apostle holds to the standard Jewish conviction that each man is responsible for his own sin. Left to themselves, people are "no damn good," and every human being in all history has proved it in his own case. Adam set the example of willful self-assertion, but he did so only because he was the first man who had the opportunity to do so. His descendants were not obliged to follow his example. Aided by the grace of God, as their Creator had intended them to be, people could be good. But since people had been given *free will* it was a simple matter of observation that none of them had accepted the guidance of grace with constancy. Each for himself, by turning from grace to sin or self-assertion, has defaced the image of God in himself. So it may be said that Adam defaced the image of God in himself and that each of his descendants has done likewise. But Adam's "Fall" was not responsible for the manifestation of self-will on the part of his heirs. We all have fallen short of, or deprived ourselves of that which God intended for us, and each of us is responsible in his own case. This position would certainly seem Pelagian to Augustine, but in reality it is not so. Left to himself, every human being will go to the devil. God did not create him in such a way that this is inevitable, but God did give the freedom that would make it possible. Aided by grace, man could avoid the natural result of his own self-will, but no man has done so. The distinction between this and Pelagianism is the fact that Pelagius did not recognize that people are "no damn good"; he supposed that man could attain to righteousness by himself. Paul recognized, as Augustine perceived, that if people attain to righteousness it will not be by their own efforts, but by the grace of God. If man is put in the right, it is God who effects the change in his condition, and it is never the result of human deserving. By ourselves we cannot hope for success. Yet it is not a matter of heredity or of environment that renders human beings powerless. It was never truly within our power to be righteous, and self-will has inhibited us from making use of that power from God by which we might be righteous. In this we ought not to speak of *original sin* as sin at all. Man in himself is not essentially depraved. But it would not have been possible for God to accomplish His purpose in creation if He had caused men to be other than they are. Had man not possessed the capacity for sin, not even by God's grace could he have been made righteous or declared righteous, because all his actions would have been determined for him and so they would have been morally indifferent. Admittedly this position has been condemned by eminent authority in various Christian traditions, and theological convention is shaken by it, but it does seem to set forth Paul's actual teaching when it is viewed against the background of Judaism.

There is another point to be taken into account, although it is less significant than *original sin*. This is the position held by Adam in Paul's argument. Dodd's statement that Paul probably thought of Adam as a *type* rather than as a figure of history is extreme. Paul certainly believed in Adam as the actual father of all humanity, just as the rabbinic writers did. Dodd's emphasis, however, is correct. Whatever Paul's convictions about history, his discussion of Adam here is *typological*. Adam is thought of as the *representative man* rather than as the progenitor of the human race. If we were to interpret this text as Augustine does, by analogy with Hebrews 7:10 where Levi paid tithe to Melchizedek in the person of his ancestor Abraham, if we were to say that we sinned in the person of our ancestor Adam, it would be necessary to stress the *historical* rather than the *representative* character of Adam. But here it is evident that Adam is being thought of in his character as man's *representative.* If this were not so, Verse 15, which contrasts Christ as the *representative* to restore humanity with Adam who stands for man's loss, would lose all its force. Christ in His incarnate ministry cannot be the *father* of humanity, but He can be its *representative,* and in that character He may be contrasted with Adam. In addition, Paul believes in human solidarity. In his teaching, the divisions of "Jew and Greek" have no ultimate validity. *In Christ* they are transcended. Adam represents a stage of human development prior to these infringements of solidarity, while Christ represents a stage whereby they are overcome.

Yet human solidarity is not inevitably good. Humanity can find some solidarity in the fact that all have sinned, and for Paul sin on man's part is essentially revolt against God. In this, likewise, Adam is the *representative man.* His sin is a revolt against God's purpose for him, as our sins are a revolt against God's purpose for us. The reality of Adam's sin consists in his declaration of independence of God, his grasping at the temptation to become as God. We also try to declare our independence of God. Again, Adam is our representative in the results he experiences because of his revolt. Because he had sinned and knew that he had sinned, he could only think of God as angered by his action. After his sin, when he heard the Lord in the Garden he hid himself, although formerly he had not been afraid to meet with God. In the same way, as a result of our sin we cannot but think of God as angry with us. Certainly it is common enough today to find people who shrink from contact with God.

Finally, Adam is our representative in the fact that he has defaced the image of God that was implanted in him. He has defaced it by his sin, and we have done the same by our sin. Yet it is not because Adam was a sinner that his progeny are compelled to sin. No man can be held to account for what heredity has given him, and Paul had no thought of denying human responsibility for sin. A belief in *original sin* as anything like total depravity was no part of the apostle's conviction. He was convinced that the subjective factors that had led Adam to sin were present in all men, and that they led all men to sin. In that sense he might be said to have held a doctrine of *original sin.* He felt that *sin,* in Adam and in us, defaces but does not annihilate the divine image that has been implanted in man. But Paul did not go beyond saying that Adam is our *representative* in sin to describe him as the *cause* of sin. As the apostle saw it, through the revolt of man *sin* (conceived as a cosmic demon) found ingress into a world order that had been created by God without sin. When *sin* is said to bring *death*, Paul seems to be thinking of *death* as a manifestation of *sin* rather than as a punishment for it. So in his view *Atonement* means deliverance from *death* no less than from *sin*. This is one of the many points of contact between Paul's doctrine and that which Aulén regards as the classic expression of *Atonement* in Christian belief. Paul holds that *sin* has established its power over the entire human race and that Christ's victory has broken *sin's* dominion.

Probably the most misinterpreted phrase in the New Testament is EPH HO in Verse 12. It was translated into early Latin as masculine, *in quo* or *in eo*, which would mean *in whom*. Properly speaking, it ought not to mean this. The Greek preposition EN would be needed instead of EPI in order to say *in whom*, and one cannot comprehend why Origen should have adopted the sense of the Latin mistranslation, although he did not go on from this to establish the Latin theory of the *Atonement*. The proper Greek meaning of the phrase is *because*, and in many other New Testament texts this meaning is obvious, as in Philippians 3:12. So we must say that death passed to all men *because all sinned* (or rebelled against God). As the Greek exegetes have maintained, all sinned in their own persons and on their own initiative. Paul's purpose here is to assert the unity of the human race in sin, together with the responsibility of each individual for sin. Difficulty in interpretation arises because Paul in Verse 12 has emphasized the inevitability of sin at the expense of responsibility for it. Apart from Paul there is no New Testament writer who suggests any connection between our sin and that of Adam, and in this text Paul is thinking of death rather than of sin as the heritage bequeathed by Adam. Furthermore, this is the only Pauline text that hints at a doctrine of *original sin*. Augustine's interpretation of Romans 5:12 is classic in the sense that it removes Paul's own inconsistencies, but at the same time it is a false representation of Paul's intention. Six conclusions may be set forth. First, Paul is not trying to formulate a systematic theory. Second, he is discussing Adam as a *type* rather than as a figure of history. Third, in his treatment he is carried away by his own enthusiasm. Fourth, he is thinking of sin as universal human revolt and not as tainted heritage from Adam. Fifth, he is no less insistent than the rabbinic teachers on the responsibility of each individual for his own sin. Sixth, he thinks of the Atonement as a deliverance from evil cosmic powers as much as being a deliverance from our own evil nature. For these reasons it is evident that the ransom theories of Atonement are closer to Paul's teaching than is the Latin theory of *original sin.*

After these separate notes, the remaining exegesis is relatively simple. The words with which Verse 12 opens, *for this reason,* must refer directly to something that has gone before, and most scholars are inclined to limit its reference to the statements of 5:1–11. *Sin* and *death* are cosmic powers here. The one man, of course, is Adam. Everything else in this verse has already been discussed. In Verse 13 *sin,* written without the article in distinction from Verse 12, is not a cosmic demon but merely an objective fact. Men did wrong in the period between Adam and Moses: they rebelled against God; but after the Tree of Knowledge had been rendered inaccessible there was no specific commandment to be disobeyed until the Torah was given to Moses at Mount Sinai. So the *sin* committed brought its due result in physical death and the damaging of the sinner's character, but it could not be accounted as willful spiritual guilt. So in Verse 14 *death,* again written with the article as in Verse 12 and so considered as a cosmic power, held sway over men from Adam until Moses, even though it had not been possible for them to sin in precisely the same way in which Adam had sinned, as there had been no specific commandment for them to defy. The last clause of this verse introduces the comparison between Adam and Christ as the respective representatives of fallen and of redeemed humanity, saying that Adam is a *type* of Him who was to come.

Verses 15–19 then develop the contrast. The *representative transgression* that was Adam's defiance of the one commandment God had given him is shown to have less effect than the *representative act of grace* (or the free gift) in Christ. *The many* means all mankind, both in the second and again in the last clause of the verse. Physical, not spiritual, death came to all men as a consequence of the *transgression* of the one man Adam whose rebellion against God had made the cosmic powers of *sin* and *death* actual realities in God's creation. But this is more than balanced by the *act of grace* in the one man Jesus Christ. Because of the intensity of his concern to show that this *act of grace* is a *free gift,* Paul piles up words here, making the sentence difficult to translate. Moreover, he is less clear than he might be when he says that the *act of grace abounded for the many;* the meaning is simply that Christ has had a greater effect than has Adam. Verse 16 continues this confusing prolixity, saying once more that the *free gift* is not like the effect produced by the one man's having sinned. While the judgment arising from the first act (Adam's transgression) results in condemnation, the *act of grace* arising from many transgressions results in *acquittal;* this latter word is to be preferred to *justification* here. Again one has to guard against Augustinian misunderstanding that has so long prevailed in Western Christendom. Paul is saying that Adam's transgression resulted in condemnation for Adam, not for everyone else. Others secured their own condemnation through their own transgressions. In order to redeem the totality of transgressions, or "the sin of the world," as it is expressed by other New Testament writers, God designed the *act of grace* in Christ. So this act may be said to arise from many transgressions. Its superiority is seen in the fact that where one transgression brings about one death, the one *act of grace* brings about acquittal for many, even for all. If one were to say that Adam's transgression by itself had brought condemnation to all, then it would be precisely equivalent to Christ's *act of grace.*

Verse 17 does go so far as to say that *death* (the cosmic power) exercised its rule by means of the one man Adam and through the instrumentality of his transgression, but at once Paul adds that there is all the more assurance that those who attain the abundance (or greater power) of the *favor* (act of grace) and *gift* (favor and gift are equivalent) which belongs to *righteousness* (here the abstract noun must be understood and it is shown as the source of the favor or gift) shall reign in life through the agency of the one man Jesus Christ. The sentence is too long for clarity, but it can be understood. As a result of Adam's transgression *death* (the cosmic power) exercises rule over men. As a result of Christ's act of grace those who receive its benefits because of their faith shall themselves reign in the life of the *New Age.* The idea that the faithful shall reign in the new world order is a part of the early kerygma which Paul employs elsewhere in his epistles. It is evident that Christ's act is more efficacious than Adam's, for by it the many who are redeemed are raised to an order of life yet higher than that which Adam enjoyed before his "Fall."

Paul's formula for a summary and statement of consequences, ARA OUN, appears in Verse 18. There is some question of whether *one* in this verse is to be taken as a masculine genitive pronoun (one man's trespass—one man's act of righteousness) or whether it is a neuter adjective (a single trespass—a single act of righteousness). After all that has been said above concerning *original sin,* this question loses most of its significance, but the interpretation that has been given expects that the word *one* should be interpreted as neuter. The only valuable manuscript that writes *man* with *one,* and so makes the term clearly masculine, is the original hand of Aleph. A precise translation should show the apostle's meaning. Whereas (ARA HOS) by means of a single trespass there was effected a condemnation (EIS KATAKRIMA) for all men, therefore also (OUN HOUTOS) by means of a single righteous act there was effected a justification of life for all men.

Verse 19 comes far closer than does Verse 12 to expressing a doctrine of *original sin,* for it declares that the many (meaning all men) were put in the position of being sinners by the disobedience of one man and that in the same manner the many (all men) were put in the position of being righteous by means of the obedience of the one man. The main point here is that Paul is drawing an exact parallel between the result of Adam's disobedience and Christ's obedience. Since the latter is the cause of our being put in the right in relation to God, when the parallel is drawn closely it must seem as if the former is the cause of our being sinners. Yet even here the causality of Adam's sin ought not to be understood as absolute. The apostle is not suggesting that we sinned in the person of Adam. Rather Adam has given the cosmic demon *sin* an opportunity *sin* did not have in the creation as God intended it to be. Further, by following Adam's example we have been put in the position of being sinners. We cannot transfer the responsibility for our individual sins to Adam, for with God's help it would have been possible for us to avoid those sins. So we can maintain the position adopted above by saying that we were made sinners when we followed Adam's example that we did not need to follow; and we can defend this statement even though we must admit that we cannot perfectly follow Christ's example and that if we could this would not in itself earn for us the position of righteousness. Difficulty arises from the effort to make the parallel between the disobedience and the obedience a close one, and this weakness Paul himself had clearly avoided in Verse 15. If Verse 19 is taken by itself, or if the rest of the paragraph is read in the light of Verse 19, then the Augustinian interpretation is tenable. But if this verse is read in the light of the rest of the paragraph, as it should be, then we shall be left with a teaching about an inclination to evil that is inseparable from the freedom of human will, rather than with the theory of an inheritance from Adam that must be understood as some sort of actual sin.

In verses 20–21 Paul then attempts to explain what function may be left to Torah in God's scheme of salvation as the apostle has outlined it. Whenever Paul attempts this, his treatment always leaves something to be desired, for after his conversion to Christianity he never seemed able to remember the real purposes and value the Torah had served. Here he restricts the function of Torah to revelation of the reality of *sin,* and even in this he does not express himself very well. Moffatt's translation of Verse 20 is brilliant; it expresses in modern idiom the snide comment that Paul is making. *Law slipped in,* as if it ought not to have been there at all. The Greek need not be given this emphasis; it would be enough to say *Torah came in in addition,* but Moffatt seems to have captured Paul's real thought. Law made formal sin into transgression by providing positive commandments that could be broken only at the price of guilt. Paul seems to be saying that man really would have been better off if Torah had never been given. Yet even in this situation the cosmic demon *sin,* although it can use the commandments of Torah for its own increase, is no match for the favor or grace of God. Where the *sin* increased, the *grace* increased yet more. As *sin* exercised its power by the instrumentality of *death* (the cosmic demon), so God's *favor* or *grace* exercised its power through *putting men in the right in relation to God,* with the goal that they might have eternal life; in this verse the apostle does add the adjective *eternal.* This is accomplished through Jesus Christ our Lord, through the *saving act* of God in

Christ. Perhaps Paul's argument is not completely consistent with itself, but in spite of this it is impressive. This is true however it may be interpreted, but perhaps it is most impressive of all when its emphasis is misrepresented by Augustine, and that fact may account for the popularity of the Augustinian explanation in Western Christendom.

CHAPTER 6

The New Life

6:1–14 Then what are we to say? Should we continue with sin in order that the favor might be increased? God forbid! We who have died to sin, how shall we go on living (or, still live) in it? Or are you unaware that all of us who were baptized into Christ Jesus were baptized into His Death? So we were buried with Him by means of the Baptism into His Death, in order that just as Christ was raised from among the dead by means of the Father's glory, so we also should walk in newness of life. For if we were united (literally, planted together) with Him in the likeness of His Death, so (literally, but) we shall be likewise in that of His Resurrection. For we know this, that our original human nature (literally, old man) was crucified with Him, in order that the body which belongs to sin might be abolished, so that we should no longer be slaves to sin. For in dying one has paid the debt (alternatively, been acquitted of the claims) of sin. But if we died together with Christ, we believe that we shall also live together with Him, because we know that Christ who was raised up from among the dead shall never die again, that death no longer has power over Him. For when He died, He died to sin once for all; now that He is living, He is living for God. So you also are to consider yourselves actually to be dead to sin, but in Christ Jesus to be alive to God. Therefore sin is not to exercise dominion in your mortal body with the object that you should obey its promptings, and do not present your members (or, faculties) to sin as weapons (or, tools) of immorality (or, unrighteousness), but present yourselves unto God as though made alive from the dead, and your members (or, faculties) unto God as weapons (or, tools) of righteousness, for sin shall not have authority over you; for you are not subjected to law but subjected to grace (or, favor).

* * *

Verses 12–14 of Chapter 6 are an exhortation which Lagrange connects with 15–23, but the vast majority of scholars prefer to join it with 1–11. There is a difference of opinion regarding how closely this section ought to be related to Chapter 5. Since this epistle is devoted to the theme of *justification*, one may say that Paul is developing his argument here but that there is no direct connection between this development and the statements of the previous chapter. While Dodd and Lagrange are the best guides for Chapter 5, here no one can be compared with Lietzmann, and his treatment is the basis for what follows.

The opening phrase of the chapter, *What are we to say?* naturally refers to the argument previously developed. What Paul has said about the manner in which *grace* prevails over *sin*, despite its merits, can be misunderstood. The most dangerous misunderstanding is that of *antinomianism*, the attitude that if sin demonstrates God's grace we should have more sin to demonstrate it more fully. There are other Pauline texts that refer to this *reductio ad absurdum* to which some people had carried the apostle's principles. Here, as in 3:3–8, Paul closes the discussion with the authoritative *God forbid!* While sin has demonstrated God's grace, man must not tempt God. But Paul does not leave the argument there. Throughout the next three chapters he deals with it from various points of view.

The first approach is an interpretation of Baptism as a death to sin and rebirth to righteousness. In Greek secular usage the verb here used for *baptize* means *to immerse*. When used of a religious rite it would surely imply that the candidate was immersed, and this would strengthen the Pauline symbolism. Going under the water delivers the *flesh* to death, and rising from it signifies union with Christ's Resurrection. Both the *death* and the *resurrection* of Baptism are truly *sacramental*. The rite is not a bare symbol, for it effects that which it represents. This explanation of Baptism is, in essence, the same as that given in I Corinthians 10:1–12, although here Paul is not obliged to correct a magical belief about the Sacrament. From I Corinthians 15:29 it is evident that such magical ideas were adopted by some Christians, and the appeal of such concepts has led to a suspicion of all sacramentalism that persists in some quarters even today. Paul defines the sacramental reality of Baptism as *freedom from the power of sin*. Here, as in Romans 8:11 and 12:2, the Christian rises from Baptism no longer to live in the *flesh* but in the *Spirit*. Sin should no longer have its natural power over the body of the Christian. The same thought may be discerned elsewhere in Romans, 7:4–6, 8:2 and 9–14 and 26, also in I Corinthians 6:19, II Corinthians 5:5–9 and 17, Galatians 5:24–26, 6:15.

In Verse 4, it is generally agreed that *the glory of the Father* by means of which Christ was raised is equivalent to God's power, and power is the instrument of Christ's Resurrection in other texts. There is a parallel to this in Colossians 2:11. The mention of the glory of the Father is absent from the Old Latin texts. Many scholars see Verse 5 as a reference to the exaltation of the believer that is expected in the end of the world. We have been planted in the likeness of Christ's Death; we shall enter into that of His Resurrection. This interpretation depends upon the absence of the word *likeness* with Resurrection, and upon the fact that the future tense would not strictly be needed to show that union with the Resurrection can be attained only after union with the Death, for the union with the Death is referred to in the present tense. Yet this stress upon the niceties of grammar is exaggerated. It would be sufficient to say that the future is used because Baptism has not yet taken place for some of those who are to be united with the Resurrection. Moreover, there seems to be no way of translating the genitive of *Resurrection* otherwise than as the source of *likeness*, and the latter word must be understood. With many writers the emphasis on eschatology here may be no more than an effort to escape the sacramental implications of the paragraph. The G manuscript writes *together with* instead of *but;* this is probably an error in which the two *lambdas* in the middle of the word were mistaken for a single *mu*.

Bultmann holds that there is a sharp break in personality between the *old man* and the *new*. Lietzmann disagrees. Certainly the *new man* lives in a new situation that is created by his possession of the Holy Spirit. He now has the power from God to perform God's will or Christ's law, as in Romans 12:2, Galatians 6:2, or I Corinthians 9:21. Yet the new man is still the redeemed sinner, and he cannot alter the facts of the past. As all Christians know, *sin* results in *death*. Paul is saying that the *life* mediated by the Spirit should result in *freedom from sin*, even in *inability to sin*. Of course, sinlessness is not found among Christians. In Romans 8:11–13 Paul speaks of it as something for the future; in this chapter and in I Corinthians 6:20 it seems to be an imperative for the present; in II Corinthians 5:20 it is a matter for exhortation. In Philippians 3:12 he does not even make the claim to sinlessness for himself, but is content to say that he is striving for it. Yet he does affirm that the Christian's life is contrary to sin, for the body of *flesh* that was subject to the cosmic demon *sin* has been buried in Baptism. The baptized person is now a member of the redeemed *Body of Christ*. Of course, a power of *sin* persists, not heritage from Adam but the *inclination to evil* that is inseparable from human free will, that which Latin theologians call concupiscence. This existing power of sin creates an antinomy between the Pauline demand for sinlessness and the observed facts of Christian life. As Lietzmann puts it, *sub specie divina* the sacramental theory applies, but *sub specie humana* the sacramental theory is only in the process of being realized. Dialectical theology would make the baptismal teaching with its accompanying antinomy rational, but it does not achieve self-consistency in doing so. Paul is attempting to improve upon a primitive Christian explanation of the fact of Christian experience. No one can account for the concept of a death with Christ in Baptism solely from Jewish lustrations for purification such as the baptism of proselytes. Points of comparison must be sought rather in the Mystery Cults, and there were so many of these that one cannot deal with them in detail. A definitive study of such matters may be found in *Psyche* by Erwin Rhode. Here it is enough to say that the Mystery concepts appealed to those Christians who knew them as satisfactory descriptions of their experience *in Christ*. Early Gentile Christians employed Hellenistic terminology to explain the meaning of Baptism, and Paul simply brought the Gentile Christian theory (based as it was upon mythology) to clearer expression. So Verse 4 asserts that death or burial with Christ in Baptism is a necessary prelude to being raised with Christ to newness of life.

The *body of sin* in Verse 6 is a phrase also found in Wisdom of Solomon 1:4. This does not mean that the body is essentially evil, but only that it is a necessary instrument for many types of sin, and that it is more susceptible to sin in general than is the human spirit. When one is crucified with Christ in Baptism, this susceptibility of the body to sin is destroyed and newness of life becomes possible. Naturally the figure of being crucified is metaphorical, not literal. Verse 7 is open to misunderstanding because of Paul's use of the phrase *has been acquitted from what belongs to sin.* In this instance the verb cannot mean to *justify* in the usual Pauline sense; it must stand for *set free from sin.* The same usage appears in Acts 13:38–39, in Ecclesiasticus 26:29, and in some of the Hermetic writings. Here one cannot be sure whether Paul is thinking of *sin* as a cosmic demon, but this is at least a possibility. The formula *with Christ* in Verse 8, and in Colossians 2:20, properly speaking is mystical; it describes the union with Christ effected by faith. In this context it is set in terms of baptismal practice, and so in a secondary sense it may also be described as sacramental. Generally the phrase has an eschatological reference when it is used by Paul, but here the apostle is discussing present experience rather than future hope. In Verse 9 *death* is clearly a cosmic power, even though it is written without the article. The primitive Christian understanding of the Resurrection obviously went beyond any observed facts, even if these are held to include every Resurrection appearance and every account of the empty tomb. At His Resurrection Christ was *exalted* to a heavenly life. His Incarnation inevitably had meant subjection to *death,* but *death's* claim could be legitimate only where *sin* had established dominion. Since *sin* had failed to do so in the Person of Christ, both cosmic demons had exceeded their rights and by exceeding them had forfeited them. This is clear in verses 10–11, where *sin* and *God* are set in antithesis. As Christ's Death has ended the claim of *sin* upon Himself, so the Christian's *union with Christ* ends the claim of *sin* upon him. In Verse 11 the infinitive *to be* is found in various positions in differing manuscripts, and is absent from A, D and G; since its presence adds nothing to the meaning of the verse, and is so poorly attested it should be eliminated.

Verses 12–14 are a brief ethical exhortation to put into practice the spiritual power outlined in verses 1–11. In Verse 12 AUTOU is neuter; the desires to be resisted are those of the body itself rather than the desires which belong to *sin* itself, because for *sin* a feminine pronoun would have to be used. This is in line with Paul's thought that *sin* exercises its power chiefly over the body of man, a thought which is also found in rabbinic teaching. Most scholars hold that HOPLA in Verse 13 is to be taken in its primary sense as *weapons* rather than as *implements,* and while this is not absolutely necessary, the thought of a Christian warfare is certainly congenial to Paul. Because of the life Christians possess by the indwelling of the Holy Spirit, they should not be taking their stand on the side of *sin,* but should take a stand or present themselves once for all on the side of God. Their members or faculties should be weapons to be used by *righteousness,* not by *immorality.* The argument of Verse 14 is strictly Pauline. Where law or positive command no longer applies there is no more *sin.* Barrett expounds further that *sin's* strength resides in law as "the upward striving of human religion and morality, whereas Christians are now under grace which is humble waiting upon God. Justification by faith, then, is living under grace a life beyond simple morality. The paradox of Christian life, Christian Sacraments, Christian eschatology is that men are at once *justified and sinners,* righteous in Christ by a mystical union but sinful in themselves by their human solidarity with Adam. So those who claim to discern a tension between justification by faith and Baptism as an obligatory Sacrament are in error. Justification and Baptism both anticipate the eschatological life in which sin is impossible; they both express the same relation with God." But, as Barrett says, "when faith is regarded as a *work* or Baptism as a rite effective without reference to its setting, perversion of the Christian life is inevitable."

* * *

6:15–23 What then? Should we sin because we are not subject to law but subject to grace? God forbid! Do you not know that to whom you offer yourselves as slaves in service (or, obedience) you are slaves to him whom you serve (or, obey), whether to sin which ends in death or to obedience which ends in being in the right? But thanks be to God that you who were formerly slaves of sin became obedient from your hearts to that pattern of teaching which you were given, and being set free from sin you were enslaved to righteousness. I speak in human terms because of the weakness of your flesh. For just as you offered your members (or, faculties) as slaves to uncleanness and to extreme lawlessness (literally, to lawlessness unto lawlessness) so now you are to offer your members (or, faculties) as slaves to righteousness (or, being in the right) for sanctification. For when you were slaves to sin you were free in regard to righteousness. So what fruit did you then obtain (or, have)? It was in things of which you are now ashamed. For the end of those things is death. But now you are set free from sin and enslaved to God, and you have your fruit for sanctification, and the end is life eternal. For the wages of sin is death, but the free gift of God is life eternal in Christ Jesus our Lord.

* * *

The opening question here is parallel to that in Verse 1, but is less formal. Paul is not calling upon his readers to review his argument in detail; he is merely discussing possible consequences of his teaching. The misunderstanding of antinomianism that was stated in Verse 1 is now set forth in another way, in pagan rather than in Jewish terms. Since we have passed from the realm of law to that of grace, are we not in the position of initiates in the Mystery Cults who consider their salvation assured by a sort of sacramental union with the god completely apart from their personal conduct? To this, as to other suggestions of the same sort, Paul replies with the usual *God forbid!* Verse 16 seems to deny the possibility of human independence. Men must belong to some power beyond themselves, whether it be God or *sin*. This statement means that human loyalty cannot be shared. As in the words attributed to Jesus, no man can serve two masters. But the verse does maintain human free will. Men must make the choice. They must offer themselves freely to obey either God or *sin*. Paul assumes that Christians, whether in Rome or elsewhere, ought to know this. They ought to know, also, that the service of the cosmic demon *sin* results in *death* while that of God results in *being in the right*. The parallel is somewhat weakened by the substitution of the term *obedience* for the divine Name, but the suggestion that the thought of obedience represents a retreat from the Pauline idea of grace to the Jewish one of performance of Torah would create unnecessary complication here.

Verse 17 is an aside, a thanksgiving for the new order of life in which Christians have been established. Servitude to sin is now a thing of the past. Freely or from their hearts the faithful become obedient to the pattern of teaching to which they have been delivered. This pattern of instruction is not Pauline Christianity; the apostle has had no opportunity to teach in Rome. Paul is simply discussing the primitive kerygma that has been the heart of the Gospel wherever it has been proclaimed. In Verse 18 it is through Christ that the believers have been set free from sin. Yet this freedom from sin is not necessarily permanent. It can be preserved only by continuing service to righteousness, which here is definitely related to the performance of commandments unless it is a symbol for God as obedience was in Verse 16. Paul had to insist that there was a pattern of conduct that a Christian must follow even under the dispensation of *grace,* for to abandon this would have been to surrender to the antinomians.

Dodd has said that Paul perceives the weakness of his argument and in Verse 19 apologizes for it, but such a statement is an exaggeration. Admittedly the words are, "I am using a human (not divine) argument because of the weakness of your flesh." But in essence this treatment is rabbinic. The *inclination to evil,* as the Jewish teachers believed, found its principal opportunity in the physical element of man. As Paul understood it, even when one had died to the world in Baptism and had risen with Christ to an *exalted Life,* temptation was still present. It was always possible that the regenerate man would lapse, and Paul seemed to find the temptations of the flesh more of a problem than those of the world and the devil. This, probably, would depend upon the temperament of one's congregations. Clearly Paul suspected that flesh was a primary problem in Rome, and the Roman history of the period indicates that he was right. In the past, as the tense of the verb indicates, the Roman Christians did offer their members as slaves to uncleanness and lawlessness. Barrett's assertion that *members* here is an inclusive term embracing all one's faculties rather than referring solely to the limbs of the body seems appropriate. In Jewish usage *lawlessness* means a willful disregard of Torah; despite Paul's insistence that a Christian lives not under law but under grace, he did acknowledge a certain norm of conduct that could not be violated without sin, and *lawlessness* seemed to him a fitting term for the defiance of this norm. The further words *for lawlessness* are absent from the B manuscript although found in others. Lietzmann holds that they are necessary to balance *for sanctification* at the end of the verse, but this is doubtful because if something were needed for balance it should not have been a repetition of the word *lawlessness.* The present behavior of the Roman Christians Paul expects will reverse the tendencies of the past. So the aorist imperative calls upon them to present their members or faculties as slaves to righteousness, to the principle that puts one in the right or more probably to the active righteousness of God. In doing this their goal is to be sanctification or consecration. *Justification* is the necessary first step in the Christian life, but *sanctification* is its final goal, and this is reached only through the service of righteousness. Some scholars hold that Paul is carrying on his military metaphor of Christians serving under God and using their members or faculties as weapons in the struggle against the cosmic demon *sin.*

Next comes a contrast between the two kinds of service. Slaves of *sin* are free in respect to (God's) righteousness; that is to say they have no share in it. As Paul contends, there was no fruit or profit in this past slavery to *sin;* in their new life as risen with Christ the memory of such a past is only a cause for shame. Moreover, the apostle repeats a point he has already made, namely, that the final reward of slavery to *sin* is *death.* Now, however, Christians have been set free from *sin* and made slaves to God. The thought is that a man must serve some power beyond himself but that he has a choice of which master he shall serve. By their exchange of masters Christians secure the fruit or benefit that leads to sanctification, and the final reward of sanctification is eternal life. In a sense this eternal life is already begun when one rises with Christ in Baptism, but whenever Paul writes *eternal life* instead of *life* he is thinking of the final consummation and the return of Christ in glory and the new creation of heaven and earth. Verse 23 then forms a summary of the chapter with its statement that servitude to *sin* earned a wage, but since evil is always deceitful it was such a wage as no man would desire, namely, *death.* On the other hand, what comes from God is not a wage but a gift, a gift that does not depend on human deserving and is indeed beyond human imagining, namely, eternal life. In saying that this eternal life is attained *in Christ,* Paul probably is thinking of the *mystical union* that at the beginning of this chapter was related to Baptism. There is a possibility, however, that the concept of incorporation into the Church as the mystical Body may also be included. Barrett's treatment of the verse adds further ideas, but neither *law* nor *grace* is mentioned here, and it does not even seem necessary to say with Lietzmann that the person to whom God has given His Spirit has passed beyond the casuistry of *law* to do what God demands simply because he is inspired by the Spirit. Assuredly the doctrine of grace is central to the Pauline Gospel, and to the Johannine as well, but there are other portions of Romans that express it more fully than this contrast between the results of yielding oneself as a slave to the cosmic power of *sin* or of embracing the service of Almighty God and the *free gift* that is its reward. No one will ever understand the richness of Paul's thinking who reads everything the apostle says in the light of this contrast between *law* and *grace*.

CHAPTER 7

The Experience of Sin

7:1–6 Or are you unaware, my brethren, for I am speaking to men who understand law (or, Torah), that the law exercises authority over a man for as long as he is alive? For the married woman is bound by law to her husband while he is alive; but if the husband should die she is set free from the responsibility to (literally, the law of) the husband. Whereas while the husband is alive she will be called an adulteress if she should be married to another man, nevertheless, if the husband should die she is free from the responsibility (or, law), so that she is not an adulteress when she is married to another man. So, my brethren, you also were made dead to the law (or, Torah) through the Body of Christ, that you might belong to another, to Him who was raised from the dead, in order that we might bear fruit for God. For when we were in the flesh, the inclinations to sin which by means of law (or, Torah) were aroused in our members (or, faculties) resulted in our bearing fruit for death (alternatively, the inclinations to sin by means of law were aroused to bear fruit for death in our members). But now that we are set free from the law (or, Torah), we are dead to that by which we were controlled, so that we may serve by the new service (or, newness) of Spirit and not by the old service (or, oldness) of letter.

* * *

There is a close parallel between chapters 6 and 7. The former outlines the manner in which the Christian is set free from *sin,* the latter how he is delivered from the authority of law generally, including Torah. There are, however, certain differences in arrangement. Chapter 6 concluded with an illustration from slavery, while Chapter 7 opens with an illustration from marriage. Like many other Pauline illustrations, neither of these is truly satisfactory, and that in Chapter 7 is obviously confused in its reference. Nor has this brief parable been helped by the tendency of so many exegetes to convert it into an allegory.

Verse 1 is an introduction. Scholars are divided on whether Paul is saying that he knows his readers to have some familiarity with Torah or whether he is thinking of their knowledge of the Roman *ius gentium.* For a married woman's responsibility to her husband, of course, the two were in agreement. Actually, there is no objection to the thought that the Gentile Christians of Rome would have had some acquaintance with Torah. One can hardly imagine any group of missionaries who would not have introduced their converts to the Old Testament. So Paul can assume at least a rudimentary knowledge of Torah on the part of his readers, and from his Jewish background it is more natural that he should appeal to this divine revelation than to the Roman *ius gentium.*

One item from Torah which the Romans might be expected to know is illustrated in verses 2–3. A married woman, Gentile or Jewish, would be under the authority of her husband as long as he lived, and bound to fidelity to him. But with his death this obligation expired. Paul is saying that the same is true with Torah. A death has occurred, and Torah is no longer in force for the Christian. Actually, the illustration is inadequate, for it speaks of the husband's death as freeing the widow, whereas in Paul's argument it is the Christian who has died to the natural order and is therefore set free. For Paul the community of disciples is the *Body of Christ,* the mystical counterpart of the Body that was slain on the Cross; by his incorporation into the *Body of Christ* the Christian has died to Torah, and his natural flesh that was subject to the sins made known by Torah has been translated to a new order of life. Before this incorporation Christians were *in the flesh* and therefore subject to Torah or to the principle of law in general; now that they are *in Christ* they are subject thereto no longer. In this way the reader is prepared for Paul's contrast between flesh and spirit in verses 5–6. In II Corinthians 13:4 and in Galatians 4:4–6 it is said that Christ also was *in the flesh,* but because in His incarnate Life He had never ceased to be *in the Spirit* neither *sin* nor *law* had power over Him. In dying with Christ to *flesh,* Christians have died also to *law,* so that they no longer serve God in accord with defined rules but by the interior prompting of the Spirit. In this way Paul explains the *bearing of fruit for God* in Verse 4.

Dodd's masterly treatment of what is meant by the *Body of Christ* is deserving of repetition: "As in Romans 6:1–11, the Christian is united with his Crucified Lord in death. There can be no sharp distinction between the *actual Body* which was crucified and the *Mystical Body* in which the Christian is incorporated by Baptism. Paul took so seriously the idea of the *Church* as embodying the *corporate personality of Christ* that in the Death of Christ on the Cross he always saw the death of the whole People of God to *sin, law* and *flesh.*" All Christians have been crucified with Christ. "As belonging to the Body of Christ you have died with Christ to the law." As a result of this Death of Christ for us, and of our own death in Him, we belong to Christ as a wife belongs to her husband, and the object of this union is that we might bear fruit for God.

There have been attempts to make the illustration more precise. Of these the most ingenious may be that of Sanday and Headlam, who suggest that Torah is slain in Christ and that the Christian is thereby freed from the obligations of his first union and may now seek the more satisfactory union with Christ. Yet such treatments deserve only the consideration of mental exercises that have no real relation to the text. The only valid exegesis must accept the inadequacies of Paul's illustration and concentrate attention upon the substance of the argument. This has been done by Dodd, and preeminently by Lietzmann. In any case the paragraph is intended to serve only as a background for the statements that follow in verses 7–25.

* * *

7:7–25 So what are we to say? Is the Torah sin? God forbid! But I would not have understood sin except by means of Torah. For I would not have known what it meant to covet if the Torah had not said, "Thou shalt not covet." Then sin took an opportunity provided by means of the commandment and accomplished in me every kind of coveting; for apart from Torah sin is without life. So I once was alive apart from Torah; but with the coming of the commandment (literally, when the commandment came) sin revived, while I died, and the commandment which was intended for life was found in my case to result in death. For taking an opportunity by means of the commandment sin deceived me, and by it (pronoun refers to the commandment) slew me. So the Torah itself is holy, and each commandment (literally, the commandment) is holy and just and good. Then did what was good become death in my case? God forbid! But sin, in order that it might appear as sin, by means of what was good brought about death for me, in order that by means of the commandment sin might become sinful beyond measure. For we know that the Torah is spiritual; but I am a creature of flesh sold into slavery to sin. For I do not understand what I am doing; for the thing I do is not what I wish, but the thing I hate is what I do. Then if I am doing the thing which I do not wish, I am giving my assent to the Torah that it is good. So now it is not longer I who am doing this, but sin which dwells within me. For I am aware that what is good does not dwell within me, that is within my flesh. For the will is present with me, but the accomplishing of what is worthy is not so. For I am not doing the good which I wish, but the evil which I do not wish I am performing. But if I am doing that which I do not wish, it is no longer I who am accomplishing it but the sin which is dwelling within me. Whereas I find the rule (or, law) for me when I wish to do what is worthy that the evil is present with me. For I give my approval to the Torah (or, law) of God in terms of my interior nature (literally, inner man), but I observe another principle (or, law) in my faculties (or, members) which is in conflict with the principle (or, law) of my mind and is making me a captive to the principle (or, law) of sin which exists in my faculties (or, members). I am a miserable man! Who shall deliver me from the body of this death? Thanks be to God through Jesus Christ our Lord! Whereas I myself render service to the Torah (or, law) of God with my mind, nevertheless with my flesh I render service to the principle (or, law) of sin.

* * *

Before one attempts to treat this section of the epistle, it is necessary to come to some decision regarding what is represented here by the pronoun *I*. For this there are as many opinions as there are possibilities in human imagination. Dodd takes it as autobiographical, holding that the apostle is discussing chiefly his own experience prior to his conversion. Barrett considers that it represents the experience of man generally rather than that of Israel or of the preconversion or postconversion Paul. Bardenhewer refers it to Paul himself in his regenerate state. Michel considers it as a rhetorical device that sets forth the experience of the regenerate man, although he recognizes a possibility that it may represent the experience of the individual Jew. Augustine set forth two ideas: that it represented the experience of man before and after the coming of Torah, and that it described the experience of the individual Jew in the course of his upbringing under Torah. Origen, although inclining to the second of the opinions later developed by Augustine, suggested that Paul's words were applicable to any sort of divine commandment, even to *natural law*.

Taking the text as it stands, Paul appears to be speaking of man generally. This is supported by the variation in language between the words *law* (standing for Torah) and *commandment* (which can represent the morality accepted by the Gentiles). Paul's purpose here is not to present an autobiography but to discuss the situation in which all men find themselves. The treatment transcends matters of race and of individual religious experience, whether as expressed in a struggle to observe Torah or to keep natural law. The literary practice of the period would give an author ample justification for describing in the first person an experience that he regarded as universal.

Yet Paul is not arguing from an ivory tower. He, too, is a human being. If the experience is universal, he too has known it, and it is from his own share in this universal experience that he derives the terms in which to describe it. He gives the account of an individual Jew who once knew no sin (although he did things that were actually wrong) in the experience of his childhood. When he reached the age of reason, he was given an awareness of the demands of Torah and of his personal responsibility to fulfill them, and thereafter he had entered upon the seemingly endless struggle of living up to what God demanded of him. Whatever innocence or responsibility Paul's readers may have known, however, was not directly related to Torah; most of them were Gentiles. If this account is worth relating to them, it must be because it answers to something in their own lives.

What could a Gentile Christian know that would be comparable in any way to a Jewish initiation as an adult member of the Chosen

Nation with the duty of observing Torah? Obviously his conversion to Christianity. So one must say that Paul is speaking of the experience of regenerate man, of the Christian. The discussion, however, embraces his entire life, both before and after conversion. The apostle can think of the Christian who had accepted the Gospel in mature life. Once he lived in paganism, not without sin but without consciousness of sin. This would be parallel to the experience of the Jew in childhood, and so parallel to the experience of Paul himself. Through hearing the Gospel, or by some other means, he has come to the conviction that his pagan manner of life is wrong; in other words, he has come to see that God sets a standard before him and that his conduct is not worthy of it. Thus he comes to a consciousness of sin. This can have the spiritual value of a Jewish initiation of the sort described by Josephus and by Rabbi Eleazar; the modern ceremonies of the *Bar-mizwah* have ancient roots. Escape from this predicament by man's own effort is impossible. It is Christ who effects the escape for man by breaking the power of the cosmic demon *sin* that has dominated him and by establishing his relationship with God on a new basis that does not depend on *law*. This can correspond to Paul's own conversion. There may be some doubt whether Paul's account of spiritual or ethical life is truly representative, but for the person converted in mature life, as the vast majority of early Christians were, it has some validity. There is, however, no evidence that it represents the attitude of the vast majority of Jews in Paul's time, and there is no need to consider it as the spiritual experience of the person who has no memory of what it means not to be a Christian. Indeed, the apostle may be justly accused of treating his personal experience as if it applied necessarily to all men without distinction.

Augustine and many later exegetes have tried to remove this objection by saying that Paul is describing the internal struggle against sin that all men face whenever they attempt to serve God. Such explanations of the text were offered long before there was any pretense of scientific psychology, but the techniques devised to explore human emotions have made possible a much more complex approach to the question. So one must ask whether Paul is describing merely the history of moral struggle for himself and others, or whether he is considering a condition present even after the reception of grace and the acceptance of Christ's justifying work. Ideally the regenerate man ought to be sinless, and this not only in acts of which positive law can take cognizance, but equally in the internal disposition that are known only to himself and to God. Actually it is not so, unless the regenerate are so few in number that human experience cannot take them into account. Not even the great saints of Christian history, not Paul himself, lived without sin; indeed, the greater the apparent attainment, the more intense is the consciousness of sin. So the struggle is continued after justification or regeneration, as Paul recognized in his own case.

In this context Paul is speaking for himself and for all men, specifically for those who have known justification. Whenever the service of God is understood in terms of obligation, in terms of *law*, the struggle is present. The more accurately the obligation is defined, the greater is one's sense of inadequacy. So the Christian, any Christian, must never think of himself as other than a sinner, and he must never regard his attainments as in any way fulfilling God's demand. Yet he should not go to the opposite extreme and think of himself as damned. Left to himself, he would inevitably be the author of his own spiritual destruction, but he is not left to himself. Christ puts him in the right apart from his own deserving by means of the saving act of Calvary, and God keeps him in the right apart from his own attainment by ever-renewed supplies of divine grace.

Does this mean that the regenerate man is *actually righteous*, or that his standing with God now depends upon performance? Latin theology tends to stress the need for accomplishment and to say that God makes man *actually righteous* by giving the grace to do what is demanded. The Reformers maintained that *actual righteousness*, even in the regenerate man, was nonexistent, that justification was not a single moment that effected a change in man but an experience continually renewed; this is set forth in the formula *simul iustus et peccator*. Thus for the Reformers justification tends to embrace all that the Latins mean by sanctification. But what does Paul himself say here? Certainly he demands performance, and he expects his converts to demonstrate the fact that they have been justified by the quality of their lives. Just as certainly he insists that neither the observance of the Old Law nor of the New Law will earn salvation for any man. The psychology set forth here ought to be disregarded, for it is Paul's own understanding of the matter and it does not necessarily apply to other Christians; the issue is theological. It is the struggle with *sin* as a cosmic power that has enthralled the natural man (whom Paul calls man in the flesh) that is to be regarded as universal. For the regenerate man this dominion of *sin* has been broken, not by his own efforts or his own deserving, but by Christ who in this deliverance expresses the scope of divine love. Thanks to this redemption sin is no longer inevitable for man. Yet while the power of *sin* is broken, its attraction to man is not destroyed. If the regenerate man stands against the attraction of *sin*, he must remember that the victory is the Lord's and not his own. Whenever he thinks of what he does himself rather than of what Christ does in him, whenever he relies on his own righteousness rather than on God's grace, religion becomes once again a matter of legal contract, and the power of *sin* revives even over the regenerate man. From this, as from what has been said above, it is clear that deliverance can be received only as a gift, an undeserved redemption mediated either in Sacrament or through the response of faith.

The historical problem, from the standpoint of Biblical study, is that both the Latin and the Reformation theologians have made the mistake of taking their own propaganda too seriously. The Catholic's demand for some degree of performance, especially when it is described as *infused justice,* seems to the Protestant to be a revival of legalism with all its faults, and no Catholic emphasis upon the work of grace in this connection seems sufficient to allay his suspicion. The Protestant's stress upon the gift of justification without consideration of the recipient's merit, especially when this is expressed as an *imputation of righteousness,* seems to the Catholic to be a legal fiction, unworthy of God, that can open the way to a divorce between religion and morality, and the actual virtue so commonly found among Protestants does not appear as an adequate guarantee against the evil results to which in theory such a teaching might lead.

Paul himself insisted that salvation can never be other than the gift of God, which no man can earn. Yet he was no less emphatic concerning the need of the man who was saved by a gift to show actual righteousness in his life. The professing Christian who was obviously unrighteous, in Paul's judgment, was a man who had turned away from his salvation. Nor did Paul intend to say that God's gift could ever be conferred without human response. If man is justified by faith, that faith involves the complete commitment of oneself to God, a perfect trust in His love and power. If this faith or trust is itself a gift of God and not an achievement of man, at least man must be free to choose whether he will or will not respond to God's prompting. If God is not to be an arbitrary despot, exalting to favor or consigning to destruction by caprice, then the response of man must play some part even in justifying faith. This holds true even though Romans 9:20–23 can be interpreted as if God were capricious. But the fact that man's response is essential to faith does not mean that faith is itself a *work;* it means only that when faith is recognized as a gift of God one must remember that a true gift requires not only the generosity of the giver but also the grateful acceptance of the recipient.

One cannot expect this explanation of Paul to commend itself to a person who is emotionally committed to the position of Luther; while it is admitted that no man can truly be deserving of salvation, it is also declared that every man must strive to be as nearly deserving of salvation as God's grace can make him. Nor is this account likely to be accepted by the modern defenders of the Council of Trent: it is here denied that God's act in justifying man can be thought of as imparting an actual righteousness, whereas the Latins do not contemplate that God might accept a sinner who is not already in the way to redemption. If one desires consistency he will turn to the Tridentine doctors or to Luther, not to Paul. Yet with all his inconsistency Paul is probably closer to the truth of God than are his classic interpreters. One may fairly suggest that finite human minds cannot hope to reduce God's dealing with man to the terms of a system of their own devising.

After this general essay one may proceed to the text. The question with which Verse 7 opens marks the beginning of a new stage in the argument. What is the function of Torah in man's salvation, and what is its connection with man's sin? Is Torah itself sin? God forbid! Yet there is a connection between Torah and sin. Sin comes to be recognized, and so man becomes guilty or responsible, only where *law* generally (the statement is too far extended to apply to Torah alone) has been proclaimed. But there is more to be said. The very existence of *law* constitutes a sort of temptation. This is nowhere more evident than in the internal sin of covetousness which is the final prohibition of the Decalogue. Paul, or any other Jew, or any Gentile who strives for ethical attainment, not only would not have recognized coveting as sin but probably would not have come to the desire for what belongs to others if it had not been defined for him in terms of *law*. Even apart from the existence of *law* the cosmic power of *sin* was real. But by means of commandment, a term that indicates that Paul is not thinking of *law* exclusively in terms of Torah, this power of *sin* has found opportunity to incite to covetousness. So Paul declares that if it were not for *law*, *sin* would have no strength. He even goes so far as to say that *sin* is dead apart from *law*.

Once Paul, once every Jew, once all men lived apart from *law*, which is here thought of as responsibility, in a state of innocence. But with the arrival of *law* (for a Jew at the time of his initiation, for a pagan at the time when he came to consciousness of moral responsibility, for a modern Christian at Confirmation or its equivalent) the cosmic power of *sin* revived. The Latins, believing in *original sin*, claim that circumcision effaced it for the Jews and that Baptism does so for the Christians, and that the moral struggle of the Jew really began when he reached the age of responsibility. But if this is the experience of mankind in general, one cannot make such precise references. For Paul, when one becomes conscious of moral responsibility *sin* gains new power. The man who strives for righteousness by his own effort finds himself helpless; his consciousness of failure is such that he may be considered dead. So law or commandment, which ought to have led to life, in reality leads man to spiritual death, to the admission of the futility of his struggle. The thought that Torah should lead to life is found in Genesis 2:16–17 and 3:3. Lietzmann describes this as the psychological experience of guilt. Verse 11 then combines the teaching of verses 8 and 10, giving them a stronger statement. Yet it is not *law* itself that is responsible for this disaster, but the cosmic demon *sin* that makes use of *law* as an instrument. So in Verse 12 Paul can describe law or commandment as holy and just and good. Lagrange defines this as *holy* in regard to man's relation to God, *just* in establishing due order or in punishing the wicked and rewarding the virtuous, *good* because of its character and because its performance leads to what is good. So this *law* that is good in itself is not the cause of spiritual death. Rather *sin* perverts the *law*, and by using this good for an evil purpose *sin* shows its own evil nature clearly. One may say that the real trouble with the principle of *law* is *people*. Men are so easily misled.

Many scholars believe that Verse 13 belongs with verses 7–12 rather than beginning anything new, but the fact that it opens with a question shows that a further advance in the argument is intended. Did what was good at least in intention come to be death for man? Paul still is speaking of *law* as a general principle and is referring to *man* by the first-person pronoun. This question must not be answered in the affirmative. Again Paul exclaims, *God forbid!* Instead he must say that the cosmic demon *sin* has misused the principle of *law*. Through man's consciousness of good and evil, which is itself a good thing, the cosmic demon *sin* has brought *death* into man's experience. In doing this, *sin* reveals its own heinous character more clearly than could be done in any other way. Yet the apostle holds that this whole development has taken place by the will of God. God gave the principle of *law* in order that *sin's* true nature might be revealed to the men whom God has created for eternal bliss. So Paul declares that the Torah, God's own expression of the principle of *law*, is spiritual; it is intended to lead man to true spiritual life.

Human nature, however, is not equal to the principle of Torah or *law*. Paul says *I* as representative of every man; I am a creature of flesh. The English does not have an adjective that can translate precisely the Greek word used by Paul, but *creature of flesh* is an adequate term for it. As flesh man is dominated by the demon *sin*. *Sold* here means no more than *dominated*, for nothing is said of who did the selling. The principle of *flesh* here is related to the rabbinic concept of an *inclination* to evil; it is an innate tendency on the part of every man to misuse his free will for his own aggrandizement. Yet it is not an intentional misuse of freedom. Paul holds that man does not understand what he is doing, that man does not accomplish his own will but finds that he does what he hates. From what he consciously approves, man recognizes that Torah or law generally is good. But because of his innate inclination to evil, man is not good enough for law. At least in many instances wrong is not a conscious choice, and therefore it does not properly belong to the man himself but to the power of *sin* that operates within him. As long as religion and morality are thought of in terms of *law*, it remains true that we have only human beings out of which to make Christians and that the material is not adequate. So some other way of thinking of religion and morality must be found. Paul has already stated the alternative way of understanding religion, and he will repeat it in verses 24–25; it is the principle of *justification by faith* that is made possible through God's saving act in Christ. In the meantime it should be observed that many modern writers, and some as ancient as Augustine, overstress Paul's psychological interest here. Evil inclination and its effects Paul understood; he knew nothing of Jung and Adler. The psychology set forth here is far from technical. It goes no further than to show that conscious intention falls far short of being a complete explanation of man's activity. Like Aristotle, Paul considered that the conscious intention of man is directed to what is good. He did not probe so deeply as has since been done into the reasons why that intention of good is often perverted to evil purposes.

In order to follow this argument with accuracy, one ought to give consideration to Pauline anthropology or psychology. Lietzmann is the most helpful writer on this subject, but in certain respects his work should be enlarged. Through the Septuagint, especially in Genesis 6:3–12, Isaiah 40:6 and 66:16 and Psalms 51:6 and 57:4, Paul's vocabulary can be related to that of conventional Judaism. Apocryphal parallels appear in IV Esdras 3:20–26, 7:92, 8:53, and in Ecclesiasticus 15:14 and 21:11. The closest parallels, however, are from Philo to whom Paul probably owed no debt. For the mention of an *inner man* there is a striking point of comparison in Plato, although the philosopher uses ENTOS rather than ESO for *inner*, and does not give the same recognition to God. Apparently Paul has effected a creative expansion of current rabbinic teaching concerning the evident power of sin in man. The language used is that of first century ethical teachers, who owed much to Pythagoras and Plato, but the thought of *sin* as a cosmic power against which man is helpless comes to Paul from his own experience and from his study of the Old Testament. There was ample rabbinic precedent for saying that *sin* (as a cosmic demon) gained power over man through the *flesh*, but neither Paul nor the Jews before him ever said that *flesh* was inherently evil. *Flesh* was weak and could not respond properly to divine guidance, but while it was in need of redemption it was not beyond hope.

The chief difficulty in understanding Paul's teaching on human nature is the widespread belief that the apostle was a systematic theologian. So far from being systematic, he was not even consistent in his own use of terms. Nor was the Hebrew language consistent. RUACH was the *Spirit* or *breath* of God, but when referred to man it could be *human spirit, breath,* or *animating principle. Human spirit* could also be described as *mind* or *heart,* while human *breath* or *life* could be called *soul.* Moreover, Hebrew could refer to a human being or personality as *soul* or *life* or *body,* while it failed to draw a linguistic distinction between *flesh* as a synonym for *body* or *person,* and *flesh* as the strictly physical element in man that was prey to evil. With this background it is not surprising that Paul's use of terms varies. He has the Greek words PNEUMA, NOUS, NOEMA, KARDIA, PSYCHE, SOMA, SARX, together with adjectives derived from them. Sometimes the first five of these terms are used interchangeably and at other times they are distinguished. The fourth and fifth are sometimes equivalent to and sometimes distinguished from the sixth, while the sixth and seventh are sometimes the same and sometimes refer to different aspects of man.

Thus it would seem that Paul defines human nature as tripartite, although this is not admitted by everyone, and even among those who accept the idea there is disagreement as to whether the apostle regards man as composed of *body, mind,* and *will,* of *flesh, life,* and *soul,* or of *body, soul,* and *spirit.* This much consistency may be established. Whenever Paul wishes to speak of that in man which is morally weak or susceptible to sin, he refers to SARX (flesh). When he wishes to describe that in man which is perishable he may use either SARX (flesh) or SOMA (body). In speaking of that which is capable of will or decision the terms may be NOUS (mind), NOEMA (thought), PNEUMA (spirit), KARDIA (heart). Both PNEUMA (spirit) and PSYCHE (soul) may be used of what is imperishable. The element in man most immediately open to God is usually called PNEUMA (spirit). But always the *whole man* must be redeemed, not merely an *immortal soul.*

For Romans as for the other epistles, Paul's anthropology may be explained as follows. Human nature is tripartite. That which makes this nature *human,* as distinct from animal, is the *spirit* that God has imparted. Paul sometimes calls it the *inward man,* and it is roughly equivalent to what the Greek Fathers and the French devotional writers called the *soul.* In addition to *spirit,* man is endowed with *conscious mind.* Mind is the realm of *will* as well as of *reasoning.* Paul sees it as normally in agreement with the *human spirit,* but capable of being turned aside to *sin* by the demands of *flesh.* In unredeemed human nature the *conscious mind* is under the dominion of the cosmic demon *sin.* Properly *conscious mind* cannot be called spirit, but Paul's words for *mind, thought, heart,* or *soul* may fairly be applied to it. The third element in human nature is the *physical,* in which Paul would certainly include what today is described as the *unconscious* (containing drives that seek physical expression). Paul calls it SOMA (body) or SARX (flesh); when thinking of its animate character he may even say PSYCHE (soul), and when thinking of its lack or responsiveness to *reason* and *will* he calls it the *outward man.* Usually when its propensity for sin is considered he uses the term SARX (flesh); when thinking of it as morally neutral he prefers SOMA (body). This element in man is subject to desires, but incapable of self-regulation or of rational choice; these latter elements must be provided by the *conscious mind.* The *physical element* may be destroyed in death, but it is as much an object of God's redemptive action as is *spirit* or *conscious mind,* and since the whole human personality must be truly redeemed the *outward man* must by some means be included. While a psychologist may regard Paul's account of human nature as less than complete, it must be acknowledged that the apostle's theory is adequate at least to the most significant facts about man. In the course of this explanation it has been necessary to touch on the problem of *free will.* For Paul *will is free,* but it can only escape the domination of the cosmic demon *sin* when empowered by the *grace of God.* In relation to *grace, free will* must respond before *grace* can become operative, but even in the true response it is God's *grace* and not man's *will* that initiates all right action and likewise all right thought.

Once these facts have been acknowledged, it becomes clear what Paul means when he says that in man as *flesh* no good thing dwells. Verse 19 repeats and gives greater emphasis to the content of Verse 15, and Verse 20 does the same for Verse 17. Verse 18 drew a careful distinction between *I* and *flesh,* and practically identified *flesh* with the *inclination to evil* of Judaism. Conscience, like Torah, is blameless, but the cosmic demon *sin* still dwells in man's *flesh.* Then in Verse 21, where Paul is speaking of his own experience as representative of the condition of all mankind, he declares that in a life under the principle of *law* when man desires to do good he discovers that he is accomplishing evil. The inward man or conscious will acknowledges that God's *law* is good, but at the same time this conscious will observes that it is not in control of the person as a whole. There is an unconscious will, in Verse 23 also described as a law, which successfully disputes the direction of the conscious, and as a result man yields to the prompting of the cosmic demon *sin*. Commenting on this paragraph, Jerome here distinguished four separate *laws*. One is the law of God, the dictate of external morality. The second is the law of the mind, the conscious choice of reason. The third is the law of the members, the unreasoning choice of man's unconscious. The fourth is the law of *sin*, the prompting of the demonic principle. The essential battle is between God and *sin*, but it is a struggle internal to man because the conscious and the unconscious are both involved and on opposite sides. Lagrange would prefer to consider only the first and last of these "laws," and to say that Paul's law of the members (or of the flesh) is merely the result of *original sin* that has already corrupted man's faculties. Barrett defines the law of the members as a perverse imitation of Torah that is the work of the cosmic demon *sin*. Since the treatment of Chapter 5 above has provisionally rejected the Augustinian concept of *original sin*, we are virtually compelled here to accept Jerome's explanation, an account that seems to conform to general human experience of the difficulties encountered in righteous living. While Barrett identifies the *inward man* here with the *new man* of other Pauline texts, and therefore understands it as the redeemed man who already belongs to the *New Age* but is still forced to struggle with the conditions of an unredeemed world order, Jerome's version of the question seems more satisfactory. Whether redeemed or unredeemed, human nature is possessed of that conscious mind which may be called the *inward man*. Modern Latin theology denies that these verses apply to *regenerate man*, but the whole paragraph will lose much of its meaning if the application of its teaching is restricted to the unregenerate. Paul is speaking of Christian life as a continuing struggle, not as a victory which has already been won.

Moffatt, with Dodd's approval, rearranges the text of verses 24–25, making 25*b* follow verse 23 and leaving 25*a* as the conclusion of the whole chapter. For this there is no manuscript authority. Other writers, feeling that 25*b* is an anticlimax, would eliminate it as a gloss. Lagrange, however, analyzes 25*b* and concludes that it must come from Paul himself, and declares that the safest procedure is to follow the manuscripts and treat it as it appears. With an admitted prejudice against conjectural emendations of the text, we may try to interpret the words in the order in which they have been preserved.

Verse 24 states the climax of man's helplessness. The phrase translated in the King James Version as "the body of this death" is sometimes questioned. Moffatt and the Revised Standard Version translate it "this body of death." While Greek word order is flexible, as the text is written it is far more natural to take *this* with *death,* as in the King James Version, and this is in closer agreement with Paul's thought as well. By "the body of this death" Barrett understands the human nature which has fallen under the dominion of the cosmic demon *death* by the operation of the cosmic demon *sin* and of the principle of *law.* In his account it is not clear whether *law* goes before *sin* as its necessary condition or follows after *sin* in order to unmask its character. But however the words may be interpreted, they show that *religion* as the last hope of mankind is not effective; religion has not brought deliverance. When man has finally acknowledged the helplessness of his own striving, however, he is able at last to receive his deliverance from a source outside himself. While the inward man (conscious mind) gives allegiance to the principle of God's law, flesh (the unconscious) can give allegiance only to the cosmic demon *sin's* perversion of the principle of law. These last four sentences are expressed in terms borrowed from Barrett, but they set forth a somewhat different point of view.

Once man has recognized his own predicament, God Himself brings the deliverance from this condition in and through Jesus Christ. There are some variant readings for Verse 25*a.* The true text is CHARIS TOI THEOI, which probably means *thanks be to God,* although in terms of grammar it is a clumsy way of saying it. In efforts to make the phrase clearer, Chrysostom and the A manuscript and one citation of Origen substitute EUCHARISTO TOI THEOI, *I give thanks to God.* With the emphasis so often found in Latin Christianity, the D manuscript and the Vulgate and Theodoret have it HE CHARIS TOU THEOU, *the grace of God.* Any of these expressions would be a thanksgiving to God for the power He has imparted to men through the agency of

Jesus Christ. Any of these forms of saying it will make clear that it is through God's power that man's problems are overcome. Once man has admitted his own defeat, then God can act, and in Christ God has acted. All that now remains is for man to accept God's gift with thanks.

If the manuscripts are right in adding Verse 25*b* here, Paul must be looking forward to continuing difficulty for man even in the regenerate state. An accurate translation will be, "Whereas I myself with my mind give service to a law of God, nevertheless with my flesh I give service to the law of sin." This would form a good summary of the argument after Verse 23, as Moffatt suggests. Yet in its present position it may prove even more helpful. God has delivered man, in and through Jesus Christ, whereas if he were left to himself man would continue in the old way. Salvation is a free gift of God, but from this second part of Verse 25 one gathers that it is not given once for all in a moment of *justification*. Instead the gift of salvation must be received continually in those fresh supplies of grace that are available in and through Christ. For that renewal man must continually give thanks because he knows that all the achievements of his new state are the Lord's doing and not his own. A word of praise ought to be given for the inclusion in Michel's German-language commentary at the end of this chapter of helpful notes on the history of interpretation of Romans 7:7–25, on the theological interpretation of the Old Testament by Paul and by Luther in commenting on Paul, and on the religious and historical background of the section. The plan of these notes is well conceived, but there is an equally good case for presenting their substance along with other comment on the text, as has been done here.

It is essential, however, to give separate consideration to the concept of abrogation of the Torah, and for this Lagrange is the most reliable authority. No study of the history of the estimation in which Torah was held in Israel can justify the belief that in some forms of Judaism the functions commonly ascribed to Torah had been transferred to the person of the Messiah. Neither the Dead Sea Scrolls nor any other sectarian Jewish writing will support such a theory. Even where Messiah is not strictly a political figure but is expected to play a part in the Last Judgment, he is seen as *judge* rather than as *saviour,* and Torah is the basis on which his judgment will be given.

In Judaism salvation was to be sought only in Torah, and this was scarcely more true of the Pharisees than of other factions.

But for Paul salvation must be sought in Christ. The apostle could not preserve Torah while putting his trust in Christ, because to do so would have meant misunderstanding the proper function of Torah in God's purpose. Paul did not see Torah as a *secondary* instrument for salvation, but as a *provisional* instrument, one that pointed to salvation without providing it. Therefore, once salvation had been provided in Christ, Paul saw no reason for the continued existence of Torah. Beyond this, it must be recognized that Paul held Torah to have been abrogated *in toto*. He drew no distinction between its moral and its ceremonial precepts. He could have assented to the dictum of Thomas Aquinas that nothing remains of the *Old Law* excepting that which conforms to *natural law*. Illustrations may be taken from the Decalogue, for the actual *day of rest* was altered, along with the manner of its observance, even in the first Christian generation; for a very large part of Christendom the prohibition of images has also been abandoned, although this did not take place so early in Christian history. For Paul, Torah is the legislation communicated by Moses, and in the face of the cosmic power of *sin* it has proved impotent, for it has only revealed and multiplied transgressions. The religion of Jesus, on the other hand, is the salvation brought by the Son of God, and it both effaces past sin and confers the capacity to avoid sin in the future. Torah is thus a discipline imposed upon slaves, while the religion of Jesus is a manifestation of paternal love.

The basis of Paul's contention is that men are saved through *union with Christ* and that no one has ever been saved by performance of Torah. So God gave Torah as a temporary expedient that was to serve until His Promise had been fulfilled. By faith in Jesus men obtain the righteousness Torah cannot give. Therefore to continue seeking righteousness in Torah is to say that Christ's Death has served no purpose. Such is the assertion of Galatians 2:21. So to place trust in Torah is to reject salvation. Since all the faithful are now *One Body in Christ*, there are no longer Jews and Gentiles, and Torah is no longer in force even for Jews. The demonstration in Romans that Torah is abrogated has two parts, a practical one set forth in 2:1–3:20 and a rational one in 7:7–25. Torah has been the occasion of numerous sins, but it has brought better understanding of the power of *sin* and has shown that *law* as a principle is ineffective. Thus it has revealed more clearly the need of *grace*. By means of Torah, then, God has brought good out of evil.

There are possible criticisms of such an argument. As presented by Lagrange it assumes that the believers are given an *actual righteousness*, while most non-Roman scholars would deny that this is true in Paul's mind. It also gives to *natural law* a place in determining moral life that few Protestants would accept, and even some who find the idea of *natural law* congenial have doubts about the degree of recognition Paul would have given it. There is also lacking here due consideration of the question whether religious practice ought to be divorced completely from *any* legal principle rather than from the Torah of Israel alone. Yet although these criticisms are real, they are secondary, and Lagrange's argument deserves careful study. Only through analysis of the varying ways in which Paul has been interpreted can one hope to come to a true understanding of his thought today.

CHAPTER 8

Adoption

8:1–11 Whereas now there is no condemnation to those who are in Christ Jesus. For the law of the Spirit of life in Christ Jesus set you free from the law of sin and of death. For what was impossible for Torah, in the fact that it was weak because of the flesh, God did when He sent His Son in what was like the flesh of sin, and to deal with sin He condemned sin in the flesh (Christ's flesh), in order that the righteousness which belongs to Torah might be fulfilled among (or, by) us who live (literally, walk) not in terms of flesh but in terms of Spirit.

For those who are in accord with flesh give their minds to what belongs to the flesh, but those in accord with Spirit to what belongs to the Spirit. For to give one's mind to what belongs to the flesh is death, but to give one's mind to what belongs to the Spirit is life and peace. For this reason to give one's mind to what belongs to the flesh is hostility toward God, for it is not being in subjection to the law of God, for indeed it cannot be so. Then those who are in flesh cannot be pleasing to God. But you are not in flesh but in Spirit, providing that the Spirit of God dwells in you. Now if anyone does not possess Spirit of Christ, he does not belong to Him. But if Christ is in you, the body is indeed dead in relation to sin, but the Spirit is life in relation to righteousness. Then if the Spirit of Him who raised up Jesus from among the dead dwells in you, He who raised up Christ Jesus from among the dead shall also give life to your mortal bodies by means of the indwelling of His Spirit in (or, among) you.

* * *

One might prefer to divide this chapter after Verse 13, with Dodd, instead of after Verse 11 as is done here, but however it is to be divided Dodd's comments will prove helpful in understanding it. Since the beginning of Chapter 5 Paul has been dealing with the life of the regenerate man. He has contrasted it with the life of the unregenerate under the forms of peace compared with enmity, of freedom compared with slavery, of life eternal in contrast with death. Now an even more significant distinction must be drawn, that between life in the Spirit and life in the flesh. While many interpreters have refused to say that Paul is speaking of the regenerate man in Chapter 7, it is universally admitted that he is doing so here. The opening verse is one more example of forensic language. The condemnation that the fact of having committed sin has brought upon the rest of the human race does not apply to those who are *in Christ* through the *mystical union* inaugurated by faith and completed in Baptism. The second word of the verse, ARA, is a legal term much used by Paul. When it is coupled with OUN it should be translated *whereas,* and although OUN is absent here ARA certainly indicates the beginning of a new Pauline summary. A textual variant in Verse 2 has been given diverse resolutions. The Revised Standard Version takes the pronoun as first singular, which would mean that Paul was claiming that he himself had been set free and that he was speaking in the name of Christians generally. Many patristic writers prefer a first plural pronoun, which would stand for all Christians without special reference to Paul. The Nestle text follows B and Aleph in reading a second singular pronoun, and since this is the reading that scribes would be most tempted to clarify it is probably the original. Here the regenerate and unregenerate states of life are represented by two *laws*, that of the Spirit of life in Christ Jesus and that of sin and of death. Neither of these laws should be equated with Torah. The former represents the fact that the believer is possessed by the Holy Spirit, and the latter expresses the assertion that the wages of sin is death. Neither sin nor death is here to be regarded as a cosmic power.

In Verse 3 *law*, without any qualifying phrase, does mean Torah. Torah is said to be powerless to deal with human infirmity because it is physical. This is essentially the criticism voiced by Jesus Himself. Torah can take account only of visible actions, whereas what is needed is a change of man's will. Since Torah is in fact not capable of doing anything about sin, God Himself has undertaken to deal with it. It is not possible here to determine whether Paul is speaking of *sin* as a cosmic demon or as a fact of human experience, but whichever of these may be in his mind he is certain that God has provided the answer to the problem in sending His Son. Although the Death of Christ is not excluded from the apostle's argument here, the stress is upon the Incarnation. Theologically this verse is strong evidence for Paul's belief in the preexistence of Christ and in His eternal relationship to the Father. The Lord's true Humanity is less clearly set forth, although it finds place elsewhere in Paul's epistles.

The words *what was like the flesh of sin* have been interpreted in a Docetic sense, but Docetism was not a serious problem for the Church of Paul's time and the apostle would not have felt the same need to exclude such ideas as is found in third century writers. Actually, Paul is explaining that Christ who is eternally God (later to be defined as the Second Person of the Trinity) did become truly Man, that He shared the nature of mankind without sharing in man's sinfulness. Bardenhewer has defined this very precisely: "*What was assumed in the Incarnation was not the* (fallen) *human nature which is found in us* but *human nature as God intended it to be* (sinless)." Of course, this definition is misleading in some ways, for it not only uses terms that Paul himself never thought of but it also depends upon the Augustinian concept of *original sin* that was never in Paul's mind. Indeed, the best commentary on the Pauline Christology here set forth is to be found within the New Testament itself in the Epistle to the Hebrews. There it is declared that in His Incarnation Christ was completely Man; at least logically sin was a possibility for Him as it has been for all men. He was tempted as we are, with the single exception that He did not know those temptations that result from previous sin. From this scriptural account of the matter, even if we reject the concept of *original sin*, we may still agree that the Incarnate Lord possessed a human nature continually aided by grace or by union with God, and that this was what God had intended for human nature, while our own human nature differs from Christ's because the help of God's grace is so often refused by us. Yet Paul here is not discussing the difference between human nature in Christ and in us at all. He is concerned to show that the earthly life of Christ was actually sinless, whereas all other human lives are sinful, and that the reason why the preexistent Christ entered human life was in order to do something about human sin. Therefore the apostle is careful to say that God sent His Son *in the likeness of the flesh of sin*, for he means it to be understood that the *flesh* of the Incarnate Lord was without sin and yet was truly *flesh*. If He had not experienced a true Incarnation, Christ could not stand as man's representative; if He had not Himself been sinless He could not have won the victory over the power of *sin*.

Yet this effort to improve upon Bardenhewer's definition does not begin to exhaust the points for discussion in Verse 3. This is one of the primary texts that have been used in support of a substitutionary theory of the Atonement. The Septuagint in Leviticus uses the Greek words that have been translated here *to deal with sin* in connection with the sin offering. Origen, like other Christians of his day, had no comprehension of the Old Testament sin offering. He believed that it was intended to remove sin, and so he assumed that Paul was discussing Christ's Death on the Cross as a Sacrifice intended to remove human sin. From this it is but a short step to the teaching set forth in so many Christian hymns that Christ has paid the penalty we owed. Yet the source of this idea cannot legitimately be found in Paul. The only Pauline texts that might be taken as supporting it are II Corinthians 5:21 and Galatians 3:13, and even in them the substitutionary interpretation is not definite, for they may be speaking only of the Lord's submission to the direst consequences of sin. Elsewhere Paul writes of Atonement in terms of ransom rather than of substitution. The apostle's real point is that no man can obtain the status of being in the right with God as *an external blessing*. The change in human status takes place *in* man as well as *for* him, and therefore man has a vital part to play in his own *justification*.

Man's part is the response of faith, and this faith itself must be defined. It is neither the wholly objective assent to articles of belief nor the wholly subjective personal commitment that has occupied so much theological discussion. The only faith that can put a man in the right with God, at least in Pauline teaching, is a faith-union with Christ, a personal and mystical relationship. Only for those who have such union with Christ can the Lord be a true representative; only for those who are *in Christ* does *God-in-Christ* bring salvation. So the words *to deal with sin* here do not refer to a sin offering of Himself made by Christ on man's behalf. By these words Paul intends little more than the common meaning *concerning sin*, and for this slightly greater stress the translation *to deal with sin* seems appropriate. Paul is expounding the new order of life in which the Christian is placed by Christ, an order in which freedom and hope find their expression in *adoption*. This new order is contrasted with the old order of sin, and its freedom is presented as freedom from the principle of *law*, for Christ's Death shows that the cosmic power of *sin* is condemned, and henceforth the Christian is endowed with the capacity to perform God's will that had never been provided by the Torah.

Whenever Paul states a theological principle, he relates it to man's life. Such principles entail consequences, and the consequences are studied in Verse 4. God has sent His Son in order to deal with sin, intending that the righteousness of law might be fulfilled by men. Lietzmann holds that *law* here is the working out of God's judgment on human sin, while Dodd sees it as the fulfillment of Torah's requirements in our lives in so far as the commandment is holy and just and good. Perhaps these views may be reconciled through Lagrange's idea that the Torah has been abrogated excepting as an expression of the principle of *natural law*, but if a choice must be made between them Dodd's view is the more reasonable. Certainly the verse contemplates a standard of performance on the part of Christians, for the believers are not living in accord with the principle of *flesh* but in accord with that of *Spirit*.

This introduces another of the apostle's vital contrasts, that between *flesh* and *spirit*. Here and elsewhere in Paul the rabbinic term *walk* is used for a manner of life. Verses 5–6 then turn from the outward concept represented by the word *walk* to the inward one that can be represented by the term *mind*. Paul holds that the inward and the outward correspond, that there can be no dualism of theory and practice. Those who act in accord with *flesh* do so because they give their minds to what belongs to *flesh*; the same correspondence applies with those who act in accord with *Spirit*. In Verse 5 Paul is probably thinking of the human *spirit* rather than of the Spirit of God; in Verse 9 he is certainly thinking of God's Spirit; and in Verse 6 it is impossible to decide between these two possibilities. The Greek word that was translated *mind* in Verse 6 could as easily stand for *will*. To set one's will upon what belongs to the principle of *flesh* means death; here the apostle is speaking of the physical experience and not of the cosmic demon. In contrast to this, when the will is devoted to the things of the *Spirit* man enters into that new order of which the characteristics are (eternal) *life* and *peace* (with God). This is further developed in verses 7–8 with the standard Jewish teaching that concentration upon physical things is hostility toward God. In modern terms, worldliness cannot be reconciled with the law of God, whether God's law is represented by Torah or by natural law or in any other way. Therefore the people who give their wills to worldliness, the unregenerate, can never by their mode of life be acceptable to God.

Verses 9–11 complete this paragraph by setting forth in more detail the internal characteristics of the regenerate life. Looking back to the baptismal teaching of Chapter 6, Christians have died to the principle of *flesh* or of worldliness and have risen with Christ to a new life dominated by God's Spirit. Because of their union with the risen life of Christ, the Spirit of God dwells in the Christians, and if there is any supposed Christian of whom this is not true his membership in the Body of Christ is an illusion. The person in whom the Spirit of God does not dwell can have no true union with Christ and so cannot be regarded as a Christian at all. The modern Church has lost much in not demanding some reasonable proof of the presence of God's Spirit in all its members.

Verse 10 then equates the indwelling of the Spirit with that of Christ Himself, a thought that appears frequently in Paul. While it must be admitted that Paul did not make any sharp distinction between Christ and the Spirit *in* the believer, there is no need to regard this as theological confusion between Christ and the Spirit; historically the Church has regarded the accomplishing of Christ's presence in the disciple as an essential phase of the Spirit's work. Moreover, whether one speaks of Christ or of the Spirit in the believer, the reality is the same. The physical element of man which in Verse 11 is called *body* but which might just as well be represented by the word *flesh* is dead because of *sin*. Regenerate man has mortified the *flesh* because it had been overpowered by *sin*. It is not clear whether the apostle is now speaking of sin as a cosmic power or as a human experience. The human *spirit* of the regenerate man is made alive because of righteousness, not a righteousness earned by the disciple himself but *the righteous act of God* who sent His Son to fulfill the inexorable moral law of God's universe. After God's Son had fulfilled it, God raised Him from the dead. Thus the Incarnation of Christ has brought true life to the human spirits of the Christians.

Lietzmann's comment on Verse 11 is worthy of quotation. He sees the verse as a summary. "If the Holy Spirit of the God who raised Jesus from the dead dwells in the disciples, the God whose most significant action has been the raising of Jesus from the dead shall also give life to the mortal bodies of the disciples by means of that Holy Spirit who dwells in them." For Paul the experience of the Holy Spirit virtually defines the meaning of being a Christian. Lietzmann then adds a note on the relation of flesh and spirit, but the vital features of his treatment have already been set forth in the account of Pauline anthropology connected with Chapter 7. The whole man must be redeemed or given life, body as well as spirit. But the body is weak and prone to sin, and for that reason the Spirit of God must operate first of all through the human spirit of the believer in order to accomplish redemption by making the life of God present in the whole man, spirit and mind and body.

* * *

8:12–30 So, my brethren, whereas (this word refers not to verses 12–13 but to the first clause of Verse 14) we are persons obligated not to the flesh to live in accord with flesh. For if you should live in accord with flesh you shall die. But if by spirit you mortify (literally, slay) the deeds of the body you shall live. For all those who are led by God's Spirit are sons of God. For you did not receive a spirit of servitude for a renewal of fear (literally, to fear again), but you received a spirit of adoption by which we exclaim, "Abba, Father." The Spirit itself (the Greek word for spirit is neuter in grammar; sometimes but not always it is represented by a masculine pronoun when used of God's Spirit) testifies together with our spirit that we are children of God. But if we are children we are also heirs, actually heirs of God, and joint heirs with Christ if indeed we suffer with Him, in order that we may also be glorified with Him. For I consider that the sufferings of the present time are not worthy of comparison with the glory which is about to be revealed for us. For the anticipation of the creation is waiting for the revelation of the sons of God. For the creation was made subject to vanity (or, meaninglessness), not of its own free will but for the sake of him who put it in subjection, with a hope that the creation itself also might be set free from the servitude of corruptibility for the freedom of the glory (or, glorious freedom) of the children of God. For we know that the entire creation groans and labors in pain together with us (with us is not expressed in the Greek) until the present time. And not only so, but we ourselves also who possess the first fruits of the Spirit groan together within ourselves as we await adoption, namely, the redemption of our body. For we were saved by hope; but a hope which is observed is not hope, for what someone observes why does he also hope for it (it not expressed in Greek)? Now if we hope for what we do not observe, we wait for it patiently. In like manner also the Spirit comes to the aid of our weakness. For the thing we should pray for, we do not know how we ought to pray for, but the Spirit Himself makes intercession on our behalf with sighs which are beyond speech. And He who searches the hearts knows the intention of the spirit (man's spirit), because He (the Holy Spirit) by God's will makes intercession on behalf of saints. Now we know that He (God) works all things out for good to those who love God, to those who are called in accord with His intention. Because those whom He (God) foreknew He also preordained to be conformed to the image (or, appearance) of His Son, in order that He might be the first-born among many brethren; and those whom He preordained He also called; and those whom He called He also put in the right (or, justified); and those whom He put in the right He also glorified.

* * *

In view of the complexity of the chapter, this section probably should be divided after Verse 17. The use of ARA OUN in Verse 12 marks one of Paul's characteristic summaries. Since the point made in verses 1–11 is to be the basis of further exhortation, it is repeated.

The words translated in the King James Version *we are debtors* mean simply that we have an obligation. Lietzmann notes that the first clause in Verse 13 is simply a variant of Jesus' saying that he who would save his life shall lose it. Evidently this idea was established in Christian tradition before Paul. The second clause of the verse is a matter of dispute. What does Paul mean by saying that we must put to death the deeds of the body by means of spirit? It is fairly easy to find in the phrase a demand for ascetical practice, for what the medieval writers called "mortification of the flesh." Yet this is not Paul's meaning. The apostle was not a medieval ascetic, and many who believe in *mortification* as a salutary discipline have declined to support it by this text. First of all, *by spirit* must be recognized as an instrumental dative, and since it lacks both article and adjective it may be taken as referring to the human spirit rather than to the Spirit of God. Whatever the people to whom Paul writes are to do, it is a step they must take for themselves rather than one that God is to work in them. The verb is emphatic. The readers are to put something to death, and since they are to do this in order that they may live, it cannot even metaphorically be a counsel of suicide. So one must determine what Paul means by the needs or activities of the body, the things that in some way are to be slain. The term is more inclusive than sins or lusts, but it does not amount to asceticism. Paul's counsel here, as elsewhere, is to beat down one's inclination to yield to the demands of the body, to be able to take or leave any natural desire as shall best serve God's purpose. It is simply the reverse of living in accord with *flesh*, and thus it is the willingness to resign one's life for Christ's sake. With this fact again brought to the attention of the readers, Paul can go on with his argument.

The first step is to define the meaning of *adoption*. Those who are sons of God, who have received the *adoption*, are the people who are led by the Spirit of God. Here there is no possibility that Paul can be speaking of man's spirit rather than God's. The people who are being led are the Christians, and Paul would not have thought of including anyone else. The contrast drawn in Verse 15 is not entirely clear. Most scholars hold that servitude and fear in Paul's mind were always related to Torah, but this is not necessarily the case. Jews did not regard obedience to Torah as slavery, and their chief motive in obeying it was not fear. Even Paul did not think of it in such terms except when it was made a prerequisite to Christian faith. In paganism, however, there were fear and slavery to sin, and there is good cause to look upon the contrast from this point of view. Christians are delivered from their former slavery to sin, and the relationship with God that they have now received is no longer one of servitude but of adoption. It is a relationship dominated not by fear but by love. It is made effective by the indwelling of God's Spirit, and from the Spirit's presence with them Christians know the meaning of adoption and learn to call upon God as "Father." The Semitic word ABBA is an example of the early Christian tendency to use the words spoken by Jesus as liturgical terms. Other examples that still persist are AMEN, HOSANNA, and ALLELUIA. Actually, in Jewish usage ABBA was colloquial rather than liturgical. There is every reason to believe that Jesus used it in His own prayers. Paul could not be sure whether it was in use among the Christians of Rome, so he provided a translation. Even for his own Gentile congregations of Galatia he did the same. Perhaps it had fallen into disuse even in his time; certainly it did not maintain the same popularity as did the other Aramaic words that have been mentioned. Paul declares that the Christian can be sure of his adoption because he feels free to call upon God in this way. God had been known as "Father" in Israel, and to some extent in pagan religions, but the title had more significance in Christianity than in other cults.

Some scholars have pointed out that the Greco-Roman concept of legal adoption was not known in Israel. This fact, of course, would not have prevented the apostle from using it as an illustration of man's relationship to God when writing to a Gentile Christian congregation. Verse 16, however, goes beyond the legal concept of adoption, using a word for *children* that applied only to physical relationship and was not used of a relationship in law. But when Paul does this he is not implying that Christians are children of God by nature rather than by adoption; his point is that the *adoption* is so real that it brings about an actual likeness to God. This may be interpreted as a recovery of the *image of God* that man has defaced by his sin, but Paul is thinking rather of attaining resemblance to Christ. Here one must reject the assertion that God's Spirit anticipates the adoption rather than effecting it. If we are the children of God, and the presence of the Spirit within us bears witness that we are, then *adoption* is a result of God's love for us; it is a *gift* from God. But as gift it is certainly conferred in the imparting of the Holy Spirit, and *adoption* is made effective simply because the Spirit is given.

In Verse 16 the human spirit or the practical experience of the Christian testifies that we are children of God, and the Spirit of God within us unites His witness with ours. Verse 17 explains further the meaning of this *adoption.* The first clause speaks of Christians as *heirs,* but in this there can be no question of inheritance as it is commonly understood. God cannot die in order to bequeath to us that which is now His. In relation to God, men can be heirs only of a promise they are destined to receive. In their present possession of the Holy Spirit Christians already have a gift from God, but there is yet more to come. Here as elsewhere in Paul there is a blend of present and future eschatology, but as usual in the apostle's writings the future idea predominates. The goal will soon be described. The second clause of the verse goes into more detail about *adoption.* Christians look for the fulfillment of a promise of which they themselves have some foretaste in the possession of the Spirit, but the fullness of that promise even now exists in Christ. It is with the exalted Lord that Christians are to be joint heirs. In some way they are to share in His Exaltation. In the words of the First Epistle of John, *we shall be like Him.* In I Corinthians Paul indicates that our resurrection bodies will be like Christ's Resurrection Body and that we shall reign with Him. Yet for this privilege we must pay a price. We can share the inheritance with Him only if we also share in His suffering. This might mean martyrdom, but not necessarily so, for Paul expects the return of Christ in glory while many believers of the present generation are still alive. It might mean sharing in the *messianic woes,* the final cataclysm that many Jews expected as the prelude to the establishment of God's reign. Perhaps even closer to Paul's thought is the suffering involved in putting to death the deeds of the body. When He went to the Cross, Christ slew the deeds of the body, but each Christian must do the same for himself whether in death or in continued life in this world. He must die to the world as Christ died in order that he may live to God. He may never be called upon to meet physical death, but unless with his Lord he has died to the world so that neither cross nor fire nor sword nor wild beast can any longer bring real terror to him he is not truly joint heir with Christ. Paul may be thinking here of death with Christ in Baptism as discussed in Chapter 6, although that is not explicit. Of course, the child of God will be baptized; Paul has no doubts on that point. But *adoption* is not a mechanical result of Baptism; rather Baptism is an expression of the reality of *adoption*, of the spiritual relation with God established by faith and proved by the death to the world of which Baptism has been the outward expression and has marked the point in time at which it took place.

Lagrange, who in many ways is the best authority for verses 18–27, takes Verse 18 as a transition and divides the rest into three subsections. One point that Verse 18 should make clear to everyone is that Paul does not consider virtue as its own reward. The current sufferings, with their central feature of mortifying the deeds of the body, can be weighed against an expected recompense. The verb used means to calculate or count. The sufferings are real. Paul is sufficiently a naturalist to see the mortification of physical desires and interests as a real deprivation. But he sees such mortification as leading to a reward from God in the light of which all deprivations are insignificant. The sufferings belong to the present time, the existing world order that Paul considers to be passing away into a *New Age*. Certainly future eschatology is in his mind here, for the present is contrasted with a glory to be revealed in a time of fulfillment. Perhaps in Romans the change is no longer thought of as imminent, for the verb used stresses the certainty that the future glory will be revealed rather than its near approach. Because of the apostle's variable use of his prepositions, one cannot be sure whether the glory is seen solely as revealed *in* us Christians or whether it is something revealed *for* us, in our interest; it seems that the majority of scholars are right in placing their stress upon the former concept.

Verses 19–23 hold together, and offer teaching of extreme complexity. The first issue to be considered is whether KTISIS means the entire creation of God, animate and inanimate, or whether it is to be limited to the rational creation, to angels and men. The Genesis story of Adam would favor the more inclusive interpretation, for there God's judgment on man's sin includes the declaration, "Cursed be the ground for thy sake." With this as a background, Paul could very well contemplate a restoration of the conditions of the Garden of Eden as a phase of the final fulfillment of God's purpose. Many in Israel before Paul had looked forward to such restoration. This thought would naturally imply some sort of consciousness in the inanimate creation, an idea found both in Stoicism and in Gnosticism. Augustine, however, preferred to limit the meaning of creation here to the human race, to say that for the apostle the only world to be considered was the world of men, perhaps even to restrict the term to the righteous. In support of Augustine one must observe that Jewish apocryphal writings do not speak of the present subjection and future deliverance of the inanimate creation; instead they look for its replacement. But since creation here is clearly distinguished from the *sons of God*, Paul cannot be referring only to the righteous. Creation here certainly embraces the entire human race, and it seems appropriate to follow the majority of the Greek Fathers and to make creation as inclusive as possible. Paul has advanced upon the teaching of the Jewish Apocrypha, and he says that just as fulfillment for men will involve the survival of personality, so the fulfillment of the inanimate creation will mean the restoration or advancement to new glory of that which God has already established.

What has here been translated as *anticipation* is probably rendered even more accurately in the King James Version as *earnest expectation*. Clearly the word is emphatic. It implies an eager desire for a fulfillment that can be accomplished or manifested only in the attainment by the righteous of all that God designs for them. Of itself, however, it does nothing to show whether this anticipation is experienced only by the rational creation or by the entire order that God has made. Attention must also be given to the identification of the *sons of God*. In Job 38:7 the phrase is used of the angels who witnessed the creation of the world. For Paul the words must mean those whom Christ redeems so that the verse is a further reference to *adoption*. But since these *sons of God* are not yet manifested, the apostle cannot be thinking of their present state but of the future glory that shall be theirs when the *New Age* is established. It will then be apparent that Christians are the *sons of God*, for they shall come to be as Christ is now when they are in possession of their resurrection bodies and are sharing in His reign. In this event all creation shall rejoice because its true destiny will therein be realized.

Verses 20–21 are a single sentence, and they can provide as many problems of interpretation as verses 18–19, even when one has determined the meaning of KTISIS. Creation has been put in subjection to vanity, and not of its own free will. Since the participle is feminine, it must refer to the unwillingness of creation itself rather than to the purpose of God or to that of man. Paul seems to suggest that God deliberately imposed this subjection upon creation for the sake of mankind. One of the few rules of Greek grammar strictly observed by Paul is the distinction between the preposition DIA with the accusative meaning *for the sake of* and DIA with the genitive meaning *by means of*. Looked at from another point of view, the subjection of creation is not God's work but man's. Man made creation subject to vanity by his sin. Adam, the representative man of Genesis, initiated the process. Creation was a victim of human rebellion against God. Yet this was so only because God allowed the perversion of creation from its original goodness in the hope of man's restoration. One should translate the Greek here *for a hope* rather than *in hope*. God has given man free will, and this gift opens the possibility that man may frustrate God's purpose by rejecting the glory of *adoption*. The subjection of creation to vanity is a step taken by God to teach or prompt men, but this will not compel men to make the desired response to God's love for them, and so it has been permitted by God only for a hope and not with any certainty of result. Verse 21 apparently equates vanity with corruptibility, but even the patristic writers have shown themselves dissatisfied with this explanation. Corruptibility in its classical sense of change and decay does not imply moral deterioration, and for that reason many have insisted that the vanity to which creation has been subjected is the misuse to which it has been put by sinful men. One must, however, avoid overemphasis on moralism in treating the New Testament. The inanimate creation of which Paul seems to be speaking is not an object of moral categories. Permanence is its good. Therefore one must acknowledge that its present slavery, occasioned by human sin, is simply slavery to decay. This fact can be observed. But Paul affirms with confidence that such slavery will be ended. Creation shall be delivered. God's purpose is not to be frustrated. The glory of *adoption* must be attained because Christ's victory over *sin* and *death* is already a fact. With the glory of *adoption* for the redeemed there will be joined the freedom from corruptibility that is the proper glory of the inanimate creation.

Naturally, creation's longing is not conscious. Only the redeemed are truly aware of it. So Paul speaks for Christians generally in Verse

22 when he declares that we know even now how the entire creation labors and groans together. In the light of the following verse we may assume that creation groans together with us. The verb translated *labor*, while it can be used of childbirth, could be rendered in the modern vernacular as *to be in a bind.* Creation unconsciously suffers from the acuteness of its desire. But Christians suffer consciously, not so much because they possess the faculty of reason as because they have the far more important gift of the indwelling of God's Spirit. Other people are in a condition not much different from that of inanimate creation, but Christians have received the revelation of that glory for which they are destined. They look for the *adoption* that is likeness to the present exalted state of Christ Himself, the redemption of their bodies from the corruptibility that has afflicted all creation, as they look forward to the change of those corruptible bodies into the resurrection bodies that shall be theirs. Paul is fond of the word *redemption;* elsewhere he uses it for the act of Christ Himself, while here it stands for the effects of that act in us. When used of Christ it bears the meaning of *ransom* and when used of Christians it means the state of *being ransomed* from the demonic powers of *sin* and *death.*

Perhaps the chief controversy here has to do with what Paul means by *the first fruits of the Spirit,* for the phrase can be taken as a statement that we already possess God's Spirit in some degree and that we look forward to a further endowment later. Alternatively it may mean that the Christian's present possession of God's Spirit is the first installment of the totality of God's gift in the *New Age.* The majority opinion, and the one that should be chosen without hesitation, is that the Christian possesses the fullness of the Spirit now and looks for other gifts from God later. It is always doubtful to make sharp separations between the individual Persons of the Trinity, and it is absolutely out of the question to divide the Holy Spirit into parts. One receives the Holy Spirit, not a fragment, although the gifts of the Spirit that one may be able to employ with profit will be determined by the reality of response to the Spirit's presence. The ideal Christian would be able to employ all gifts. In this context the future blessings can be summed up in the term *adoption,* the sharing in Christ's Exaltation that shall be ours in the *New Age.* This blend of an eschatology already realized in what Christians have obtained from

God, and one that looks for perfection in the near future, was part of the kerygma of the Church even before Paul, and it is reflected in one way or another by almost every writer of the New Testament, but few have given such force to the combination as has the Apostle to the Gentiles. There can be no doubt here that the glory is something to be expected in the very near future; the apostle is anticipating that the day of fulfillment will arrive without delay.

Verses 24–25 are devoted to an account of the meaning of hope, perhaps the most complete statement on the matter that may be found in Paul. But before approaching this, it is necessary to establish the meaning of the verb which is literally *we were saved.* Some take this as a proof text for the proposition that salvation is a present possession according to Paul, something already complete. It is true that if the apostle had been thinking solely of future salvation in the *New Age*, he should have used a future passive instead of a past tense. Yet this argument loses most of its force when one remembers how little precision is shown in the New Testament with regard to tenses. As Jews accustomed to a Semitic tense structure, the earliest Christian writers never mastered the distinctions of the four tense systems of the Greeks. Appealing as it might be to say that Paul is stressing a present possession of salvation and is declaring that it has been ours potentially since the moment of Christ's victory and actually since the moment of our own conversion, we must admit that such an account of the apostle's intention can be no more than probable. Furthermore, the meaning of hope in this clause is not certain. One may understand the words as, *we were saved by hope,* although Paul more often used a preposition to show the instrument by which something was accomplished. Most English translations have taken it, *we were saved in hope,* but for this also a preposition would be desirable. A third alternative is to take the clause as parallel to Verse 20, and to translate it, *we were saved for a hope.* This would not require a preposition, and it is in conformity with the context. We were saved by God *for a hope* that we might attain the glory of *adoption.* This glory is what God designs for us; it has been the final cause or goal of every saving action He has performed in our behalf.

Paul adds that this hope has not yet been realized, that the very nature of hope is that it should be more than one can observe. This makes it clear that the hope in question is for *adoption,* the manifestation of the *sons of God.* This is something that must await the *New Age,* but which by Paul is soon expected. In Verse 24 there is also a problem of text. The reading favored by von Soden and the later editions of Nestle must be translated, *what someone sees, why does he also hope for it?* This is not literary Greek, and some texts have improved it by the removal of two words, leaving what would have to be translated, *who hopes for what he sees?* This expedient gives good Greek but little meaning. Paul is often clumsy in his style, but never banal in his thought, so the longer form of the text must be retained. Its meaning is that *adoption* is not a present fact but something to be looked for in the future. So in Verse 25 the Christians are hoping for what they do not yet see, and are waiting for it with patience. As a rule the Greek word stands for *perseverance,* but here *patience* is a more satisfactory translation. Vincent Taylor has worked out a scheme of salvation in which *adoption* comes between the initial *forgiveness* and the final *sanctification,* but Paul's intention here cannot be fitted into such a scheme. Here *adoption* is itself the final goal, the object of a hope that is more than faith because it adds to complete confidence in God's goodness a clear picture of the content of expectation even as it recognizes that the fulfillment has not yet been attained.

Verse 26 is difficult in itself, and historical controversy has rendered it more so by prompting many of the Church Fathers to say that Paul is not speaking of God's Spirit here. But the only alternative to Holy Spirit here is the human spirit. Paul declares that Christians, like the inanimate creation, are in need of help from outside themselves. We Christians show a weakness that would be fatal to us if *spirit* did not come to our aid, and since we cannot procure our own salvation Paul must mean the Holy Spirit. The Church Fathers who have taught otherwise have not understood the apostle correctly. Our weakness has to do with our life of prayer. When accented, the Greek word τι asks a question, either *what* or *why* or *how.* But Paul cannot be saying that we do not know *what* we are to pray for; he has already made it perfectly clear that we should be praying for *adoption.* Nor can the words be made to apply to the object of our prayers as saying that we do not know *what* to pray for as well as we ought to know it. So the statement must be translated as follows: *For the thing we should pray for* (aorist subjunctive) *we do not know how as we ought.*

This is clumsy, but it makes a point. Paul is dealing with mental prayer, with the inmost aspiration of the Christian. We pray for the proper object, for it has been revealed to us, but the manner of our prayer shows weakness. We lack the sincerity, the singleness of purpose that should be ours. Therefore God's Spirit comes to our aid and makes good our weakness. The Spirit does this in sighs that are beyond speech. Paul is not speaking of a *gift of tongues;* he is declaring that human speech is not adequate to the true desire of the human spirit in prayer.

The proper subject of Verse 27 is God. It is He who searches the hearts of men, He who knows what is within us. One might argue that the second clause of this verse is strictly parallel to the first, that God both searches men's hearts and knows directly what is the intention of the human spirit. On the other hand, one may say that the second clause of the verse refers to the Holy Spirit, that God knows the mind or intention of the Spirit because that intention is internal to Himself. This is the interpretation put forward by Lagrange, and the final clause shows that it ought to be accepted, for in that final clause it is assuredly the Holy Spirit who intercedes for the saints, and one can scarcely believe that Paul would vary his use of terms within a single sentence. So the apostle says that God searches men's heart and knows the intentions of the Holy Spirit who is interceding for the saints, even though the saints themselves cannot properly express the objects of their own intercessions.

The complexity of the chapter continues into Verse 28, where the King James Version translates, *we know that to those who love God all things work together for good.* This is an appealing thought, but it depends upon a misunderstanding of the Greek on the part of the first Latin translators, and it is not justified either by Paul's experience or by that of anyone else. Clearly God is the subject of the verse, and the two most reliable manuscripts, Papyrus 46 and B, have added the word *God* to avoid confusion. So the Revised Standard Version gives a better translation, *we know that for those who love God, God works for good in everything.* Yet there is one question even with this translation, for the Greek really means that God works *all things* out for good to those who love Him, rather than that God works for good *in all things.* The apostle is not so naïve as to affirm a conscious or unconscious cooperation with the righteous in everything that happens; what he does affirm is that God is in ultimate control no matter what may happen. For Christians God will effect the fulfillment of their true destiny, the *adoption.* Many of the Greek Fathers have misrepresented Paul and have said that he is speaking here of *grace* and not of *glory,* but Augustine and the Latin Fathers have explained the text correctly. Throughout this section Paul has been speaking of the future state of *adoption* as the Christian's goal, and he is still doing so here.

Verses 29–30 are the primary statement in this epistle regarding *election.* Lietzmann notes the ascending scale of importance in the terms used: foreknowledge, preordination, vocation, justification, and the climax of glorification. In defining foreknowledge one may begin with Barth's claim that the concept of predestination safeguards God's initiative in the working out of His own plan, and that in its Biblical form predestination should not be seen as a quantitative limitation of God's action but as its qualitative definition. Viewed in this light it is a way of saying that salvation is provided only by God's grace. For Christians of the present time the only satisfactory explanation of foreknowledge and preordination must be in relation to God's saving purpose. For Paul and his contemporaries, however, the thought of God's foreknowledge may have served chiefly as an apologetic for the refusal of many (especially among the Jews) to accept the Christian preaching. One could explain apparent failure from God's foreknowledge or insight into human nature, and could say that those who refused were the people whom God recognized as unworthy to accept. Such an explanation would have been significant in the first century, however little it would mean today.

Thomas Aquinas described *calling* as "a predestination following foreseen merits," but there is little evidence for such an idea in Paul's own writings, and it can only be reconciled with the text by restricting such predestination to the fulfillment of God's purpose that there should be other *sons of God* to share with Christ in God's glory. Paul himself declares that for those who are worthy God has already appointed a glorious destiny that is "likeness to the image of God's Son" and that was explained in Verse 23 as *adoption* and as the *redemption of the body.* It will become possible truly to describe Christ as "the firstborn among many brethren" only as and when Christians attain this likeness. Actually, the *calling* of Verse 30 looks back to that of

Verse 28; it indicates that the initiative, even in man's proper response to the Christian preaching, lies with God. There is no need here to add that Paul's *calling* is always effectual, for the apostle had seen its effect in his own conversion. For every Christian conversion will lead to a right relationship with God, to *justification* if one wishes to use that word, and while it involves a status of righteousness it need not mean present attainment of actual righteousness. Much of this has been dealt with in the previous chapter. The status of right-Fathers used the word *deified* in the same sense that Paul here uses eousness itself is a prerequisite to glory. At a later date the Greek *glorified;* by either term one would understand the fullness of *adoption.* Since this will have to await the day of redemption, its attainment must be in the future, although in a sense it has already begun. Paul's purpose in employing a past tense here consistently is to show the certainty that God's purpose will be fulfilled. Its accomplishment has been initiated in Christ's saving act, and no power temporal or spiritual can prevent its completion for those who have responded to God in *faith.*

* * *

8:31–39 Therefore what shall we say in answer to these things? If God is on our side, who is against us? He who did not keep back His own Son, but surrendered Him on behalf of us all, how will He fail to grant us every favor in addition to (or, along with) Him? Who shall bring a charge against those who are God's Chosen? God is He who puts them in the right! Who is he that shall condemn? Christ Jesus is He who died, and rather who was raised up, who is at the right hand of God, who also is making intercession on our behalf! Who shall separate us from the love of Christ? Tribulation or difficulty or persecution or famine or nakedness or danger or sword? Just as it is written, "For thy sake we are slain the whole day, we were reckoned as sheep for slaughter (or, sacrifice)." But amid all these things we do more than prevail by the aid of (or, by means of) Him who loved us. For I am convinced that neither death nor life nor angels nor principalities nor things present nor things to come nor powers nor height nor depth nor any other created thing shall be able to separate us from the love of God which is in Christ Jesus our Lord.

* * *

The discernment of a rhythmic structure and of the quotation of hymns and liturgical phrases in the New Testament is a study to which much has been added in recent years. Thus the most complete treatments of such hymns are to be sought in recent commentaries such as that of Michel. Yet the rhythmic structure here was perceived more than half a century ago by Lagrange, and it is of such importance that no interpretation can be satisfactory unless it recognizes that Paul has formed the conclusion of this outline of redemption from quasi-liturgical material. Michel would make four strophes of this paragraph. The initial question of Verse 31 should not be included in the hymn, for it is a Pauline formula already encountered in Romans and in other epistles. Here it serves to introduce the poetic lines. What Michel considers as the first strophe runs to the end of Verse 32. It declares a confidence that cannot be shaken. If God is on our side, no opposition can be effective. Paul is thinking especially of the opposition of Satan, for he believed too firmly in the power of God to consider the Roman state or army as a force of real resistance. Moreover, he declares that Christians have proof now that God is on their side. He has given His own Son to death for us, so we may be sure He will not withhold from us anything that would serve our welfare. If these words form a liturgical text, they must be an expression of primitive kerygma, the material with which every Christian would be familiar. Among other things, this paragraph bears witness to the fact that Paul's advanced Christology was widely accepted in the Church even at this period.

Verses 33–34 form the second strophe in Michel's arrangement, with verses 35–37 serving as the third. Perhaps this scheme should be modified. Verses 33, 34, and 35 are all introduced by questions, and in many ways these questions are parallel, although the third demands a longer and more complex answer. It is no cause for surprise that a hymn should be organized in sections of unequal length; one may compare the Nicene Creed or the Gloria in Excelsis. This hymn may once have possessed a balanced structure of three strophes with four hexameter lines and a final trimeter line each, but to arrive at such an arrangement one would have to eliminate many vital ideas from the present text. During the first century there was rapid growth in Christian thought, and ten years might have sufficed for the sort of expansion found here. Verses 33–34 can be understood best as a series of questions and answers. First there is a full line, "Who shall bring a charge against God's Chosen?" The answer occupies only half a line, "God puts them in the right." The second question takes the other half of the line, "Who shall convict them?" Probably the original answer formed a third line, "Christ died and was raised up." The phrase is an answer because Christ's saving act has eliminated the possibility of conviction for all who make it their own. This much of the answer as it appears in Romans is almost a perfect hexameter line. In the Final Judgment Christ has left no possibility for anyone to bring a charge. But this one line in itself did not say all that the Church desired to have said about Christ. For that reason it was expanded, probably even before Paul, with the declaration which rests upon Psalm 110:1, the affirmation that Christ is now at the right hand of God. Yet even this is not enough. A further expansion is made, perhaps by Paul himself, to the effect that Christ makes intercession on our behalf. This serves to develop a parallel between the work of the exalted Lord and that of the Holy Spirit as mentioned in Verse 26; if this is not Paul's own addition, it is surely a good expression of Paulinism. Finally a need was felt to stress the identity of the exalted Lord with Jesus of Nazareth. This expansion may have been later than Paul, for the Name of Jesus is not found in the B and D manuscripts.

The fourth line of the presumed original would have posed the third question, "Who (or what) shall separate us from the love of Christ?" The variant reading here, *love of God,* is probably an assimilation to Verse 39, and in Paul's mind there was no real distinction between God's love and Christ's love. The original answer was probably a short line, "In all things we prevail." The verb the King James Version translates *we are more than conquerors* can be understood simply as an emphatic form of *we overcome.* The first expansion would be to relate this closely to the exalted Lord, to say that we prevail by means of Him who loved us. Next would come some examples of possible causes of separation. That which appears in Verse 35 is formal, a series of seven perfectly natural difficulties, things that could happen to anyone and certainly to any member of an unpopular minority. Elsewhere Paul declares that he has had experience with all of them. The point is that none of these things can affect spiritual relationship with God and that none of them would indicate that the spiritual relationship had been damaged. The citation of Psalm 44:22 in Verse 36 would be yet another expansion of the original hymn, and it is probably the addition of Paul himself, since the apostle uses the same verse twice in I Corinthians and once in II Corinthians. Probably this Old Testament text had a place in most of the primitive Christian collections of *testimonia.* In contrast to the doubts felt by saints of the Old Covenant, the present trials and persecutions of Christians can never cause them to feel separated from Christ's love. Here, of course, it is Christ's love for us and not ours for Him that is being discussed. As in Verse 17 Paul is saying that to share in the tribulations unites the Christian with his Lord. Verse 37 explains why it is Christ's love rather than God's that is mentioned here. We Christians win our victory by means of the new powers communicated to us in Christ's presence within us. Scholars are divided on whether the scriptural background for this teaching is to be sought in the Genesis story of Isaac's sacrifice or in the Suffering Servant texts of Isaiah. The word *chosen*, which is plural, does not help in the decision, for it refers to the faithful and not to the Lord and is equivalent to the phrase *those whom He called* in Verse 30. Perhaps the stronger case is for a reminiscence of Isaac than of the Suffering Servant, but neither concept can be excluded.

Verses 38–39 bring the chapter to its close. Probably they formed the original third stanza of the hymn. Three questions have now been answered. Who shall accuse? Who shall convict? Who shall separate? A statement of unfaltering faith is to be expected. The list of realities that might separate Christians from what this time is called the *love of God* consists of ten terms. This is as formal as the earlier list of seven. It is doubtful whether there were more than five realities mentioned in the original hymn, namely, *death* and *life* as states of man's existence, and three classes of spiritual beings, *angels, principalities,* and *powers.* Efforts have been made to remove all that is mysterious or supernatural from the list, and to interpret it as follows. Death with its terrors, life with its enticements, the angels and principalities as powers of Heaven, present facts and future possibilities as anything in time, height and depth as anything in space, powers as the forces of nature, and any other created thing: none of these can separate us from God's love.

While it may be admitted that some of Paul's terms are merely rhetorical, mystery cannot be eliminated, and all ten terms must be recognized as spiritual forces. Paul often speaks of *death* as a cosmic demon, and if he had adopted a list in which death was included he could readily have interpreted it in that way here. Then the term *life* that he had also taken from his source could be considered as the spirit of worldliness. Both of these realities could be accounted as hostile to God and to man. In the same way the *angels* and *principalities* would be classes of spirits either subservient to God or in revolt against Him. In I Corinthians *present* and *future* describe a contrast between the present age and the *New Age*. Here, however, a different picture may be in the apostle's mind. In Rome as in other places during the first century there was a widespread interest in astrology, including a belief in planetary and astral deities. Thus it is possible that *things present* may be understood as the present positions and influence of the stars, and *things to come* as their future positions and influence; certainly Paul was thinking of more than present and future events. The next term, *powers*, elsewhere in the epistles is joined with such names as *thrones* and *dominions*, and stands for spiritual beings. There is no reason to suppose that Paul has varied his usage here, either to speak of the forces of nature or of civil magistrates. In the language of the time *powers* usually meant astral spirits, and it is likely that the word was so understood both by Paul and by his readers. Such hypothetical beings were not usually thought of as subservient to God, and they were almost always considered hostile to man. This is especially clear in the later literature of the Mandaeans. Here we may believe that Paul regards them as in rebellion against God, or at least as trying to maintain their own independence of Him. In view of these facts, *height* and *depth* would probably be taken as zenith and nadir in the courses of the stars, although it is sometimes said that Paul was speaking of spirits above and below the earth. Holding a Jewish doctrine of creation, Paul would regard all spiritual beings as creatures of God, in the same way as human beings and the various entities of nature. So the apostle concludes that neither these nor other created beings or forces shall be able to separate Christians from the love of God they possess in Christ Jesus. Nor can such realities in the last resort separate Christians from the final glory of *adoption* to which God's love shall bring them. This is the measure of the apostle's confidence in the victory of Christ.

CHAPTER 9

Divine Election

9:1–5 I am speaking the truth in Christ, I am not lying, when my conscience bears joint witness with me in the Holy Spirit, for I have great grief and unceasing pain in my heart. For I myself have longed to be separated from Christ by Anathema for the sake of my brethren, my kinsmen in physical terms, who are Israelites, to whom belongs the adoption and the glory and the covenants and the giving of the Torah and the worship and the promises, to whom belong the fathers, and from whom in physical terms is Christ, who is God over all (things or men) blessed to eternity. Amen. (Alternatively, Christ, who is over all, may God be blessed to eternity. Amen.)

* * *

Dodd suggests that chapters 9 to 11, which state the place of Israel in God's plan of salvation, may have been composed apart from the rest of the epistle and that they may represent a standard lecture or sermon by the apostle on this subject. In favor of this claim it should be noted that one might pass directly from Chapter 8 to Chapter 12 without any sense of an omission. Yet Dodd also wisely cautions that while these chapters may represent an earlier composition of the apostle, he certainly intended to include their substance. For that reason he had felt free to treat Israel as briefly as he did in Chapter 4. Paul also seems to refer back to this material in later portions of the epistle. Assuredly it was a subject on which he would have found it necessary to express an opinion in many places, and it would have been in order for him to work out such a discussion. It would have a place in his appeal to Rome because Paul suspected that some Christians there were accusing him of apostasy from Judaism. Had he written this out following the hymn with which Chapter 8 concludes, he probably would not have made such an abrupt transition from praise of divine love to the expression of his own grief concerning Israel. If we think of it as something prepared on another occasion, we can understand the way in which this treatment begins.

The discussion is introduced by a solemn affirmation of Paul's care for his own People. Among other things, he feels a need to account for the refusal of Israel as a whole to accept the Gospel. Paul can explain that refusal from the fact that, to use Barrett's words, "the Jews were content to evaluate their privilege on a purely human level. To them Torah was a claim on God's favor showing their superiority to other races rather than a judgment upon their failures. In the same way they saw the worship of the Temple as an expression of their own holiness rather than of God's." Thus they were unable to recognize their own Messiah. The style of Stoic diatribe dominates this whole block of material. In Verse 1 Paul shows that to speak the truth *in Christ* is the same thing as to speak *in the Holy Spirit*, but there is no need to move from this to a complete theological treatment of these concepts.

The apostle's sorrow and grief are real. Verse 3 echoes the prayer of Moses in Exodus 32:32, "If thou wilt, forgive this people . . . but if not pray blot me out of the book which thou hast written." In rabbinic literature a similar phrase expressed the highest degree of affection, "I wish to be sin on behalf of . . . ." In modern Catholic devotion it is considered a heroic act of love to call upon God to credit one's own merits to the poor souls in purgatory, although Protestants question the possibility of such a transfer of merit. Paul is saying that he would trade his own hope of salvation for that of his compatriots. Presumably he recognizes that the wish is not possible to fulfill, but it stands as an expression of the attitude proper to every Christian in regard to those who are in need of being saved. In the Septuagint of Deuteronomy the Greek word ANATHEMA is used to translate a Hebrew word which means *doomed to extermination*; in Christian usage it seems to be equivalent to *damned*, to being eternally separated from Christ.

Verses 4–5 outline the historic privileges of Israel. The term *Israelites* is itself a title of religious honor. The *adoption* that is said to belong to Israel implies that this Nation was chosen in order that its members should become *sons of God*, but here the idea is to be explained in terms of Exodus 4:22 and Deuteronomy 14:1 rather than by the definition of Chapter 8. As in Exodus 16:10 and elsewhere, *glory* represents the evident presence of God with His People in the appearance of the Shekinah during the wanderings of Israel in the wilderness. *Covenants* are mentioned in the plural as including those with Abraham and the other patriarchs as well as that with Moses, and so the word describes God's choice of Israel; the past covenants naturally point to the *New Covenant*. The *giving of the Torah* needs no explanation. The divinely ordained rites of the Temple are described under the term *worship*, which rabbinic thought united with Torah and the performance of righteousness as the three pillars on which the world was established. Paul believed that both Torah and worship, when rightly understood, pointed forward to the Gospel. The *promises* first had been understood as the inheritance of the land of Canaan, later as its recovery by the Chosen Nation, but in Paul's mind they had come to be thought of as the blessings brought by the Messiah. The *fathers* are the patriarchs of Genesis whom Paul now counts as spiritual ancestors of all the Christians. The crown of Israel's privilege is the fact that the physical nature of Christ is derived from the Nation; as Lietzmann points out, in His spiritual nature He is Son of God. The fact that God has chosen Israel as the scene of His saving act in Christ makes the rejection yet more culpable.

The translation of the final words of Verse 5 is debated. The King James Version, the Roman Catholic scholars, and Lietzmann all refer the ascription of praise to Christ. The Revised Standard Version and most Protestant writers refer it to God the Father on the ground that Paul would not have called Christ *God*. There are three possibilities. By transposing two monosyllables that are similar in sound, Dodd arrives at the sense "to whom (the Jews) belongs the God who is over all blessed to eternity," but he acknowledges that this transposition is sheer conjecture. Since Paul previously has made the point that God does not belong exclusively to the Jews, this must be rejected. The Revised Standard Version places a period after the Greek word for *flesh*, so that its translation is, "and of their race, according to the flesh, is Christ. God who is over all be blessed forever. Amen." Since the most reliable manuscripts were written without punctuation, one cannot quarrel about where periods are to be placed, and it is to be observed that many of the Greek Fathers have taken the words in this sense. Yet Lagrange's argument against this interpretation is decisive. In Paul, and in Jewish writings contemporary with

Paul, doxologies regularly begin with some sort of predicate, but if this doxology refers to God the Father it begins with the subject. Thus we must accept something equivalent to the King James Version, "to whom belongs Christ according to the flesh, who is God over all blessed to eternity." If Paul does not elsewhere describe Christ as God, he does so here, and evidently he feels that he is able to do so without detracting from the glory of the Father. Actually, there is a very similar ascription of praise to God in Romans 1:25, and yet another which might refer to Christ in II Corinthians 11:31, while in Philippians 2:6–11 it is obvious that Paul is saying that in His eternal nature Christ is equal with the Father.

* * *

9:6–13 Now this is not to say that the word of God has failed: for not all those who are derived from Israel constitute Israel, nor are all his children the seed of Abraham, but "by Isaac shall thy seed be called." This means that it is not the children of the flesh who are the children of God, but the children of the promise are accounted as the seed. For this is the word of promise, "according to this time (the meaning is forty weeks hence) I shall come and Sarah shall have a son." And not only so, but Rebecca also conceived from intercourse with one man, with Isaac our father; for when they were not yet born and had not done anything either virtuous or base, in order that the purpose of God might be established (or, might remain) in terms of choice (or, election), not as a result of performance (or, works) but from the purpose of Him who gave the vocation (or, who calls), it was said to her, "the elder shall be servant to the younger." Just as it has been written, "Jacob I loved, but Esau I hated."

* * *

Barrett's treatment of *election* as set forth in verses 6–13 might stand as the last word on the subject. Verses 1–5 bring a problem before us. Since God so obviously intended His plan of salvation to be fulfilled through Israel, does not Israel's defection mean that God's purpose has been frustrated? In Chapter 11 Paul will try to circumvent the difficulty with the assertion that the Nation's fall is only temporary. Here, however, he attempts a more profound solution. What actually constitutes *Israel?* If it were simply human descent, the idea of blood and soil, an external limit would be set upon

God's freedom. In the Nation's actual history it is clear that God has not been so limited. Therefore Paul defines *Israel* in terms of God's promise, much as the Fourth Gospel speaks of those who were born "not of blood nor of the will of the flesh nor of the will of man, but of God." Here as in Galatians Paul refers to Messiah as the one true seed of Abraham. So it is only *in Christ* that the promises can be fulfilled. For an example Paul turns to Genesis 21:10–12 where Ishmael is rejected in favor of Isaac; one should compare with this Galatians 4:21–31. Isaac's birth depended upon the divine promise, which indicates that the *seed* is to be defined in terms of God's creative freedom. But this example is not sufficiently clear to establish the point about which Paul is concerned. Isaac as the son of a free woman could be taken as representative of legitimate descent, and so could be proposed as a defense for the claims of Israel in contrast to Paul's assertion that by grace the Gentiles could share in the inheritance. So in verses 10–12 a better example is set forward. Jacob and Esau were not the sons of different mothers. They were twins. As in the Septuagint of Numbers 5:20 or Leviticus 18:20, here KOITE has to be understood as an act of sexual intercourse. In this instance God's choice is influenced neither by prior ancestry nor by subsequent virtue; it is completely arbitrary. To quote Barrett directly, "from the human side this means that not works but the call of God is decisive. God, if indeed He is GOD, must choose in accord with His own purpose and without regard to other influences. The promises must be seen as depending not upon anything that man does but upon God's will." So Verse 11 can serve as the answer to any suggestion that God has failed. In such a context there can be no thought of merits, foreseen or otherwise. Everything depends entirely upon God's *calling*. Paul seeks further justification from Scripture for all that he has said by the citation of Malachi 1:2–3. But the justification of this argument will require more than a text from the Bible.

* * *

9:14–29 Therefore what are we to say? Surely not that injustice exists with God? God forbid! Indeed He says to Moses, "I shall have mercy upon whom I have mercy, and I shall have pity upon whom I have pity." Since this is true it does not depend upon him who has the desire nor upon him who has the performance (literally, who runs), but upon

God who shows mercy. For the Scripture says to Pharaoh, "For this very purpose I raised thee up, that in thee I might demonstrate my power, and that my Name might be made known (or, proclaimed) throughout the whole earth." Since this is so, He has mercy upon whom He will and He hardens whom He will. So then you will say to me, "Why does He still find fault? For who withstood (or, was able to withstand) His will?" But, man, who are you indeed that you are carrying on a debate with (literally, making an answer to) God? Shall the thing formed really say to him that formed it, "Why did you make me thus?" Has not the potter the right with the clay to make of the same lump one vessel for a noble use and one for a menial one? And if God in wishing to demonstrate His wrath and to make known His power in His great patience produced (literally, bore) vessels of wrath set in order for destruction, and in order to make known the riches of His glory upon vessels of mercy which He prepared in advance for glory, upon us whom He also called not only from among Jews but also from among Gentiles? As it also says in Hosea: "I shall call that my People which was not my People and her that was not beloved beloved; and it shall be that in the place where it was said to them, 'You are not my People,' there shall they be called sons of the living God." Isaiah also cries aloud in reference to Israel: "Although the number of the sons of Israel be as the sand of the sea, the remnant shall be saved; for fulfilling and hastening (or, abbreviating) His word the Lord shall do this upon the earth." And as Isaiah said before this: "Unless the Lord of Hosts had left us a seed, we should have become as Sodom and have been made like to Gomorrah."

* * *

The apostle realizes that objections may be raised against what he is saying, perhaps that his words can lead to serious misconceptions about the nature of God. Such objections and misconceptions he attempts to answer in a section of diatribe that runs from Verse 14 to Verse 29. He introduces this with a general question. *What are we to say?* Is a God who predestines one unborn child to glory and another to servitude not arbitrary and capricious? As one might expect, Paul answers this, *God forbid!* But in this instance the assertion of apostolic authority cannot bring satisfaction to the reader. Comparison of the various commentaries will show this. Dodd confesses that he is helpless here, that a man is not a pot and that the whole argument is unsound in many ways. Michel makes a clear analysis of the section, and then explains it with a complexity resembling double talk.

Bardenhewer looks this particular peril in the face and rushes off to deal resolutely with other dragons of less forbidding aspect. Lagrange does likewise in his exegesis, and his appended note on the question is far removed from Paul. Barrett adopts what is essentially the theory of Augustine, and does his best to make it acceptable. While Lietzmann tries to face the problem, in the end he admits defeat. This, probably, must be the fate of the present effort as well. The Augustinian explanation is logical. It holds that all men have been corrupted by Adam's sin. All stand justly condemned. God has no need to predestine any to damnation, for the doom of each has already been determined by the fault of the ancestor of all. There can be mercy exercised upon this company of the damned, a mercy perfectly illustrated by the choice of one unborn child in preference to another because this choice is absolutely free from the influence of merits present or foreseen. No man can earn salvation, no man can deserve salvation, and it is perhaps particularly clear that those who are accounted the *saved*, Jacob, David, Elisha, had no legitimate claim upon God's choice. A crowned caprice sits on the throne of heaven, and each new favorite chosen proves more clearly than the last that God is blind. Barrett tries to make this tolerable, for he is fundamentally Augustinian in his thought. He declares that *election* takes place always and only *in Christ* and that even the vessels of wrath or of ignoble use have their place *within* and not *outside* God's purpose, which is a purpose of mercy. Like Augustine, Barrett fails to show how this mercy becomes evident to Ishmael driven into the desert, to Esau cheated of his father's blessing, to Pharaoh mourning his son, or to the medieval Jew in his ghetto.

But we have rejected the Augustinian theory of *original sin*, at least as an expression of Paul's thought. The human race may be totally unworthy of God's love, but the God who is revealed in Christ is not more vindictive than the beings He has created. If God loves the undeserving, He loves all of them and not merely individuals who have been selected in accord with no principle of merit whatever. To consider living persons, God loves Albert Schweitzer and Mao Tse-tung, Thurgood Marshall and Orval Faubus, Rafael Trujillo, Kate Smith, Pope John, Therese Neumann. One cannot say that God loves any one of these more or less than the others, that He is more interested in the salvation of any one of these than of the others. Yet God's love cannot be expressed in the same way to such diverse persons, and the differences in the expression of God's love will be accounted for by the differences shown in their individual responses to His love. With some God's love must take the form of wrath, even of punishment. With others it will take the form of approbation and reward. But it is contrary to the moral nature of God as revealed in Christ to suggest that He is directly responsible for any evil action. In other words, if we are damned it is our own doing. It is not God's will that anyone should be damned, but if we insist on it God has such respect for our freedom that He will allow us to work out our own damnation even while He overrules the results of our sin for the fulfillment of His wider purpose. On the other hand, if we do attain salvation it is God who is responsible for the fact. In Aristotelian terms, God is the Final Cause of salvation because He created us with a possibility of responding to His prompting; He is the Formal Cause because of His saving act in Christ that provides the necessary conditions in which the response can be made; and He is the Material Cause because He confers upon us the grace by which alone we may be enabled to persevere in following out His purpose. For ourselves the most that we can say is that the Efficient Cause of salvation is the response we may make to the divine prompting. So while we are the authors of our own damnation we cannot be considered the authors of our own salvation; we can do no more than cooperate with God who is its author, while knowing that if we do not cooperate through the response of our faith we shall not receive the salvation for ourselves.

Yet it is not possible to say that Paul understood the paragraph in this way. The apostle was the victim as well as the beneficiary of his own conversion. He knew that God had chosen him at a time when he stood in opposition to God's purpose. God had had mercy upon him when there was not even cooperation on his part, still less deserving. He knew that others had not been so favored. That this might imply injustice on God's part was unthinkable, but he was too closely involved in the situation himself to be able to explain its consequences with precision, or even to understand the small share that he did have in the work of his own salvation. On Damascus Road it had not seemed possible for him to refuse God's call, and subsequently he had given himself so completely to the work of the Gospel that he had never considered the possibility of apostasy. Yet the possibility was there for him, as it had been for Judas and as it is for us.

In some degree this may be a solution for the problem of predestination. Obviously it is very far from final, but it is sufficient to serve as a groundwork for the discussion of the text. The question, *then what are we to say?* introduces the diatribe proper. God's dealing with Jacob and Esau must not under any circumstances be regarded as a proof that God acts in a manner contrary to justice. Perhaps this can be illustrated from later incidents of what may be called "salvation history." The first citation chosen by Paul is from Exodus 33:19, a word of God addressed to Moses; the apostle by his word order shows his emphasis. The consequence of this assertion that God will show mercy in accord with His own purpose rather than because of any man's desire (willing) or performance (the Stoic term of running which meant performance is also used by Paul in I Corinthians), is that salvation depends entirely on divine mercy. In this we may agree with Paul. There comes a further illustration from the story of Pharaoh in Exodus 9:16; in the same chapter it is also declared that God had hardened Pharaoh's heart. From this Paul draws the conclusion that God's mercy and His permission to anyone to stand in opposition to the divine purpose are determined solely by God's sovereign will. In this we cannot follow the apostle. While it must be said that in this context mercy and hardening of heart do not refer strictly to salvation and final reprobation, it remains true that we are here confronted with a primitive religious concept that has no real place in Christianity. The God revealed in Christ does not prompt anyone to sin simply in order to win fame for Himself. He permits sin because of His respect for the freedom of those whom He has created, but He never prompts sin. An arbitrary choice of Jacob in preference to Esau may be regarded as a step in the fulfillment of a grand design, and the history of the Exodus may represent a further development of that design, but both of these stories come to us through fallible human beings, and neither of them represents a perfect understanding of the divine nature. On this point Paul's fundamentalist approach to Scripture has brought him into error.

In true diatribe style Verse 19 states the obvious objection. If God were to act in such a way as has been suggested, it must mean the end of all moral responsibility. The man who is compelled by God to do evil is no longer a *person* but a *thing*. The spade that should be employed in cultivating land cannot be held to account if it is used as a weapon of assault. Paul here seems to have missed that point entirely. He simply declares that man must not argue with God. Yet God's action can be immune to man's question only when it is good from every possible point of view. Paul's appeal to authority is bolstered by a citation of Isaiah 29:16 in Verse 20, and with this there seems to be joined something from Wisdom of Solomon 12:12 as well. The weakness of the apostle's argument lies in the fact that God has not given personality to clay. While it may be true that people have no more claims in relation to God than clay has in relation to the man who forms it, it remains true that human beings have received personality and for that very reason their situation is different as a result of God's own action. The quotation from Jeremiah 18:6 in Verse 21 adds nothing to this. Pots may be designed for varied uses, but unlike men they can never be the objects of moral judgment. As Dodd notes, when Paul argues an untenable case his intellectual confusion comes to be reflected in linguistic obscurity. So here verses 22–23 state the protasis of a conditional sentence, and the apostle never does supply the apodosis. In sense the verses may be compared to Romans 3:6–8. There *sin* had demonstrated God's *righteousness*, although not very clearly. Here *wrath* demonstrates God's *mercy* in a manner yet more obscure. It is evident that the *glory* referred to is that of the Day of Judgment. Paul has done a bad job with a worse case, and now he simply lets the matter drop and turns to an issue of greater importance to him, the fact that believing Gentiles are members of the *true* or *spiritual Israel*.

This theme occupies verses 24–29, which consist chiefly in texts of Scripture, Hosea 2:23 and 1:10, Isaiah 10:22–23 and 1:9 in that order. We who belong to this *spiritual Israel* have been included within it solely because of God's call. To this we can agree. If God had not called us, given us revelation, helped our response by His grace, assuredly we would not have turned to Him. As in rabbinic usage, Paul pays no regard whatever to the context of his citations from the prophets. Hosea had meant that at the restoration of the Nation God would again call Israel *His People*, although all claims upon His love had been forfeited by sin. Paul has it that when Gentiles come to faith in Christ, God will call them *His People*, although formerly they had no Covenant relation to Him at all. Isaiah had been making a threat of judgment; of all the great number of the sons of Israel only a remnant would be spared or saved. Paul adds a few words from Hosea 1:10 to the first Isaiah quotation. The other text in Verse 29 is important for the development of Paul's teaching of the *saved remnant*. Isaiah makes a threat of judgment that is relieved by a promise that some portion of the Nation is to be spared. This time *seed* in the singular is used as equivalent to *remnant*. From this Paul derives the picture that is employed more directly in Galatians, the scheme of a gradual or progressive restriction of what is meant by "God's Chosen," an ever purer and more homogeneous *remnant*, until all is expressed in a single individual, the one true *seed of Abraham*, Christ. Then *in Christ* that *seed* becomes expanded into the *spiritual Israel* which in theory might embrace the entire human race, all who are *in Christ* whether Jew or Gentile. This forms the basis of Barrett's defense of a doctrine of *election* as something that is not arbitrary because it takes place always and only *in Christ*, that even the "vessels of wrath" have a place *within* and not *outside* God's purpose of mercy. Perhaps one should note that the D manuscript in Verse 28 adds after *hastening* the words "in righteousness that His purpose may be swiftly accomplished"; in the face of the combined witness of Papyrus 46, Aleph, and B this addition cannot be accepted, and it does nothing to clarify the text.

* * *

9:30–33 Therefore what are we to say? That Gentiles who did not strive for (or, pursue) a status of being in the right received a status of being in the right, a being in the right which comes from faith; while Israel in striving for (or, pursuing) a principle (or, law) of being in the right did not accomplish it as a principle (or, law). Why so? Because it (Greek has no pronoun, Paul means the principle) was not derived from faith but as it were from performance (or, works). They stumbled at a stone of stumbling, as it is written, "Behold I set in Zion a stone of stumbling and a rock of offense, and he who believes in it (or, Him) shall not be put to shame."

* * *

After a weak argument it seems perfectly natural to ask once more, "Therefore what are we to say?" At least one clear consequence can be drawn. The Gentiles, at any rate the Christian Gentiles, without trying to earn a status of being in the right with God nevertheless attained it as a result of *faith*. On the other hand, Israel, which had sought to follow a principle or law designed to bring about a status of being in the right with God, had come short of what the Nation sought. Verse 30 looks as if Paul were saying that Israel had failed to live up to the law, but this cannot be the apostle's intention because it would imply that if Israel had lived up to its Torah it would have attained the status of being in the right with God. Such an implication would be contrary to Paul's thought generally, and in particular to the idea of Verse 32 that the status of being in the right with God can be attained only through *faith* and never through *accomplishment*. Israel had been seeking the right goal by the wrong means. The Gentiles who did not recognize the goal had no preconceived notion of how it should be sought, and therefore they had not been drawn away from the path of faith when it was shown to them. In verses 32–33, Isaiah 8:14 and 28:16 are combined as a proof text on this issue. A similar interpretation of Christ's work appears in Matthew 21:42, Acts 4:11 (where it is ascribed to Peter), I Peter 2:6–8, and two texts in Luke. Thus the importance and wide acceptance of the figure of Christ as the stone chosen by God is clearly established, although it was not regularly used to support the argument that being in the right with God depends upon *faith*. As "stone of stumbling" Christ creates *offense* for some and *faith* for others. Thus Paul concludes his second section on the place of Israel in God's plan of salvation. He has given a satisfactory proof of the fact that Gentiles may be included in the *true Israel* by means of their *faith*, and this has more significance than the fact that he has failed in his effort to show how God's action in this matter may be reconciled with the claims of justice.

CHAPTER 10

Israel

10:1–13 My brethren, the longing of my heart and my prayer to God on their behalf is for salvation. For I bear them witness that they have zeal (or, aspiration) for God but not in accord with guidance (or, knowledge). For not knowing the righteousness (or, status of being in the right) which comes from God, and seeking to establish their own (by this Paul means a righteousness that depends upon themselves), they did not submit to the righteousness which is from God. For to everyone who believes, Christ is the conclusion of Torah in righteousness (or, being in the right). For Moses writes that the man who performed the righteousness which comes from Torah shall live by it. But the righteousness which comes from faith speaks thus: "Thou shalt not say in thine heart 'who shall ascend into the heaven'—that means to bring Christ down; or 'who shall go down into the abyss'—that means to bring Christ up from the dead." But what does it say? "The word is near to thee, in thy mouth and in thine heart." That means the word of faith which we preach. Because if thou shalt confess with thy mouth that Jesus is Lord, and shalt believe with thine heart that God raised Him up from the dead, thou shalt be saved. For with the heart a man believes in order to be in the right, and with the mouth a man makes his acknowledgment with the purpose of salvation. For the Scripture says, "Everyone who believes in it (or, Him) shall not be put to shame." For there is no distinction either of Jew or Gentile. For there is the same Lord of all, who is generous (or, rich) for all those who call upon Him. For everyone who shall call upon the Name of the Lord shall be saved.

* * *

While no sharp division should be made between chapters 9 and 10, there are distinctive developments here that must be taken into account. These will be understood most clearly from Lietzmann's critical note on the *righteousness of God* that appears at this point in his commentary. There it is said that the fault of the Jews lies in their disregard of the *righteousness of God.* Instead of seeking to be comprehended within it, they have attempted to set up in its stead *their own righteousness.* The same concept is set forth in different words, and with such clarity as to exclude all misunderstanding, in Philippians 3:9. There the apostle speaks of himself as "not having my own righteousness which is from the Torah, but that which is by means of the faith of Christ, the righteousness which is from God in response to faith." This *personal righteousness* is that which one has acquired for himself by performance of Torah, while the *righteousness of God* is given by God in response to the faith of the believer, as in Romans 10:4–6. So Paul sees *their own* and *of God* as absolutely parallel. In both cases the possessor or bearer of the righteousness is the man to whom is credited the "imputed" righteousness of Romans 4:11, or the "status of being acquitted" of Romans 3:28. In the second instance the Person who acquits is God, as is clear from Romans 3:26. On the other hand, in Romans 3:5 the *righteousness of God* is contrasted with *our unrighteousness,* and from its whole context there it is recognized as a *divine attribute.* In Romans 1:17–18 the *righteousness of God* is contrasted both with God's *wrath* and with man's *unrighteousness.* Yet in opposition to this the clause *from faith unto faith* of Romans 1:17 raises a difficulty, and if it is combined with the phrase *righteousness from faith* one is forced to acknowledge that the *righteousness of God* is a quality for men. Thus it may be clearly established that from Romans 1:17 onward *God's righteousness* has a dual meaning. When it is taken up in Romans 3:21–25 it designates a *divine attribute* by which grace may be conferred upon men who have faith. This is especially clear in the earliest Pauline text where this formula is encountered, II Corinthians 5:21, "For us God has made Christ to be sin." This means that God made Christ to be the bearer of sins in order that we might become the *righteousness of God* in Him. It is only as we are *in Christ* that we can become bearers of *God's righteousness.* Thus it is clear that Paul, using a term that commonly denoted a divine attribute, converted it into a human attribute, and in this Pauline sense the words *of God* as applied to *righteousness* must be a genitive of source, meaning from God, divine, spiritual, or some similar idea. But in most Pauline texts the two meanings are present at once. In II Corinthians 1:12 Paul says, "because in the holiness and sincerity of God, not in worldly wisdom but in the love of God, we conducted ourselves in the world." Here the holiness and sincerity that are *from God* stand in contrast with the personal wisdom *of the flesh*. With this one may compare Odes of Solomon 25:10, "I was strong in the truth and holy in thy righteousness." An alternative idea defines God's righteousness as a divine attribute transferred to the believer as a result of mystical union with Christ. The phrase itself appears outside the Pauline writings only in James 1:20 and II Peter 1:1.

Beginning with a repetition of his longing for Israel's spiritual welfare, Paul now attempts a further explanation of the Nation's failure. First he commends the zeal for God that his compatriots have shown, however misguided it may be. The word EUDOKIA is not good Greek, but it was frequently used by Jewish writers instead of the correct EUDOKESIS. While acknowledging this loyalty of Israel to God, Paul adds that its negative results show that in some way it is in error. Here the apostle addressed the Christians as *brethren*, and he refers to the Jews as *they* as if he were not one himself. The fault of Israel's religion is stated in Verse 3. Failing to comprehend the *righteousness which comes from God*, they have attempted to put in its place their *personal righteousness* which comes from performance; by this action they have been trying to put themselves in the place of God. Barrett's explanation of this point is very satisfactory: "Virtue can become rebellion against God whenever the person who possesses virtue turns it into a standard for the judgment of others. Only the person who is content to wait upon God's decision truly accepts his proper status as a dependent creature." The extent of Israel's error on this point prompts Paul to use the emphatic word EPIGNOSIS to show how far the Jews were from true knowledge.

Yet the Jews were not entirely wrong. Indeed, they were right in their conviction that no man can come before God unless he has some sort of righteousness, and wrong only in their belief that man had to acquire this for himself. By His saving act in Christ, God already has made available to everyone who will respond with faith the *righteousness* which He Himself can confer. Thus one may describe Christ as the TELOS of the Torah, but there is debate regarding what Paul meant by this term. Most of the Fathers took it that Christ is the *goal*, the *absolute fulfillment* of Torah. Yet when this text is compared with Romans 3:21 or Galatians 3:25, it seems rather that Paul is calling Christ the *termination* of Torah, and is saying that the man who believes in Christ has no need of Torah in order to attain *righteousness*. Then Verse 5 may be seen as strictly parallel to Romans 2:13 and to Galatians 3:12 in which Leviticus 18:5 is also cited; the thought is that to perform Torah truly means to turn to Christ and so to find life in Him. In verses 6–8 Paul offers an inexact quotation of Deuteronomy 30:11–14 and makes use of some of the rabbinic exegesis to which that text had previously been subjected. This rabbinic exegesis had taken the Torah as an eternal reality in God's will, and had declared that Moses ascended into Heaven in order to bring it down to the world of men. This is far removed from the original intent of the compilers of Deuteronomy who had meant to say only that the requirements of Torah could be fulfilled. But because he could draw upon this exegetical history, Paul felt free to develop his own application of the text, and he made it the basis of a positive appeal for response to God. It may be that the application of these words to Divine Wisdom in Baruch 3:29–30 gave further encouragement for the apostle to substitute his own personification of the *righteousness which is from faith*. This divinely given righteousness is set almost in opposition to Moses, and when the words from Deuteronomy are ascribed to such a *righteousness* they become a typological reference to Christ. Like most typological treatments, this is obscure, but one can discern its meaning. There is no need to bring Messiah down from Heaven as the Jews had sought to do by their performance of Torah, nor yet to bring Him up from the grave. Incarnation and Resurrection have both taken place. The eschatological conditions have already been realized. Christ is even now present and He can be known in the preaching of the Christians. In Him at this very moment men can receive the *righteousness which comes from faith*. Much of the language here is decorative, and perhaps it should be noted that Paul's version of Deuteronomy 30:13 differs from any form of that text known elsewhere.

While the *word of faith* in Verse 8 certainly is the Gospel, it seems that the following verses relate the appropriation of salvation to the act of Baptism. The formula of salvation is stated in Verse 9 and is given an explanation in Verse 10. It is the inward conviction or self-commitment of faith in one's heart that puts one in the right with God in the first place, but Paul finds the actual acknowledgment of this conviction with one's mouth equally necessary if one is to attain final salvation. This must mean that there can be no hidden Christians and no invisible church. It is also a declaration of the significance of Baptism as the outward proof that one is a Christian. Clearly the baptismal confession of Paul's day was no more than the recognition of Jesus as *Lord*, and as a title *Lord* had displaced *Messiah* in the Gentile churches even within the second decade after the Crucifixion. Barrett gives great importance to the other term of this confession, the assertion that God had raised Jesus from the dead, as something needed to protect divine unity and to show that Christ was what He was because of His union with the Father. It is no less important to relate this to what Paul says of Baptism in Chapter 6. The confession one makes must include the statement that God raised Christ from the dead *because* Baptism means reigning with Christ. Eschatological salvation has already begun, although its completion in what Paul in Chapter 8 had called *adoption* must await the Last Day. Verse 10 is a brief summary of Paul's conviction, and Verse 11 reinforces it with a quotation of Isaiah 28:16.

Verse 12 then looks back to the statement that all without distinction have sinned, both Jews and Gentiles. Now Paul shows that all without distinction have the same Lord, the same divine resources, the same call to faith. Verse 13 adds to this a citation of Joel 2:32, which originally had meant that everyone in Israel who called upon the Name of God would be delivered, but which for Paul becomes a declaration that the Gospel is to be extended beyond the limits of Israel. The Septuagint had frequently used the Greek word *Lord* to translate the Hebrew Name *Jahveh* or *Yahweh*. In the same way the Septuagint had used *Lord* as a title of the Messiah in some of the apocryphal writings it included along with the Hebrew canon. This latter use of the word *Lord* had been appropriated by Semitic-speaking Christians years before the public ministry of Paul began. In divine providence this use of the same word to stand both for God and for the Messiah helped to prepare for the doctrine of the Trinity. Yet for Gentile Christians the title *Lord* probably was understood less from the Septuagint than from analogy with the Mystery Cults. To call Jesus *Lord* was to refer to Him as *Lord of the Cult*, and so the words *Lord Jesus* would declare the truth of which the imperial cult's *Lord Caesar* was a demonic caricature.

* * *

10:14–21 So how are they to call upon Him whom they did not believe? And how are they to believe Him whom they did not hear? And how are they to hear apart from someone to preach? Or how are they to preach unless they shall be sent? Just as it is written, "How seasonable (or, beautiful) are the feet of those who proclaim good things." But not all were obedient to the Gospel. For Isaiah says, "Lord, who believed our report?" Whereas faith proceeds from a report (or, hearing) and the report is by means of a word of Christ. But I say, Did they not hear? Assuredly: "Their voice went forth into all the earth, and their words into the ends of the inhabited world." But I say, Did Israel not understand? First of all Moses says: "I shall provoke you to jealousy with what is not a nation, with a foolish nation shall I provoke you to anger." And Isaiah even dares to say: "I was found by those who did not seek me, I became manifest to those who did not ask for me." Then to Israel he says: "All the day long I stretched out my hands to a People that was disobedient and contrary."

* * *

Lietzmann joins verses 14–15 with the prior paragraph, but the alternative arrangement seems to agree better with Paul's meaning. The argument is formal, even artificial. Verses 14–15 take up the statement that those who call upon the Name of the Lord will be saved, and they set forth a scheme that begins and ends in God. One can call upon God only if one first comes to faith, and one can come to faith only from hearing the Christian Gospel in the present time or from hearing its equivalent in God's promise as contained in prior revelation, and one can hear only if someone preaches, and one can preach only if duly commissioned thereto by God. Like the Fourth Gospel at a later date, which declared that belief through the word of a witness was in no way less significant than that which came from the preaching of Jesus Himself, so here Paul indicates that wherever Christ is faithfully preached it is Christ Himself who is to be heard. This holds true both of the anticipatory preaching of Israel's prophets and of the testimony now being declared by the Christian missionaries. A citation of Isaiah 52:7 tells of the grace or beauty of the task of preaching God's revelation.

Paul's question, then, is why Israel has failed, what link in this chain of testimony has not held. Verse 16 states the obvious fact that the majority in Israel has not been responsive, and supports this with a statement from Isaiah 53:1. Verse 17 repeats the claim that faith results from hearing and that the only thing worth hearing for this purpose is the word or revelation of God in Christ. But Israel has heard. While this was not the original meaning of Psalm 19:4, Paul presses the text into service to set forth the idea that the message of the Christian missionaries has been carried into all lands. The trouble has been in the will of Israel. The Nation heard and refused to understand. Deuteronomy 32:21 was frequently quoted by the Christians to make this point, although its original meaning was that Israel had provoked the jealousy of its God by worshiping unreal deities and that in the same manner God would provoke the Nation's jealousy by means of that which was not His own People. For Christians this became a way of representing the Church that was not a People at all but was composed of men from every nation. The text was an obvious one to use in this way. Isaiah 65:1 is then employed to support a point Paul had already made in Chapter 9, namely, that those who did not seek God found Him because they were not hindered by their own preconceptions of the manner of His calling. At the same time Isaiah 65:2, originally a complaint against the disobedience of Israel, is used to state the converse of this, to show that it was Israel's self-will that had made obedience impossible. Paul describes this as a bold statement on the prophet's part, and it would have been so if the original author had intended the precise application the apostle made. For modern Christians this section has very limited value, but as addressed to Jews under rabbinic influence it formed an argument that would be difficult to refute.

CHAPTER 11

God's Purpose

11:1–10 In consequence I ask, surely God did not reject His People? God forbid! For I myself am an Israelite, from the seed of Abraham, from the tribe of Benjamin. God did not reject His People whom He foreknew. Or do you not know what the Scripture says in Elijah, when he intercedes to God against Israel? "Lord, they slew thy prophets, they broke down thine altars, and I alone am left and they are seeking my life." But what does the oracle say to him? "I have left for myself seven thousand men who did not bow a knee to Baal." So likewise also in this present time there has been a remnant in accord with the choice (or, election) of grace (or, favor). But if by grace (or, favor) it is no longer from performance (or, works), since if it were, grace (or, favor) would no longer be grace (or, favor). What then? What Israel was seeking, this it did not obtain, but the chosen (or, elect) obtained it, while the rest were hardened, just as it is written: "God gave to them a spirit of stupor, eyes not to see and ears not to hear, until this present day." And David says, "Let their table become a snare and a trap (literally, a hunting) and a cause of offense and a recompense to them, let their eyes be darkened not to see, and bow down their back forever (or, continually)."

* * *

The word OUN in 11:1 takes up the ARA of 10:17. Specialists are at odds as to whether the first major division of this chapter should come after Verse 10 or after Verse 12. Here the former scheme has been chosen only because the structure of Verse 11 is parallel to that of Verse 1. It is generally agreed that a lesser division may be made after Verse 6. The paragraph is relatively simple, and may be regarded as a sort of expansion of 9:30–33, the declaration that Israel failed to attain that for which it strove while others attained without striving. The verb LEGO can have an interrogative sense, and Verse 1 will be more clearly understood if it is so interpreted. There is a loose quotation from Psalm 94:14, which Paul casts in the form of a question expecting a negative answer: So I ask, has God really cast off His People? The answer is the emphatic negative, *God forbid!* Some Jews have not been cast off, for Paul himself has every claim as an Israelite and he is prepared to name his own tribe. Benjamin had remained part of the Southern Kingdom, although its earliest ties had been with Ephraim. Thus it was seen not only as a true part of existing Israel but also as a pledge of the recovery of the Northern tribes. So it was especially appropriate that God's Apostle to the Gentiles should belong to Benjamin. In Philippians, Paul deals at even greater length with his Israelite heritage.

Paul's own life proves that God has not abandoned His People whom He foreknew; the mention of foreknowledge here should not be made a defense of *election,* for it merely implies that Israel's eventual salvation has been God's purpose throughout history. This goal the Almighty has long worked to accomplish, and since there can be no change in God no purpose of the divine will can be abandoned. The apostle adds that a proper understanding of Scripture ought to convince anyone of this truth. The citations chosen are from I Kings 19:14 and 18. In Jewish writings of the period there are references to what Scripture says *in Elijah,* meaning in those chapters dealing with the first of the line of prophets since no individual book had been ascribed to him. Even in the past Israel had been disobedient. Paul changes the word order of the text; the breaking down of altars is a more direct attack upon God than is the killing of prophets, for the man who slays a prophet might have other motives besides hatred of God. As Elijah at the Mount of God felt that he was alone, so the faithful Jewish Christians now might feel themselves to be a helpless minority. Yet it was not so. Paul was sure that there were some whose hearts were steadfast, although for the moment they might not themselves be aware of the proper consequences of their loyalty.

The word CHREMATISMOS in proper Greek meant the answer of an oracle, and it has been so translated here. From Maccabean times it had been used in Israel to refer to the words of God. Paul revises the Septuagint form of the text to make it more useful for his present purpose. The feminine article with *Baal* can be explained from history. In Israel the name of this fertility god had been regarded as unmentionable, and it had become customary to replace it with the noun *shame* which in Greek is grammatically feminine. Evidently Paul had started to say *shame* and had decided that *Baal* would be understood more clearly by his readers, and he failed to make a correction. In Elijah's day there had been a faithful *remnant*, and the apostle declares that there is one likewise in his own time. He hastens to add that now as then the *remnant* exists by the choice of God's favor. This must be so if salvation is to be a gift and not something that man earns for himself. There is some textual uncertainty in Verse 6. The Nestle text, following Papyrus 46 and the D manuscript, reads "if by favor it is no longer from works since in that case favor would no longer be favor." The harder reading, supported by the B manuscript, is "since in that case work would no longer be work." The easier reading is so completely in accord with Paul's thought that it ought to be accepted here. As a gift, salvation must depend on God's choice and not on what man has done; what depends on man's performance would not be a gift but an obligation. One need not be a disciple of Paul in order to realize that no man can put God in his debt; the disciple of Jesus must say this.

The parallel between Romans 11:7–10 and 9:30–33 is obvious to all. In both sections the theme is introduced by a question, but in the present instance Paul's argument is carried a step further than it was before. Once more it is said that what Israel sought it did not obtain, but this time the apostle adds that the *elect* did get what was sought, and it is evident that Paul is thinking of a chosen group within Israel. The *elect* (the Greek word is a singular collective noun) are set against the background of the rest of the Nation, against a majority who were *made callous*. The primary meaning of this Greek verb is to turn to stone, and so it must be taken as equivalent to *harden* in Romans 9:18. Some scholars have proposed the substitution of some form of a verb for *disable* that is similar in sound to the Greek for *petrify*, and so to interpret the text here as telling of a majority who "*were disqualified*." But to justify this change one would need substantial support for it in the ancient manuscripts, and such support does not exist. The Nestle text here seems reasonable. Paul then offers a free citation of Scripture, a combination of Deuteronomy 29:4 with Isaiah 29:10, to buttress his claims. Mark cites a similar text, Isaiah 6:9–10, as an explanation of why Jesus taught in parables. In both instances the motive clearly is apologetic. Christians had to account in some way for the fact that many of the Jews were exposed to the truth of Christianity and yet refused to accept it. Paul finds additional evidence that Israel's failure was foreseen in the divine will from Psalm 69:22–23. Such support in Scripture should be enough in rabbinic treatment for any theory, for all three divisions of the canon are represented, the Law, the Prophets, and the Writings.

Paul's teaching concerning sin is that it feeds upon itself, that the initial act of rebellion against God must inevitably lead to further acts of rebellion, that if one chooses sin God will not stand in the way of that choice but will allow the sinner to go on to wickedness which increases continually until the full horror of the cosmic demon *sin* becomes manifest in him. This teaching is the fruit of the apostle's experience, and it is supported by the experience of other people. Paul seeks to make it plain that nothing less than this has happened to the bulk of the Chosen Nation. Yet he has too much faith in the power and love of God to draw the conclusion that Israel's fall, or the fall of anyone else, is beyond recovery. His hope for the restoration of his own compatriots to God's favor is about to be described. In the meantime, mention of the *elect* here must not be understood as a predestinarian concept. As far as may be seen, *elect* is no more than a name for the *remnant*. Certainly those who belong to that *remnant* owe their position to God and not to their own choice. In that sense the *remnant* can be described as the *elect*. But Paul does not define this more closely here than in his general description of the process of salvation.

* * *

11:11–24 So I ask, did they really stumble in order to fall? God forbid! But by their transgression there is salvation for the Gentiles, that they may be provoked to jealousy. Now if their transgression is welfare of the world and their lapse welfare of the Gentiles, how much more will their fulfillment mean! Now I am speaking to you, the Gentiles; therefore in my capacity as Apostle to the Gentiles I exult in this service of mine, if somehow I may provoke my own People (literally, flesh) to jealousy and may save some among them. For if their destruction is a reconciliation of the world, will not their acceptance be actually life from the dead? Now if the first fruits be holy, so also is the mass; and if the root be holy, so also are the branches. Now if some of the branches were broken off, and you who were a wild olive were grafted in among them and became a partaker of the root of the fatness of the olive, do not be arrogant in regard to the branches. But if you are arrogant, it is not you who support the root, but the root supports you. So you will say, "Branches were broken off in order that I might be grafted in." True. They were broken off for want of faith, and you by reason of faith are established. Do not be conceited but be fearful: for if God did not spare the natural branches, neither will He spare you. So consider (or, behold) the kindness and the severity of God; severity toward those who fell, but toward you the kindness of God providing that you shall continue in His kindness, since He may cut you away also; while they, if they should not continue in lack of faith, shall be grafted in. For God is able to graft them in again. For if you were cut from what is by nature a wild olive and contrary to nature were grafted into a good olive, how much rather shall they be grafted according to nature into their own olive!

* * *

Verse 11 repeats the question of Verse 1 in another way. Recognizing that God's Chosen Nation, apart from a *remnant*, has made an error and so has forfeited its privilege, is it an irreparable error? The answer is the same as before. *God forbid!* This is amplified by a statement of the results of this temporary departure from the divine purpose by Israel, a departure which has provided the occasion for Christian preaching to be offered to the Gentiles. Yet the last clause of Verse 11 does not set forth the only motive for a Gentile mission. It is true that Paul held the turning to the Gentiles was undertaken so promptly because Israel had proved disobedient, but the apostle's writings make it clear that he regarded this extension of salvation as a part of God's eternal purpose. The thought of provoking Israel probably is included because Paul remembers that he has already quoted Deuteronomy 32:21 in the previous chapter. He considers that this desire for emulation will be a useful by-product of the work to which God has called him among the Gentiles. God has overruled the evil involved in Israel's *false step* (Goodspeed's brilliant translation of PARAPTOMA) and *falling behind* (HETTEMA) for the benefit of the entire world, specifically for the benefit of the Gentiles. But if evil can be overruled for good, good itself will prove yet more useful for God's purposes. The restoration of Israel to its destined relationship with God will mean *life from the dead*. There have been many who regard this benefit of the restoration of Israel as limited in its effects to the Chosen Nation. Others insist that the benefit is for all mankind. On this Lietzmann's argument is decisive. The pronoun AUTON is used three times in this verse, and its meaning cannot vary within a single sentence. Therefore the benefit is not for Israel alone but for all. Thus *life from the dead* is not a spiritual revival for the bulk of the Nation that is dead in sin, but it must refer to the consummation of the divine purpose, to the reality of *adoption* considered in Chapter 8, to the revival of God's creation as a whole.

Verses 13–15 are closely connected with 11–12. Taking up the thought of provoking Israel to jealousy, Paul attempts to explain it more fully to the Gentile members of the church in Rome, and to make the idea more acceptable to them. In his capacity as Apostle to the Gentiles he claims a special right to speak to these people. This vocation or service to God which has been given to him will be further glorified in leading to the conversion of some who belong to the Chosen Nation. Evidently Paul's expectation is a modest one; he anticipates that individual conversions will result from his own work. The restoring of Israel as a whole he expects as a consequence of the total Christian mission in which his part (however great) is only a minor fraction. Verse 16 then moves from this to introduce the allegory of the wild and the cultivated olive trees. There is a reference here to Jewish sacrificial customs, with a reminiscence from Numbers 15:17–21. A cereal offering was made from the first fruits of the grain. This had the effect of making the rest of the year's harvest ceremonially clean, and therefore proper food for members of the Holy Nation. It represented a primitive stage of religion in which the deity by accepting the first fruits removed the taboo from the entire crop; it was not a real offering to God.

In this text one must not think of the *first fruits* as meaning the Jewish Christians, the *remnant;* here both *first fruits* and *root* stand for the patriarchs of old, men who have been accepted by God and whose acceptance guarantees the holiness of their descendants. The divine purpose has not changed. In essence Israel is still beloved. It is through the Nation that God's saving purpose is made manifest. Gentile Christians have been grafted into Israel, not Jewish Christians into paganism. The significance of this root of the Old Testament patriarchs is about to be defined for those Gentile branches who have been grafted upon it.

Verses 17–18 state a warning. Anti-Semitism was not unknown in the ancient world, and Paul may have heard some report that the Gentile Christians of Rome tended to look down upon Jews generally if not upon Jewish Christians. Such an attitude has appeared often enough in the centuries which have followed. While Paul feels bound to make the point that certain branches have been broken off from the true stock, and that in this way room has been found for the grafting in of newer branches, yet the fact remains that Israel is the true stock. Among other advantages of Israel, the Bible that Christianity has received from the Jews continues to be the repository of God's revelation. Rabbinic writers had used the figure of the olive tree to represent the Chosen Nation, just as they had used that of the vine. The allegory here ought to be compared with the Johannine picture of the vine and the branches in the development of any New Testament doctrine of the Church. Actually these botanical illustrations are more helpful for the understanding of the nature of the Church than is the other Pauline idea of the Body of Christ. A body that has lost one of its members is forever a maimed body, but a tree or a vine can compensate for such a loss without damage to its life and function. For the point that Paul is making here, the tree is an especially happy choice, for branches can be added that did not originally spring from it and such grafting can stand for the incorporation of new converts. Revelation is through Israel. The Christian preaching itself comes only through the witness of those earliest Jewish disciples of Jesus. Christianity can never be truly a Gentile religion, for all that it can offer is derived from the true stock. The phrase *root of the fatness of the olive* is Semitic idiom; it means simply the fat root, the root that gives fatness to all the branches whether they are its natural growth or whether they have been grafted in from extraneous sources. Perhaps Paul's comment to the Corinthians is appropriate here: "What hast thou that thou didst not receive?"

In view of this, if the Gentile Christians presume to boast of their privilege they will find themselves in precisely the same position as rejected Israel, rejected because it had insisted upon boasting of the privileges it had formerly enjoyed. One might say that branches had been broken off the stock in order to make room for these new shoots which were grafted upon it. This was true; KALOS is idiomatic and means *this is a good argument*. But what follows from this? One must remember the reason why such branches had been pruned away from the tree. They had been removed because of a lack of faith, or one might say because of disobedience to God's demand for faith. In consequence it must be remembered that the new branches hold their position solely because they have the faith or the obedience that the others lacked. Moreover, they can hold that position only for as long as they manifest the faith or obedience. God who refused to spare the natural branches will assuredly refuse to spare others that have no such historical claim, if they show the same disobedience that caused members of the Chosen Nation to be rejected.

The stress on faith in verses 21–24 is probably the strongest argument for free will in all Paul's writing. At the same time it is a complete refutation of the claim that once saved means always saved. As turning away from faith has meant the loss of salvation for the Jew, it will mean the same for the Gentile who does not persevere in faith. As the Gentile could be grafted into God's Covenant contrary to nature, so if the Jew does not continue in his unbelief it will be natural for him to be restored to his proper position. Paul is realistic in his account of God's nature, for he says that it is expressed both in kindness and in severity, and that the way in which God may deal with anyone will depend on the person's faith or lack of faith. At the moment Gentile Christians are the recipients of God's kindness and the unbelieving Jews of His severity, but these positions could be reversed. This does not mean that man is the author of his own salvation. Man's relation to God always depends upon God's grace, but Paul is saying that grace is not arbitrary. God is severe only to those who fall away from Him, while to those who remain in His grace by their faith His kindness is unfailing.

The horticulture here set forth is erroneous. There is no profit from grafting wild branches onto cultivated stock; the reverse is what proves helpful. Yet this does not necessarily mean that Paul has no knowledge of tree grafting. It may be that the illustration in conflict with normal practice has been chosen deliberately, that it represents the unlimited power of God who can accomplish good where there is no reason to look for benefit. God can graft the wild olive upon the true stock with beneficial results for both, and at the same time He can keep the branches that He removed and can restore them at His pleasure. Thus false horticulture is not the ignorance of a city man, but is more probably the purposeful choice of an illustration that tells of the sovereignty of God even as it makes the other points that the apostle is anxious to impress upon his readers.

* * *

11:25–32 For I do not wish you to be ignorant of this mystery, my brethren, so that you may not be conceited about yourselves, because insensibility (or, hardening) has come upon part of Israel until the time when the fullness of the Gentiles may enter in, and thus all Israel shall be saved, just as it is written: "The deliverer shall come from Zion, who shall drive (or, turn) impieties away from Jacob. And this is the Covenant on my part (or, from me) with them, when I shall take away their sins." In terms of the Gospel they are at enmity for your sakes, but in terms of the choice (or, election) they are beloved for the sake of the fathers (or, patriarchs), for the blessings and the call of God are not subject to change. For just as you formerly were disobedient to God, but now have obtained mercy by their disobedience (or, lack of faith), so likewise they have now been disobedient in order that they also may now receive the same mercy as you. For God has imprisoned all in disobedience (or, lack of faith) in order that He may show mercy to all.

* * *

In approaching this paragraph one may do well to begin with a summary of Michel's note on what Paul means by *all Israel*. There are five possibilities. He may mean the Nation as a whole and as comprehending all individuals who belong to it. He may mean the Nation as a corporate being while allowing that individual members of it may be excluded. He may mean the spiritual Israel as in Galatians 6:16. He may mean the elect or *remnant* of Israel as in Romans 9:6. Finally, he may mean the elect as drawn both from Gentiles and from Jews. The first of these interpretations would commit us either to a complete universalism, which Paul certainly did not believe, or it would destroy all of the apostle's arguments regarding a spiritual Israel. The third would be out of place here in a paragraph where *all Israel* is contrasted with the believing Gentiles. The fourth would have no meaning, because Paul obviously is thinking of the salvation of some who do not now belong to the holy *remnant*. The fifth is a predestinarian misconception and is open to the objections already urged against both the third and the fourth. Thus we are left with the second, the concept of Israel as a corporate being from which those individuals who continue in disobedience will be excluded. This will serve the purpose of Paul's argument, and it has been accepted by many reputable scholars of the present century, including Lietzmann. For all who approach the text without preconceptions, this choice is inevitable.

These eight verses add little to what has gone before them. Their function is not so much to develop new ideas as to bring to sharper definition thoughts that have already been stated. Verse 25, however, begins with a phrase that usually in the apostle's writings introduces something new, "I do not wish you not to know, my brethren." The subject on which he wishes them to be informed is a *mystery*. Here the Moffatt translation brings out the meaning, although it is not precisely equivalent to the Greek. The apostle is explaining a *secret purpose* of God, something that can be understood only by those who are *in Christ*. In this instance the knowledge is imparted for the benefit of the Gentile Christian majority in the Roman church; it is a corrective for spiritual pride and is intended to prevent these Gentile Christians from despising others. Hardening or insensibility has come upon a part, indeed upon the majority of the Chosen Nation. But Paul has already made the point that this is not irreparable. It is something temporary. It has a function in the divine plan. It will continue only until the fullness of the Gentiles shall enter into God's Covenant. After that goal of the divine purpose has been attained, then Israel as a whole shall be saved. Although Paul's Greek is not especially clear on this point, this is the only satisfactory way of explaining his intention.

The meaning of the *fullness of the Gentiles* must be determined from the sense given to *all Israel*. On this, Roman Catholic scholars have provided the most satisfactory treatments. The apostle had spoken of the salvation of Israel as a corporate entity while allowing for the exclusion of individuals who belong physically to the Nation. In the same way he now speaks of the various nations of Gentiles as corporate entities, rather than speaking of individuals within them. Paul contemplates that every nation in its corporate character is to be brought into the Christian Community. Of course, this seems rashly optimistic even today, and must have appeared to be even more so nineteen centuries ago, but the Apostle to the Gentiles was never a man to content himself with limited objectives. Here, however, he is chiefly concerned with the ultimate salvation of Israel as a whole, and so he supports his statement with some phrases from Scripture. These words are rather loosely quoted, evidently from memory. Verse 26 clearly is drawn from Isaiah 59:20–21, and is given in a form closer to the Hebrew Bible as we now know it than to the Septuagint. As used by Paul, and in the Hebrew Bible, this says that the Deliverer shall come from Zion, and for Paul it indicates that Christ has exercised His ministry in Israel and that He shall turn away ungodliness from the Chosen Nation, thus accomplishing the final salvation of Israel. For Verse 27 scholars seem to be about equally divided between the belief that the apostle is making use of Isaiah 27:9 and that he is drawing upon Jeremiah 31:33–34. Perhaps the Jeremiah text is the more probable, because that prophet was the principal witness in the Old Testament for the thought of a *New Covenant* that seems to be in Paul's mind here. Verse 28 then relates this directly to the unfolding of the divine plan. In terms of the *Gospel* or current Christian preaching, the Jews have become hostile to God, and this has resulted in benefit for Gentile Christians. But God is not hostile to the Jews, and He shall never become so. In terms of God's choice of Israel (the word implies saving purpose here rather than a doctrine of election) the Jews are beloved by God because of the patriarchs who were the root and the first fruits of the allegory in verses 16–24. This divine love for the Jews is constant. God's gifts and vocation are not subject to change or recall. Here the *gifts* must mean divine favor in general terms rather than the specialized *gifts of the Spirit* discussed in I Corinthians, and divine vocation is certainly to be counted as one among such gifts. The idea that Israel's present hostility to God's purpose serves a useful function for the extension of the Gospel is present here, but it is less significant ultimately than is God's love for Israel as demonstrated in His original choice. In verses 28–29 one can then see an emphasis upon God's freedom in showing mercy to all by a choice that is not related to merits or achievements, but this will be true only if one holds to the word *choice* rather than to the term *election*.

For verses 30–32 there seems to be no way of improving upon Lietzmann's introductory statement. Ultimately the principle there set forth is derived from Wisdom of Solomon 11:23. Paul had already brought this to full expression in Galatians 3:22, saying that God has caused all men to bring themselves under judgment by disobedience in order that all may recognize their need of mercy. This is the Pauline teaching that no man can earn salvation. Judgment came first upon the Gentile. At the present time it is falling upon the Jew. The Greek word NUN is used three times in Verse 31 of events that follow one another, and Lietzmann clearly is right when he says that Paul expresses himself in this way in order to reserve words which contrast the future with the present for the return of Christ in glory. Definitely Paul expects this Second Advent within his own lifetime. Because of the contemporary disobedience of the Jews, Gentiles have come to be the present recipients of divine mercy. Yet Jews in their turn will receive the same mercy once they have been provoked to jealousy by seeing the favor now bestowed upon the Gentiles. The disobedience of Israel had arisen from failure to consider that God's demand upon mankind was for *faith* rather than for *performance*. Barrett's words must be added here: "When the religion of men of religion asserts its independent effectiveness (as it has done in Israel's reliance upon Torah) they are lost; when it denies itself they are saved." Although the sentence is difficult to follow, it will repay the attention given to it.

Because no human effort can be truly effective in establishing a right relationship with God, God brings all men into a position that deserves only to be visited by divine *wrath*. Then, when the failure of human striving becomes apparent, God offers His mercy to all who see that they stand in need of it. This much must be said by anyone who desires to give a true interpretation of the apostle's thought. But it must be admitted that Paul's manner of expressing himself has been affected by the intensity of his conversion experience, and that whenever his words are taken to mean that no one can be saved without a similar conversion they come into conflict with the experience of many of the truest disciples of Jesus. Only sinners can be the objects of God's mercy, but this is so because all human beings are sinners, and it must not be limited to those like Paul and Augustine who could think of themselves as conspicuous sinners. Only those who see themselves as separated from God can realize the boundless scope of God's love. But neither logic nor theology will permit us to go on from this to the assertion that *every man must be damned if he is to be justified.* A person can be put in the right with God when he has hope in God's mercy; all that is necessary is for him to abandon trust in his own efforts. The denial of validity to the religion of what William James called the "once-born" Christian is too high a price to pay for giving some moral value to the concept of a dual predestination which has sometimes been discerned in the apostle's teaching; therefore one must reject the assertion that damnation is a necessary prelude to justification.

* * *

11:33–36 O thou rich depth both of God's wisdom and of His knowledge! How unsearchable are His judgments and how untraceable are His paths! "For who knew the mind of the Lord? Or who became His advisor? Or who made an advance to Him (literally, gave to Him beforehand) and shall receive recompense from Him?" Because all things have their existence (there is no verb in the Greek) from Him and by means of Him and in His interest (for Him). To Him be the glory unto eternity! Amen.

* * *

Easily the best treatment to be found in existing commentaries is that of Otto Michel. Here as elsewhere in the epistle he gives much fuller consideration than the other scholars to the hymnodic elements of the text. The phrases here can all be shown to have parallels in existing Jewish literature of the period. Paul has now set forth all that he can say of the divine plan of salvation. He has shown enough to enable man to do his necessary part in cooperating with God's plan. If one tries to go beyond this, the reality is too great for comprehension. So one must end with the hymn of praise before the ultimate mystery. This Paul does. First comes an exclamation. It is not certain whether the genitive of *riches* is to be taken as an independent noun like *wisdom* and *knowledge,* or whether it is to be understood simply as qualifying *depth,* but most scholars prefer not to put *riches* on quite the same plane as the other two nouns. While in essence *riches* does qualify *depth,* it calls to the reader's mind what Paul has said previously of the diversity of divine gifts. One may compare Romans 2:4, 9:23, and 10:12. Like other neuter nouns in

Greek, *depth* has no distinct vocative ending, but since the omega particle normally introduces an address to a person or thing, it seems best to translate it in this way. This will be particularly appropriate if the verses are to be thought of as based upon some primitive Christian hymn.

Divine *wisdom* is a common concept in the Jewish writing of this period. Paul probably is using it in the same sense as did the apocalyptists. *Knowledge* for Paul is that which discerns divine secrets, and God's *knowledge* is the understanding by which He devised the plan of salvation; while the apostle is not unwilling to employ Gnostic terms, he never uses GNOSIS in a Gnostic sense. *Depth* is therefore a term that reveals the scope of God's plan or the fact that it is beyond human comprehension. The Old Testament abounds in references to God's judgments and His ways, and is not lacking in statements that these are unsearchable. Paul has said the same thing in other words elsewhere in his writings. Few statements of this sort quite catch the lyrical character of this Pauline exclamation.

The scriptural citations here are the Septuagint of Isaiah 40:13 and the Hebrew of Job 41:11. It appears to be Paul's custom to quote Job as it appears in the Hebrew Bible, although for other Old Testament books he generally follows the Greek of the Septuagint. As he makes no reference to these words as Scripture, it is clear that they are not being used to prove a point. They appear here to be used in the same way as scriptural phrases are employed in other liturgical verses or prayers; the Bible has said what the Christians of the day wish to say. The last verse is a doxology that is not taken from the Old Testament. Many have interpreted it as a Trinitarian formula, and the later Church chose to take *from whom* as referring to the Father and ultimate Creator, *through whom* as referring to the Son as the agent in creating and sustaining action, *unto whom* as referring to the Spirit who is to fill all things when they are brought to their final goal. In the next century, however, Marcus Aurelius used almost the same words in reference to nature, and it seems likely that in origin they express Stoic pantheism rather than Christian doctrine. Paul presumably is using all three prepositions here in reference to the Father.

After this there is no more to say. The doctrinal section of the epistle is concluded. There remains the moral or paranetic section that begins in Chapter 12. One question, however, must still be considered. Are these verses the composition of the apostle himself or are they part of a contemporary Christian hymn? Their liturgical form indicates the latter. These are not the words that one expects as part of a teaching epistle. There are many examples in Paul of the apparent use of hymns to give lyrical expression to the point he wishes to stress. When one voices the praise of an ultimate divine mystery, hymns seem appropriate. On the basis of those echoed in the epistles, of which this is one of the more complete examples, we must acknowledge that these earliest Christian hymnographers have never been surpassed.

CHAPTER 12

Duty to God

12:1–2 Therefore I call upon you, my brethren, by the mercies of God, to offer your bodies as a sacrifice that is living, holy, and acceptable to God, as your appropriate (literally, reasonable) worship (or, service). And do not conform yourselves to this present age, but be transformed by the renewal of the mind, in order that you may distinguish (or, make trial of) what the will of God is, that which is good and acceptable (or, pleasing) and perfect (or, fully developed).

* * *

In the chapters so far considered, Paul has come closer to a systematic presentation of Christian dogma than anywhere else in his writings. But Paul never considers dogma in isolation from Christian living. Even the Apostle to the Gentiles recognizes a need for performance, for the expression in action of the relationship to God which one may enter by grace. So in Paul's epistles moral exhortation regularly follows the theological statements from which it is naturally to be developed. Sometimes this occurs in alternating sections; at other times the whole body of dogmatic teaching precedes the mass of ethical exhortation. In this longest of Paul's epistles the relation between faith and morals is drawn on a grand scale.

This fact has a marked bearing upon the Pauline concept of justification by faith. While the apostle denies that performance can establish a proper relation between God and man, it is a gross misrepresentation to say that performance has no real place in Paul's thinking. In the teaching of the epistles, those who have faith will wish to please God by their manner of life. The true believer will unite himself with Christ, in purpose, in action, in sacrifice. Those whose manner of life is such that it cannot please God, or who offer no practical response to God's love, can make no valid claim to faith at all. Thus the ethic of Christians is not to be distinguished from that of Pharisees in any matter that can be observed. Indeed, as Jesus Himself declared, the Christian ethic is more stringent than that of the Pharisees. It deals not only with the action and word that can be subject to external command, but also with the intention and attitude that no external judge can regulate. None of the early Christian teachers accepted this approach to morality more completely than did Paul. Those modern systems of morals that are founded upon the New Testament draw more from these hortatory sections of Paul's epistles and from the Sermon on the Mount of Matthew than from all else that is contained in the twenty-seven books. Yet just because Christian morality is an internal rather than an external imperative, the Pauline principle of justification by faith is essential. It is the only motive upon which an ethic of intention and attitude can be established. Paul's own writings make clear, however, that justification by faith will ultimately lead to a more stringent standard of performance than any effort to regulate conduct by external law could create.

One characteristic of Paul's hortatory or paranetic sections ought to be recognized at once. The apostle makes no serious effort to relate the various moral themes to one another. Instead he passes from one to the next without forging links either of logic or of literary style, and he establishes no ethical system. The subjects appear one after the other, without any consideration of their interrelations or of the order in which their respective dogmatic backgrounds had been treated. While some scholars have attempted a more precise division of the topics, the threefold scheme propounded by Michel is satisfactory. Chapters 12 and 13 form the first group of exhortations, 14:1 to 15:13 the second, 15:14–33 the third. It is easy enough to find connections between the various items of moral teaching and the earlier dogmatic statements upon which they depend, but it is futile to seek any particular order in the apostle's presentation.

Verses 1–2 serve as an introduction to this whole loosely ordered collection of exhortations. They make a definite break with the dogmatic teaching that has gone before, but at the same time they indicate that what follows is the natural result of what has been said. The opening word cannot properly be described either as a request or as a command. It is a request made by one who can claim the authority to command, a counsel or an admonition. It is addressed to all the brethren in Rome, whether of Jewish or of Gentile origin. In the preceding chapter Paul has offered particular advice to the two groups of Christians separately; now his advice is applied equally to both. All Christians without distinction ought to present themselves in sacrifice to God. The appeal by divine mercies in the plural reflects only the fact that the Septuagint had used a Greek plural to translate a Hebrew word that is plural in form and singular in meaning, and this Greek word is adopted here. Yet Paul knows only the one great mercy of God's plan of salvation. Because God has shown this mercy to them, the Christians have an obligation to make the offering that is possible for them. Performance does not induce the divine mercy, but is its only proper consequence.

Here *to present their bodies* is a happy phrase, for it protects Paul's statement from any possible misinterpretation of Gnostic dualism. In classical Greek the plural *bodies* was often used to stand for what we would call *persons* or what the Hebrew Bible called souls. Here it represents the entire personality, body and mind and will, all that man has and is. This becomes clear as one continues with Paul's exhortation. The combination of the particular Greek words for *offer* and *sacrifice* does not appear in the Septuagint, but it is a standard Hellenistic expression for religious sacrifice so often used that one need not ask how Paul might have learned it. When speaking to converts whose background differs from one's own, it is perfectly natural to adopt the expressions they are accustomed to using; to do so aids them to understand. The requirements of sacrifice as defined by Paul are the usual ones accepted in the ancient world. It was proper that the victim in the principal offerings should be living when presented at the shrine. Christians were to present their living selves for God's use. The offering was holy in the sense of being set apart for God's service, and it had to be without blemish. As Paul develops his moral teaching, the Christians are to make this self-offering of lives that have been freed from moral blemish. The adjective *acceptable*, despite its Greek form, is in grammatical agreement with the noun *sacrifice*, but there can be some question of whether the words *to God* apply to the adjective or to the noun. This latter issue, however, is resolved by Lagrange's argument that the word *acceptable* requires this reference to God, and that if the other conditions have been met the offering of the Christian assuredly will be acceptable to Him. The last clause of Verse 1 has been variously translated in English versions, with LOGIKE being taken either as *spiritual* or as *reasonable*, and LATREIA as *service* or as *worship*. The noun certainly ought to be taken as *worship*; it is *service* only as offered to a god, and every service offered to a god in some sense is worship. The adjective is more of a problem. The writings of the Mystery Cults and kindred literature before Paul, had contrasted the *spiritual sacrifice* of mystic communion with animal sacrifices, and texts can be found in the Old Testament that make the same point. On the other hand, since Paul has clearly stated that the offering of the Christian is to consist in his own body, it would be bizarre at this point to draw a contrast between physical and spiritual. Therefore one must agree with Lagrange that Paul is calling upon the Romans to make a rational offering of themselves. Perhaps the term is included here simply to show that the presentation of the whole person is intended, mind as well as body.

In Verse 2, as in many other Pauline texts, *this age* stands for the present world order. It was common Hellenistic usage, and so were the words translated in the King James Version as *conform* and *transform* when they were used in connection with it. There is a variety of possible meanings for SCHEMA, one of them being *pattern*, and the related verb here has to be translated by something equivalent to *do not cast yourselves in the pattern of this present world order*. A century later the same idea was put forward by Marcus Aurelius, but long before that it had held a place in Stoic thought quite apart from Christian eschatology. Paul here is contrasting the present age with an age of fulfillment to which he looks forward in the near future. A similar contrast appears in IV Esdras. The thought of transformation played a large part in the Mystery Cults, where it stood for the passage from a death of slavery to the natural order into the new life of freedom in union with the redeemer god. Such a concept was made to order for the expression of Pauline union with Christ, and a glance at what Paul has written will show that for him the transformation is the new life in Christ that is initiated externally in Baptism. Christians are to be transformed by *the renewing of the mind,* by the fact that the indwelling of the Holy Spirit who is received in Baptism raises man's mind to the life of God instead of leaving it involved in the affairs of the world, separating the mind from sin and devoting it to God. The function of the mind is expressed by the verb DOKIMAZEIN, which is translated *prove, approve,* or *put to the test.* Whichever of these translations may be chosen, the thought of putting to the test clearly has a place in the apostle's mind. Only the renewing of the mind by the indwelling of the Holy Spirit will enable the Christian to discover what the will of God is for him as an individual, what is the precise vocation to which he has been called. The King James Version takes the adjectives in the last clause of Verse 2 as qualifying *will,* but there is a better case for treating them as a predicate, giving the translation, *that you may put to the test the will of God, that which is good and pleasing and fully developed.* Paul is appealing to the Romans to conduct themselves in a manner suitable for those who have in some degree already received the life or the powers of the age of fulfillment. He is about to give a list of those powers and to spell out the conduct he regards as proper for those who have received them. To quote Barrett, "the renewal of the mind is begun in conversion and enhanced by every Christian decision a believer may take until it ends in the glory of God," and so it is the reality that is elsewhere described as *adoption.* Yet since this glory is real, the mind's renewal likewise must be actual, and the fitting proof that it is so will be seen in moral life. This shows how Paul's ethical exhortation grows inevitably out of the dogmatic teaching he has already given.

* * *

12:3–21 For by means of the favor (or, grace; even, commission) which is given to me, I call upon everyone who is among you not to show excessive self-conceit, but to give thought to being temperate, as God has imparted to each a measure of faith. For just as we have many members in one body, and not all the members have the same function, thus we, many as we are, are one body in Christ, and individually we are members of one another. So we have gifts that differ in accord with the favor (or, grace) which was given to us, either prophecy in accord with the proportion of one's faith, or service differing in the particular field of service, or he who teaches has his gift in the function of teaching, or he who exhorts in that of exhortation; he who expends alms does so with honesty, he who engages in administration does so with diligence (or, zeal), he who shows mercy does so with cheerfulness. Love is to be without pretense. We must hate what is evil and hold to what is right. We must be affectionate to one another in love for the brotherhood, we must outdo one another in showing respect, not being dilatory in our zeal, with spirit aflame (or, burning in spirit), serving the Lord, joyful in hope, persevering in trial, continuing in prayer, imparting to the needs of the saints, devoting ourselves to (literally, pursuing) hospitality. Bless your persecutors (literally, pursuers), bless and do not curse them. Rejoice with those who rejoice, weep with those who weep. Be in agreement with one another. Do not be ambitious of the important tasks but devote yourselves to the humble ones; do not become conceited about yourselves. Do not repay anyone evil in return for evil. Give consideration to the things that are well regarded in the sight of all men. If possible, so far as it rests with you, be at peace with all men. Beloved, do not exact vengeance for yourselves, but give scope (or, place) to the wrath, for it is written, "Vengeance belongs to me, I shall recompense," says the Lord. But if your enemy is hungry, feed him; if he is thirsty, give him drink: for in doing this you will heap burning coals upon his head. Do not be overcome by the evil, but overcome the evil with good.

* * *

Since spiritual gifts may easily become a source of spiritual pride, Paul considers it necessary to give a warning against this vice before he undertakes the discussion of the actual virtues Christians are to demonstrate in their lives. Here the verb which literally means *I say* is parallel to *I call upon* in Verse 1, and it has been translated in the same way. Now, instead of appealing to the divine mercies the Christians have obtained, the apostle supports his counsel by the divine grace or commission that has been given to him. This commission is the Apostolic Office, not this time the Apostolate to the Gentiles but rather Paul's share in the primary ministry of the Church. Backed by this authority, his counsel clearly has the force of a command. He declares that he is speaking to every Christian in Rome; of course, he has been doing so throughout the epistle, but here he stresses that no one can be excluded from this warning against spiritual pride.

No ancient witness to the text gives any reason to accept the conjectural addition τι in Verse 3 and understand it, *I call upon every man who is anything among you.* The verse would lose rather than gain in meaning if one were to limit Paul's advice to those who hold some office in the Church; spiritual pride is just as common among those who hold no special position. Both the King James Version and the Revised Standard treat the verb here as a reflexive, although it is active in form. This makes good sense, for one is more likely to hold extravagant opinions about oneself than about any other subject, and the following injunction to *temperance* strengthens the idea. Temperance was one of the cardinal virtues of the Greek world, known from the writings of Plato and Aristotle as well as from those of the Stoics. Paul adopted these cardinal virtues as necessary elements in the scheme of morality, and their pagan origin did not deter him. Temperance is enjoined upon each man because God has imparted to each a measure of faith. This is not to be regarded as the faith that effects justification, but simply as the gift of God that must precede all the other gifts Paul is about to mention. The measure or proportion of faith determines what other gifts one receives, and one must be temperate in one's estimate of his Christian accomplishments because of the knowledge that all of them are gifts from God received only because of his union with Christ.

Verses 4–5 are carelessly put together, as often happens when Paul is dealing with a subject of great concern. The illustration of unity in diversity that Paul usually prefers for the Church is that of the members of a body. Verse 4 is parallel to I Corinthians 12:12. This fact explains perfectly the various functions listed in this section. In Christ the believers are one *body*, members both of the Lord and of one another; apart from Christ they would be nothing. The varying capacities that Christians possess are all gifts of God and are imparted to each by the Holy Spirit. Paul often uses the word *grace* to stand for the Spirit, just as Jews usually avoided direct mention of God, but his usage on this point is far from precise. The terms listed are not identical with those of I Corinthians 12, but many of the same functions appear. None of those set forth here are designations of particular orders of ministry; this is one point of difference between the treatment in Romans and that in I Corinthians. Prophecy is mentioned first. This really stands for the proclamation of the Christian message. While the idea of foretelling the future is not excluded, it is certainly not emphasized. The word ANALOGIA is not found elsewhere in Paul. It was a Stoic term that had found its way into the general vocabulary of moral teachers, and its meaning here is not different from that of *measure* in Verse 3. The DIAKONIA must be translated *service*, probably any kind of service to God, but if a specific thought is intended it would be the care for the sick and the poor that became a particular function of *deacons*. Here, however, Paul is thinking of it only as a manifestation of Christian work. *Teaching* would be what technically is called *catechesis*, the work of laymen rather than of clergy but a task requiring that the Christians engaged in it should be well instructed. The participle *teaching* is chosen in preference to the noun *the teacher* principally because the following term, *exhortation*, in Greek does not possess a satisfactory noun to refer to the person who practices it. Lagrange suggests that exhortation is a less intellectual function than teaching, but one that in essence is parallel to it.

The next term clearly refers to the administration of charity, but there is some difference of opinion whether it means personal almsgiving or the distribution of the corporate aid of the Church. Probably private almsgiving is in the apostle's mind, and the other two terms of Verse 8 need not be directly related to it. If so, *ruling* would be the managing of the temporal affairs of the local church, which is a lay task rather than a priestly one, and for which diligence or zeal would be the primary qualification. There are some, however, who relate *ruling* to *giving* as the supervision of corporate charity. But when this is done, then *showing mercy* must stand for personal almsgiving. It is, however, more important that *cheerfulness* should accompany the forgiveness of personal injuries than that it should go together with almsgiving, for grudging forgiveness is a complete contradiction in terms. Moreover, I Corinthians shows that the forgiving of injuries was regarded by Paul as an important part of Christian living. Thus all three activities are to be accounted as the tasks of ordinary Christians and not duties reserved for professional men of religion. Elsewhere in his epistles Paul does describe the position and functions of the Christian ministry, but it is not in his mind to do so in Romans 12:6–8, or anywhere else in this epistle. The ministry is not a subject on which it would be appropriate for him to expound at length in a church that he had not founded himself, and in any case in this chapter the duties described are intended for the entire membership of the Church.

In verses 9–16 Paul sketches the ideal of life within the Christian Community, a life which must be dominated by the virtue of *love.* The teaching on love here given is less systematic than that of I Corinthians 13, but many scholars have discerned a parallel. Love must be free from all pretense, as in II Corinthians 6:6. Verse 9 speaks first of love for one's neighbor as a general duty, and Verse 10 defines the more specific duty of love within the Christian fellowship. For the general duty, the Christian must hate wrongdoing and for himself must hold to what is right, but hatred of wrong must never be carried over to the wrongdoer. Within the fellowship itself the mutual affection must be so developed that it will be observed by all. Indeed, as in Philippians 2:3, the Christian must esteem others more highly than himself, and the members of the Community must be outdoing one another in love. Verses 11–13 mention particular duties, all of which of imperatives. Scholars differ on whether the *spirit* of Verse 11 is the Holy Spirit or the human spirit; Lietzmann prefers the latter for the are expressed by participles in the nominative case that carry the force satisfactory reason that *spirit* here seems to be strictly parallel to the other dative nouns such as *zeal.* The D manuscript has a variant reading, *serving the time,* instead of *serving the Lord* as in other early texts, and Lietzmann's account of the origin of this reading is also convincing. In early abbreviations used in manuscripts, the dative of Lord was usually written as kappa omega, and sometimes kappa rho omega; the latter could easily be taken for an abbreviation of KAIRO the dative of *time.* Verse 12 gives emphasis to the virtue of perseverance, offering hope as an answer to trial or persecution, and prayer as a method of maintaining the hope. Verse 13 draws attention to the social virtues of generosity to the poor and hospitality to all who belong to the fellowship. In this as in other texts Paul is doing what he can to encourage those qualities that make for stability in the Community.

Verses 10–13 deal with relationships inside the Christian Community, and the same appears to be true of verses 15–16. In contrast verses 17–21 speak of love of enemies. These facts have caused many to believe that Verse 14, which sets forth the correct response to persecution, is out of its proper place. Obviously persecutors would be persons outside the Church. Yet the present order of the text can be preserved, for we may say that Verse 15 does not refer to the Church but to the world. Thus Verse 14 would deal with that element of the world that impinges most directly upon the Church, Verse 15 would apply to the part of the world that takes no stand one way or the other, and Verse 16 would be Paul's way of turning from the consideration of individual relationships to communal ones. There are many New Testament texts that counsel one to bless persecutors—Matthew 5:44, I Corinthians 4:12, and most definitely I Peter 3:8–9—although it is likely that the last parallel is a conscious imitation of what appears here.

Verse 15 takes a line different from that laid down by Paul in I Corinthians. In the earlier epistle he advises that those who rejoice or weep should not take such matters seriously because the end of the world is too close at hand for them to have any real significance. Evidently eschatology has been somewhat modified in the apostle's mind, although if Paul is speaking of individual relationships with those outside the Church he could not have been expecting such unbelievers to live in anticipation of the end of history. Verse 16 then speaks of social attitudes. The demand for agreement among the believers, for thinking the same thing, has a parallel in I Corinthians. It is an obvious requirement for the solidarity of the Community. The second clause of the verse is translated in the King James Version, *mind not high things, but condescend to men of low estate*. The noun that stands for *high things* is neuter and cannot refer to persons, while in form the dative plural adjective *humble* might be either masculine or neuter, and the King James Version has taken it as masculine. Yet if we are to have a proper balance of structure here, both words should be taken as neuter. Thus the command to the Christians in Rome means that they should not be ambitious for exalted gifts and duties but instead should be willing to accept humble ones for the benefit of the Community. Then the third clause of the verse, which is a quotation from Proverbs 3:7, would fall into place as an exhortation not to become arrogant about personal accomplishments. For all this there are parallels both in Paul's other epistles and in rabbinic writings. It is reasonable to assume that most of this section depends upon primitive Christian legal codes.

In Verse 17 the apostle launches into the Church's corporate dealings with the world at large. Christians are not to adopt the standards of those who oppose them. The Greek idea of doing good to one's friends and evil to one's enemies, although it had been opposed by Plato and others since his time, was still widely accepted. Yet it could have no place with Christians. In essence this first half of the verse repeats an idea from Verse 14, but now there is added a demand based upon the Septuagint of Proverbs 3:4 to maintain the good repute of the Christian Community before the world. In view of what follows in Chapter 13, the apostle clearly intended to seek the tolerance or approval of the state for the Church, although what he has to say here is at variance with rabbinic teaching that was given not very much later than the time of writing this work. Even Verse 18, with its demand to be at peace with all men, would imply the need to maintain such credit in the eyes of non-Christians. Paul, however, has a clear enough understanding of reality to be aware that it may not always be possible to live at peace with all men, even for those who do carry out in full the general duty of love to one's neighbor.

But although peace with all may not be possible, Christians must not attempt to visit punishment on evildoers. The infliction of punishment is not their task but God's. The scriptural condemnation of revenge is probably related to Leviticus 19:18, or perhaps to Deuteronomy 32:25; whichever it may be, it is not exact and there is a good chance that the form in which it appears here is derived from an early Christian collection of *testimonia* rather than from either the Septuagint or the Hebrew Bible. Verse 20 offers a positive command of what Christians are to do when they experience an injury. This also is expressed in the words of Scripture, Proverbs 25:21–22. Originally this had been an expression of worldly wisdom, but now the apostle gives it wider reference. Actually, the mention of heaping coals of fire upon the head of the evildoer has no clear application to the case in point, but it is reasonable to expect that the return of good for evil might cause the evildoer to feel remorse. There are several instances of the use in Jewish literature of the phrase *heap coals of fire upon one's head,* but these do not seem intended to make the same point that appears here. The final verse of the chapter must be regarded as originally a prudential maxim of the sort sometimes credited to Jesus in the Gospels. The Christian must not imitate the methods of evildoers, for if they are to be converted it can only be through the steadfastness in good that others show to them. Paul's Stoic contemporary Seneca said much the same. In contemporary life, when one sees a willingness to abandon traditional liberties in the interest of a supposedly threatened national security, this advice has immediate relevance. To act in the manner of one's opponents is in essence to surrender to them. Evil will never be overcome by greater evil, but only through goodness.

CHAPTER 13

Duty in the World

13:1–7 Every person must be in subjection to the authorities. For no authority exists except by God's appointment, and those that do exist have been instituted by God. So he who opposes the authority has set himself against the appointment of God; and those who have set themselves in opposition shall bring judgment on themselves. For rulers are not a cause of fear to good action but to evil. Do you wish not to stand in fear of the authority? Do what is good and you will get praise from it. For it is a servant of God for your good (or, for good in your interest). But if you should do what is evil, be afraid; for it does not carry the sword for nothing. For it is God's servant avenging with wrath upon the man who does evil. Wherefore it is necessary to be in subjection, not only because of wrath but also because of conscience. It is for this reason also that you pay taxes; for they are officials of God giving their attention to this very matter. Give to all men what is due to them, the tax to the tax collector, the excise to the excise collector, fear to whom fear is due, respect to whom respect is due.

* * *

From the corporate relationships of the Church with individuals and groups in the non-Christian world, Paul turns quite naturally to the Church's position in regard to the state. Then as now there were diverse opinions among Christians on the matter. Many of the Jews, and of the Jewish Christians, looked upon the Roman Empire as a manifestation of demonic power. As one born to the privilege of Roman citizenship, a privilege he was willing to invoke in his own interest, the apostle held no such views. Moreover, he was able to perceive the extent to which the unity of government, the establishment of a common language, and ease of communication had assisted the missionary work of the Church. A generation later the systematic persecution initiated by Domitian drove all Christians into the attitude of resistance to the state that is expressed in the Book of Revelation. Yet even in that Christian Apocalypse something of the Pauline teaching here set forth survived. Even when they were being oppressed by the state, Christians acknowledged that order was better than anarchy, and in the midst of their intense expectation of the end of the world they looked upon the Roman Empire as in some respects a force for good that restrained demonic powers. To that extent the teaching of this paragraph survived the influence of the persecutions.

Actually, both in the Hebrew Bible and in the Jewish Apocrypha there was much teaching to the effect that the civil power owed its origin to God, that God was responsible for its establishment and therefore that it existed by a sort of divine right. The pre-Christian Jewish teaching, however, had referred to the constituted authorities of the Jewish Nation, and it had called upon the rulers to exercise their power responsibly because they had derived it from God; it had not been addressed especially to the governed as an appeal for obedience. The thought of a government controlled by the heathen as deriving its power from God could appeal for scriptural sanction to Isaiah 45:1 where heathen Cyrus is said to have been strengthened as God's anointed. Paul's teaching here, however, rests upon Gentile rather than Jewish origins. Many people in the ancient world had believed in a divine right of kings on a national level. When the local kings were conquered by the Roman Republic, something of this sentiment had been transferred to the international power, especially on the part of those who were given the privilege of Roman citizenship.

Some scholars have tried to find a justification for what Paul has written in the stability the Roman Empire showed, but that stability was largely imaginary. Roman history knew many successful rebels. The empire itself had been a successful subversion of the republic, and apart from the century of the Antonines it had no opportunity to attain even a semblance of legitimacy. Augustus had grasped the crown by force, and there was the suspicion that Tiberius and Caligula had each in turn succeeded to it by murder. The reign of Claudius had begun as a caretaker administration. Not one of these men had left a natural heir, and the electoral procedure had degenerated into a mere ratification of prevailing force. Probably Paul himself could not have written as he did if it had not been for his continuing belief in eschatology. Although he no longer expected the end of the world to come quite as quickly as he had when writing I Corinthians, he seems at this point to have been thinking in terms of five to ten years. But if one does not have to plan for a long future, there can be no real place for political revolution. The existing civil authority that Paul knew might lack legitimate title; its claim might be little more than naked force. But since God had not interfered with its establishment one could say that it had some measure of divine approval and that the Christian had no right to interfere in its operation. In the few years of history remaining, as Paul believed, there were far more pressing tasks for the disciple of Jesus to accomplish. Indeed, one could even say that the Roman Empire, despite its faults, was doing a great deal of good. Therefore Paul could feel justified in extolling submission to the state as a Christian virtue, and in this paragraph he does extol it.

In Verse 1 *every soul* is a Semitic expression for *all people*. Naturally Paul is speaking only to the members of the Church, for he has no authority in counseling anyone else. It has sometimes been suggested that the *higher powers* in question are spiritual beings rather than civil rulers, but to do this one must ignore the whole context. From what follows it is also clear that Paul is discussing authorities in the state and not within the Church. Thus the subjection demanded is civil and not spiritual obedience. Where the claims of God conflicted directly with the demands of the state, Paul counseled martyrdom rather than revolution, and so did several later New Testament writers. This also is an expression of first century Christian eschatology. Since no civil authority can exist without divine sufferance, it can readily be maintained that every authority that does exist has been established in some sense by God Himself. Since Paul believes this, he can say in Verse 2 that resistance to the government is also resistance to God's appointment. Thus the *judgment* that Paul sees as the result of such opposition to the state is God's judgment and not the penalty the state may inflict. Thus to resist is to forfeit one's salvation.

Verses 3–4 explain the social benefits the established government confers in the restraint of wrongdoing and the reward of virtue. It is the man who does what is evil, murder, robbery, and so forth, who must stand in fear of the government. The law-abiding citizen should have nothing to dread, and he may even look for some special approval. This is reflected also in I Peter 3:13. When the civil ruler in Verse 4 is described as DIAKONOS, it becomes clear that the term had not yet been appropriated in the Church as a title of Christian ministry exclusively; it must be remembered that Christian ministry was not fully organized at this early date. So the civil ruler is a servant of God for a good purpose. The Greek word for *sword* here stands for the Latin *gladius*. Both in the Roman Republic and under the empire, senior magistrates possessed the *ius gladii*, the power to enforce the death penalty. In the ancient world many crimes were regularly punished with death. So the evildoer has physical cause to dread the operation of Roman law, and the magistrate serves God's purpose in visiting punishment upon the man who does wrong. Some scholars here hold that the term *wrath* means God's wrath or eschatological judgment, but this is not supported by the context. Here Paul has in mind the displeasure of the state that is to be expressed by the infliction of punishment; for such punishment the word *wrath* is eminently suitable. In so visiting the state's wrath upon the evildoer, the magistrate will be fulfilling a part of God's own purpose.

In Verse 5 Paul adds the claim of conscience to that of physical necessity. One must obey the law, which in the Roman Empire also meant obeying men, for fear of retribution or *wrath*; this everyone understood. One must do so likewise for the sake of morality, which is here described by the Stoic term *conscience*. Since the greater part of the magistrate's work serves God's good purpose, the Christian has a duty to support it. In Verse 6 this support is extended to the willing payment of taxes. PHOROS was the primary direct tax. In Rome it was a levy upon property rather than on income. Since the majority of laborers were slaves, a tax upon productive property that would include the slaves themselves would be more effective than one upon wages. Taxes support the administration of justice, the maintenance of order, the security of the state. Each of these Paul considers to be at least a relative good, and therefore a Christian should be glad to pay his share of the taxes necessary to provide for them. This held true even though the government gave no recognition to the Christian religion. Perhaps the apostle then hoped, as did the writer of Acts some twenty years later, that if the Church showed itself a support to the state some fitting recognition would be given.

The word LEITOURGOI did not acquire specifically Christian use for many years after Paul. In Athens originally the LEITOURGOI were wealthy citizens who were "permitted" to serve the state by fitting out naval vessels or units of cavalry, or by training a chorus for the civic dramatic festival at their own expense. In the Septuagint of Isaiah 61:6, the term had been used to describe priests in their sacerdotal functions, and in Numbers 18:21 it had stood for those who were to receive the religious tax of Israel. It is evidently this last use that Paul has borrowed here. The people he is describing evidently are civil magistrates, and they are not being credited even metaphorically with a sacerdotal function. They receive tribute because they are performing a function that is necessary to God's plan, and they have a right to receive it. So there should be no thought of equating these people with "ministers" of God; at most the term here would mean *officers*. Verse 7 may well owe something to the tradition of our Lord's words that is preserved in Matthew 22:21, "render unto Caesar what belongs to Caesar," and this had been referred to the payment of the direct tax in the Gospel. The second term in this list refers to indirect taxation comparable to modern sales levies and excises. The actual recipients of taxation were not particularly exalted officials, and would not be accounted due to receive reverential fear or personal honor; the last two terms of the verse, therefore, should be reserved for governors and judges. Perhaps the best commentary of this verse is I Peter 2:17: "*Fear God, honor the king.*" Such surely can serve as a summary for all the teaching contained in this paragraph.

* * *

13:8–10 Owe nothing to anyone, except the duty to love one another. For he who loves his neighbor (literally, the other) has fulfilled Torah.

For the statement, "Thou shalt not commit adultery, thou shalt do no murder, thou shalt not steal, thou shalt not covet," and any other commandment there may be, is summed up in this word: "Thou shalt love thy neighbor as thyself." Love works no evil (or, injury) to one's neighbor; therefore love is the fulfillment of Torah (or, law).

* * *

The subject dealt with in these three verses is quite different from the duty of the Christian to the state, and the repetition of the word concerning debt from Verse 7 is a bond more apparent than real. After completing what he has to say on the corporate relations of Church and state, the apostle returns to the individual duty of loving one's neighbor. In Judaism a standard issue of debate was the proper manner of observing Torah. As a well-trained rabbi, Paul felt impelled to give a Christian answer in terms of the principles he had already laid down in the theological chapters of his epistle. It is apparent from what has been said above that as individuals the Christian believers must meet their civic obligations if the relations of Church and state are to be established in the right way. But as Verse 8 explains, personal obligations are equally important. Yet the Christian has one obligation that can never be entirely fulfilled, namely, the love of his neighbor. Debts can be paid and services performed, but love never ends. Each new act of love creates opportunities for further acts. Zahn would translate the second clause of the verse, "*he who loves has fulfilled the rest of the Torah*," but this would place an almost impossible strain upon the Greek, and in addition it is certainly contrary to rabbinic usage and to the general line of the Pauline argument. So *the other* must mean *the other person*, the *neighbor* when that term is given a reference as wide as humanity itself. One must not ask what are the limits of love for one's neighbor; as in the Parable of the Good Samaritan he is any person whose need the Christian can relieve.

Verse 9 expands this with a sampling from the second table of the Decalogue. The Commandments appear in the order 7, 6, 8, 10, and an additional clause shows that Paul knows of the existence of other statutes. This order of treating the Commandments is found in several Hellenistic Jewish sources, notably in Philo, and it may have become almost a standard. Paul then holds up the whole duty of love to one's neighbor with the words of Leviticus 19:18, which is also used in the second part of the Lord's Summary of the Law. There is also evidence that it was recognized as a true summary of the Torah by many of the rabbis of the time. Verse 10 is roughly parallel to I Corinthians 13:4, and also parallel to Hillel's statement in negative form of what is the Golden Rule of the Gospel. Love is the fullness of the Torah, because where true love for one's neighbor is present all positive injunctions become unnecessary. Love of God is not mentioned here because Paul is discussing ethical rather than religious duty, but it is clear that on the principles he has already established Christian morality cannot exist where the love of God is lacking. Barrett draws a careful distinction between this *law of love* and *legalism*, and his point is well taken. "Man is not *justified* by fulfilling the *law of love*, but the *faith* by which a man can be *justified* is bound to express itself ethically in *love*. Thus *love* is not to be accounted as a means of salvation, but as the ethical channel through which the new life *in Christ* flows."

* * *

13:11–14 Now this is true when you recognize the occasion (literally, the time), that it is already time (literally, an hour) for you to awake out of sleep. For now our salvation is nearer than at the time when we came to faith. The night is almost over (or, far spent); and the day is at hand. Therefore let us put aside the deeds which belong to the darkness, and let us put upon ourselves the weapons of the light. As in the daytime, let us conduct ourselves (literally, walk) decently, not in revels and drunken brawls, not in acts of lechery and licentiousness, not in strife and jealousy; but put upon yourselves the Lord Jesus Christ, and do not give consideration to the lusts (or, desires) which belong to the flesh.

* * *

There is considerably less eschatological urgency in Romans than in the earlier epistles, and more allowance that a few years may still be left to the present world order, but the apostle's convictions that the end is near remain unchanged. So here we find a statement of urgency. The end is so close that there can be no dallying. This is not a conclusion for Chapter 13 alone, but rather for all the moral teaching so far provided. Thus Paul here is looking back to 12:1–2 more than to 13:1–10. These words also recall teachings stated in the dogmatic section of the epistle. Roman Christians must show awareness of the present situation. It is misleading here to limit the meaning of KAIROS simply to time. There is a question of whether in the second clause of Verse 11 we should read *for you* with the B and Aleph manuscripts, or *for us* with Papyrus 46 and the African texts. On this as on many other textual points Lagrange's argument carries conviction. Paul is making an appeal to the Romans, and it is only in the third clause that he unites himself with them, but several early scribes altered the pronoun here in the interest of what they thought was greater consistency. For all practical purposes the hour is already here, so close that the interval that has elapsed since the conversion of Paul or of his readers is a significant proportion of the time that yet remains. There is no need to say the time already past is greater than that which remains. Paul had held that position when he wrote I Thessalonians, but he no longer goes so far. Rather he now sees the Incarnation itself as the dawn, and because the Incarnation has taken place the works of darkness must immediately be cast aside to be exchanged for the armor of light. In Paul's language *day* is the occasion for labor. There is still work to be done, work that must be done before the fullness of glory shall appear. This work can be accomplished only in the strength of the Holy Spirit. Paul clearly is calling upon Christians to stir up a gift that is already in them.

It was in the religion of Persia that *light* and *darkness* had first become primary figures for the conflict between good and evil, but this picture had been adopted by Jewish teachers long before Paul, and it is seen quite clearly in the Qumran Scrolls. In Christian writing *light* and *darkness* are given more importance in the Fourth Gospel than elsewhere. Yet these figures also have a part to play in Paul's teaching. Verse 13 offers a list of what ought not to be done, a sketch of the life that Augustine in his *Confessions* said that he had abandoned. The six terms here represent well-known features of pagan life in Rome and other cities, part of the former experience of many Christians prior to their conversions. But these activities are absolutely impossible for Christians. The KOMOI were uninhibited banquets; the METHAI simply eliminated the food, as do some modern cocktail parties; the KOITAI were occasions for bringing in party girls or engaging in wife trading, while the ASELGEIAI were occasions for homosexual indulgence. Paul and most other early Christian moralists were especially concerned about two sorts of wrongdoing, those involving sex and those involving personal wrangling. The first four terms here deal with the former, the last two with the latter; this is appropriate, for as a matter of observation strife and jealousy often accompany sexual impropriety. The point here is that day has dawned. In Christ's earthly ministry the powers of the New Age have been made available, and by the aid of those powers the faults here described can be avoided.

Verse 14 recalls the Pauline teaching on Baptism, and scholars of diversive backgrounds have perceived the connection. In the day that has dawned because of Christ's Incarnation, Christians are to put on Christ. Elsewhere the apostle makes the same point by saying that the believers are to put off the *old man,* and to put on the *new man.* This means a change of character, a change normally effected in connection with Baptism if one may take Paul seriously, although it is not related to that Sacrament by absolute necessity. The suggestion of Moffatt's translation that this means conformity to the character of Jesus Christ is valid in essence. It is the character of Christ that Christians must show to the world in the present situation. But if they are conformed to the character of Jesus Christ, they shall not make provision for the desires of the flesh, just as He made no provision for such desires. In the enjoyment of the powers of the New Age (their life in the Holy Spirit), it becomes possible for Christians not to yield to the flesh. By the grace of God even the most powerful instincts must be sublimated and put to work in divine service instead of in their ordinary manifestations. This may stand as a summary of Christian morality; it means a complete break with one's former manner of life, a break made possible by God's grace that is brought to the believer by the Holy Spirit. Often in Paul's writings the function of the Spirit is to effect Christ's own presence in the disciple, to make real the union with Christ that every baptized person possesses. If the union with the Lord is a fact, and Paul believes that it is, then it can only be expressed in the manner herein described. Other points remain to be dealt with in the development of Paul's moral teaching, but if this much can be attained all the rest will fall into place, both in chapters 12 and 13, which have already been developed, and in chapters 14 and 15, which are still to come.

CHAPTER 14

Unity Among Christians

14:1–12 You are to accept the man who is weak in faith, but not with a view to debates regarding principles. One man believes that he may eat everything, while the one who is weak eats vegetables. The man who eats is not to despise him who does not eat, and the man who does not eat is not to pass judgment upon him who eats, for God accepted him. Who are you to pass judgment upon someone else's servant? He stands or falls in relation to his own Lord; and stand he shall, for the Lord is able to cause him to stand. One man judges one day to be better than another, while another man judges all days to be equal. Each man is to be assured in his own mind. The man who has regard for the day has regard for it in relation to the Lord. And the man who eats, eats in relation to the Lord, for he gives thanks to God. And the man who abstains, abstains in relation to the Lord, and he gives thanks to God. For no one of us lives for himself, and no one dies for himself. For both if we live we live with respect to the Lord, and if we die we die in respect to the Lord. So both if we live and if we die, we belong to the Lord. For it is for this reason that Christ died and revived, in order that He might have dominion both over the dead and over the living. So you, why do you pass judgment on your brother? Or you also, why do you despise your brother? For we all shall present ourselves at the judgment seat of God. As it is written, "As I live, saith the Lord, to me every knee shall bow, and every tongue shall make acknowledgement to God." Consequently each of us shall render account on his own behalf.

* * *

The first question to be considered here is that of the religious practices of those whom Paul describes as *the weak*. It is also necessary to decide whether all the practices mentioned here were those of a single party within the Church, or whether the abstinences were the distinctive observance of one party and the recognition of special days for feast or fast belonged to some other group. The apostle could have used the term *weak* to refer to more than one faction. The making of this decision will also aid us in determining whether the practices at issue had any relation to Judaism or to Jewish Christianity.

From the way in which this paragraph is written, it seems that only one group was involved, that the same people were observing special days and maintaining particular abstinences. If the observance of days were the only matter at issue, one might suppose that *the weak* were maintaining Jewish customs; Israel had Sabbaths and new moons and several annual feasts, along with two days weekly for fasts. Yet no such conclusion would be demanded. While the Sabbath was a Jewish institution, a variety of feasts and days of abstinence was observed in other ancient religions, and no one would require Jewish prompting in order to regard one day as more suited for religious activities than another. There is also the possibility that some observance of Sunday as a memorial of the Lord's Resurrection is being discussed here; Sunday certainly had come to be such when Justin wrote, and in I Corinthians 16:2 Paul himself states that the first day of the week was a good occasion for putting aside what one had saved toward the Christian relief fund. It may be debated whether there should be any specific day for worship at all, or if there should be such a day whether the seventh day might not be more desirable than the first, but the vast majority of Christians have found some form of Sunday observance satisfactory, and there is much evidence in its favor from the New Testament. Actually, Paul is writing in this epistle to a local church he does not know at firsthand, and his statements may have been left purposely vague in order that his lack of knowledge on such points might not cause offense. Clearly his discussion has nothing to do with the sort of Jewish Christianity opposed in Galatians; if there is any parallel for it in the apostle's writings it must be sought in Colossians.

The abstinences seem to have been from meat and wine, and this does not correspond to the issue in Galatians at all. Judaism did not reject wine except for the duration of a vow, and it only forbade certain types of meat or meat that had been slaughtered in the wrong way. If all meat were to be refused, the reason probably would be the same as that given in I Corinthians, namely, the difficulty in obtaining meat that had not previously been offered in sacrifice to pagan deities. Yet there were other possible reasons for such abstinence. Those who followed the Orphic Mystery Cult and the Pythagoreans appear to have been vegetarians, and it was said that Paul's Christian contemporary James of Jerusalem abstained from eating that which had contained life. At the end of the century the Ebionites followed the practice of James. Less is known about abstinence from wine, and Paul says so little on that point that there may not have been any serious dispute about it. Some Gnostic cults rejected wine, while some of the Mystery Cults, such as that of Dionysos, indulged in it most freely. Thus the scruples about food and drink, like the observances of days, could have been derived quite as readily from Gentile as from Jewish sources.

Paul's real concern here is with division in the Community. There were those Christians in other cities, and presumably in Rome as well, who believed that by the power of Christ they could live in the world without being harmed by its influence. At the same time there were other Christians who felt that an ascetic withdrawal and a system of religious practice was a measure of safety if not an absolute essential. For Rome as for other places Paul felt that the former group had the better case, but he was willing to tolerate the latter on the condition that they should not seek to impose their own scruples upon others. At the same time he felt bound to condemn the members of the former party who might lead other Christians to violate their own consciences. Thus, while the person who believes that *in Christ* he has freedom to eat whatever he likes possesses a stronger faith than the one who feels bound to impose restrictions upon himself, it is not permitted for *the strong* to look down upon *the weak*. In the same way, those who maintain restraints for themselves have no right to say that others are without true religion. Believers of both sorts belong to Christ in equal degree. Christ has the power to use both for the advancement of God's purpose. Thus neither may pass judgment upon the other, for all such judgment belongs to the Lord alone.

From the way in which the chapter begins, it would appear that *the strong* form the dominant party in Rome, at least as far as the apostle knows. He who is *weak* in faith is to be accepted. Apparently *the weak* ran some risk of exclusion because of their scruples. The manner of acceptance is also explained. There must be no acrimonious debate on the matter, no effort on the part of either faction to enforce its views upon the other. All such disputes tend to disrupt the Community, and all Christians are required to live together in fraternal solidarity. Verse 2 states the distinguishing characteristics of the two parties. The prevailing faction is mentioned first, represented by the person who has full confidence to eat anything. In contrast *the weak* is a vegetarian. It seems that *the weak* avoids meat on principle, not merely for specific occasions but at all times. Paul forbids the man who has such trust in Christ as will free him from all such scruples to look upon his scrupulous brother as not adequately Christian. By the same token he forbids the scrupulous Christian to pass judgment upon the other as upon a man who makes no effort or sacrifice for the sake of religion. God has accepted both.

This is more than a simple exhortation to charity. The scrupulous is tempted to regard the acceptance of his own standards as an external test of righteousness, to think of his own acts and abstentions as the fulfillment of God's commands. But *the strong* are tempted to the comparable error of despising *the weak*, of looking upon their own confidence in Christ as evidence of personal superiority. God alone can judge this matter properly, and in His sight the claims either party may be tempted to make are insignificant. Whatever value there may be in either of these approaches to religion is derived from God. While Paul is more concerned with the prospect that *the weak* will presume to pass judgment than that *the strong* will do so, the prohibition of Verse 4 applies to both factions in equal degree. The Christian who differs from oneself in religious practice is actually a person who belongs to Christ. Here the term for *household slave* is used in preference to the more common word that would stand for any sort of slave. In every slave economy there are bonds of intimacy between the owner and the household slave that do not exist between him and those of his slaves who do not work in the house. Nowhere else in his writings does the apostle find occasion to refer to household slaves in distinction from others. Paul is saying that every Christian is a slave of Christ, and by ancient law or practice slaves had no privilege of advising their owners regarding approval or disapproval of other slaves. Thus he shows that differences in practice are for the Lord's decision alone, and he adds his own word of confidence that the Christian who asserts his freedom will indeed be justified. The sense of the verb STESAI is causative; Christ shall cause the Christian who does not choose abstinence or special observance *to be in the right in relation to God* and so to stand.

Verse 5 adds the mention of particular days to that of abstinence, and in treating of them Paul does not suggest that one form of devotion is better than another. He merely insists, as all moral theologians since his day have done, that each man must act in obedience to his own conscience. No man can disregard what he considers to be a moral or religious obligation without damage to his own soul. This is true even when his conscience is in error, when what he believes to be an obligation actually is not so. Many of the later manuscripts have added to Verse 6 a clause reading, *he who disregards the day disregards it to the Lord;* this must be eliminated not only because it is absent from the oldest texts but also because it is a clumsy parallel to the final statement of the verse. Accepting the text upon which the translation above is based, Paul refers first to the practices of *the weak* in regard to special days, then to those of *the strong* in regard to food, and he declares that both are undertaken in loyalty to God. This clearly is evident in connection with the eating, because every Christian gave thanks over all the food he ate just as every Jew did. But the abstention is no less an act of loyalty to God, and no less a matter of thanksgiving. So although both are exposed to the same spiritual danger, they also share the same positive virtue since they undertake what they do for the glory of God.

Barrett's treatment of verses 7–9 is impressive. He shows that *the strong* has no real independence while *the weak* is not abandoned to his own resources, because each disciple of Jesus is *a man in Christ* who belongs not to himself but to the Lord who has redeemed him. Thus the life and the death of the Christian must be related to Christ. Michel's analysis gives greater precision to any treatment of the section, for it shows how Verse 7 with its affirmation that we neither live nor die only to ourselves is the counterpart of the declaration in Verse 6 that the man who eats and likewise the man who abstains does so in relation to God. Then Verse 8 makes the positive statement of the same theme with such balance of structure that Michel's contention that this is part of the primitive baptismal liturgy seems to be well taken. The same liturgical balance is carried forward into Verse 9 where it is said that the real reason why every act of a Christian must be related to the Lord is to be sought in God's saving act in Christ. A comparable statement can be found in Philippians 2:8–11. Christ partook of death and now He has been raised to newness of life precisely in order that He might be Lord alike of the living and the dead. Several manuscripts, including some early ones, add the word *rose* along with *died* and *lived;* this mention of the Resurrection would be an obvious explanation of how Christ came to live in the newness of life, and for Paul such a statement was not needed. In Baptism the Christian has already died to the world and has been raised with Christ. Because of this the entire life of the disciple, which is a life risen in union with Christ, belongs to Jesus. Likewise the earthly death which has now been anticipated in Baptism belongs to Him. Nothing that can befall the Christian occurs apart from his relationship to his Lord.

Verse 10 then repeats the thought of Verse 4, adding that all will have to face God's judgment. This means that Christians are not responsible to one another. The Greek word used here for a *judge's bench* appears both in Matthew's and in John's Passion narrative, but it is not less proper when referred to God's judgment than to Pilate's. No human being can advance a claim to judge another, for all judgment belongs to God, and a favorable judgment can be accepted only by faith. When the person who claims to have risen above the rules finds in that freedom a proof of his own superiority to others, he has attempted to appropriate to himself God's function as judge. When the person who has used his own performance as the manifestation of his own effective relationship to God turns that standard into an absolute by which others are to be judged, he likewise has attempted to usurp God's function. While Paul personally preferred the type of religion of those whom he described as *the strong,* an impartial approach to the paragraph will recognize that either party may be equally right or equally wrong, that ultimately all depends upon the acceptance of God's offer in faith which can be equally real with either approach. As a matter of observation, the varied Christian traditions that have maintained themselves in the modern world on some points take the attitude characteristic of those whom Paul called *the strong* while on others they take that of *the weak;* one cannot contemplate the possibility of Christians who neither worship nor practice self-denial in any way.

In support of what he has been saying, Paul offers a citation of Scripture drawn from Isaiah 49:18 and 45:23; the latter verse is also employed in Philippians 2:11. Verse 12 then concludes this first section of the chapter with the declaration that every man must give an account of himself to God in the final judgment. The text here is not certain. The first word of the verse is certainly ARA, which may be translated *consequently*. There is stronger manuscript authority for adding OUN than for omitting it, but in this instance the weight of manuscripts alone is not decisive. At the start of a section ARA OUN, *consequently it is to be determined* is appropriate, but not at its conclusion where no immediate further consequences are to be drawn. A further point of variance here is whether the verb is simple or compound; reliable manuscripts are divided about equally, but Paul's general fondness for compound verbs should probably settle this issue. Early textual evidence is also divided on whether the words *to God* should be included at the end of the verse, and for this neither logic nor history can clarify the answer, for whether the words are included or not it is obvious that the account must be given to God. Since the combined witness of B and W has been followed in the previous instance, it seems proper to omit the words with them, as has been done in the translation. Thus Paul is saying that *the weak* ought not to claim a responsibility concerning what they regard as the laxity shown by most of their brethren. No one can answer to God on behalf of his brother, and therefore the Christian should concern himself with his own spiritual condition for which he alone can be held to account.

* * *

14:13–23 So we are no longer to pass judgment upon one another. Instead (or, but rather) you must make this decision, not to place in your brother's way hindrance or snare (or, obstacle). For I know and am fully convinced in the Lord Jesus that there is nothing profane by nature (literally, of itself), except that to the man who considers something to be profane it is profane to him. For if your brother is distressed on account of food, you are no longer behaving (literally, walking) in accord with love. Before God do not (the negative is very strong) by means of food destroy him on whose behalf Christ died! Before God do not (the same strong negative) let what is good for you (or, your good) become a cause of reproach (or, be ill spoken of)! For the Kingdom of God is not food and drink, but being in the right (or, righteousness) and peace and joy in the Holy Spirit. For he who is obedient to (literally, serves) Christ in this is acceptable to God and approved among men. In consequence therefore (ARA OUN) we are zealous (some texts read, we should be zealous) about the things which make for (or, belong to) peace and those which make for (or, belong to) mutual edification (literally, upbuilding one another). Before God you must not (again the strong negative) destroy God's work because of food! All things indeed are clean, but a thing is profane (literally, evil) to a man who eats of it while regarding it as a sin (literally, who eats it by means of hindrance). It is a good thing not to eat flesh or to drink wine or anything else by means of which your brother sins (literally, stumbles). So you keep the faith which you have to yourself in God's presence! Blessed is the man who does not bring judgment upon himself by means of that which he approves. But he who has scruples (literally, is doubtful) if he should eat has been condemned, because it does not originate in (or, is not from) faith. Now everything which does not originate in faith is sin.

* * *

If the injunctions of the first half of the chapter are addressed more particularly to *the weak*, those of the second half are for *the strong*. Both can sin, *the weak* by excessive criticism and *the strong* by a lack of charity. Moreover, their situations are not equal. *The weak* cannot harm *the strong* by his abstentions, but *the strong* may destroy the faith of *the weak* by ostentatious violation of what appear to the one faction as vital principles of religion. Yet offenses of this kind can and must be avoided. *The weak* may be destroyed when he sees the principles by which he lives negated in the name of Christianity. The worst that can befall *the strong* through practicing abstinence for the sake of charity is inconvenience. Therefore Paul, while in essence he agrees with *the strong*, must give warning that the person who takes his stand for freedom from rules will be tempted to greater sin than is possible for his brother who attempts to live by rules. So Christians are not to pass judgment upon one another. At the same time, they must pass severe judgment upon themselves. There is here a deliberate play upon words, with the same verb used first in exhortation and then in command. The believers must determine whether they are creating difficulties for their brethren. Two separate words are used to describe the offense; the first of these properly means an accidental obstacle in the road, and therefore stands for inadvertent sins against charity, while the second means an obstacle placed in the road deliberately, and so stands for intentional slights upon *the weak*. Both types of offense must be avoided. The first duty of the Christian is to promote the spiritual welfare of others within the Community.

In Verse 14 the apostle reasserts his conviction that the issues of religious practice mean nothing in themselves. As Barrett puts it, "where the whole of life lies equally under judgment and under the grace of God, it is idle to mark out areas that are in a special sense *unclean*." In Acts 10:15, Matthew 15:11, and I Corinthians 10:25–27 it is made clear that there is nothing that Christianity counts objectively profane. But whenever a person believes a thing to be profane and despite his belief indulges in it, this act is sacrilege. On this and similar verses moral theologians have established the principle that when one does something in the belief that it is a mortal sin, it is such a sin for that person even though it may not be so in itself. Therefore those who agree with Paul regarding religious observance must especially show charity for their weaker brethren. If a brother is distressed by the sight of a Christian doing what he considers to be sinful, or if the example of someone else prompts him to violate his own conscience, the action of the Christian who is independent of rules is almost certain to cause injury for the one who depends upon them. To cause a fellow Christian to be false to his own principles is to betray Christian love. No sin may equal this, for it may have an infinite consequence in the spiritual destruction of a person for whom Christ died. There is no principle or privilege of sufficient value to justify such a loss. The Christian freedom for which Paul campaigned is good, but the apostle perceived as clearly as anyone else in history has done that when such freedom is used without regard for love it causes injury to the Church. Therefore such freedom must be tempered by responsibility, and where the responsibility is lacking the consequences are far more serious than those of legalism. So Verse 16 declares that the Christian must not cause harm with something that objectively is good.

Verse 17 then sets forth a principle already established in rabbinic writings. Scholars differ as to what Paul means here by *the Kingdom of God*. Some contend that the phrase is invariably eschatological when it appears in the apostle's writings, and usually this is true. Yet there are exceptions to this general rule, and assuredly this is one of them. Here the apostle is defining Christian life for which the principles of freedom and of self-denial can never be more than secondary. What is of prime importance is the triad of concepts, *righteousness, peace,* and *joy in the Holy Spirit.* Each of these concepts, however, is in need of explanation. Roman Catholic scholars generally hold that *righteousness* is that which Christians themselves possess, an attainment that sets them at *peace* with God and is the cause of their spiritual *joy.* Obviously, when compared with these blessings matters of food and drink cannot have serious importance. Lietzmann offers an entirely different understanding of the matter. To him the vital things are *being in the right with God,* which is not possible apart from love; *peace within the Community,* which also depends upon love; and *joy in the Holy Spirit,* which is the assured possession of the person who does have love. Barrett handles the words in yet another way, making *joy* a subjective reality that determines both *righteousness* and *peace.* In this scheme *peace* will be within the Community, and it can only be preserved when love of the brotherhood is more important to its members than any private distinctions that may exist between them.

Of these three interpretations, that advanced by Lietzmann is the most satisfactory. This whole block of teaching is parallel to that given by Paul in I Corinthians 8:7–13. Love is the heart of all Christian living, and the true test of love as applied to *the strong* here is the consideration they demonstrate for their weaker brethren. If *faith* puts the believers *in the right with God* in the first place, it is *love* that preserves them in that relationship, and love for God must find practical expression in love for the brethren. In this way *righteousness* can be given the same value here that it has elsewhere in Romans, and can retain its status as a prerequisite for all the other qualities that are to distinguish a person who belongs to the *Kingdom of God.* Alternative schemes of interpretation convert *righteousness* into a consequence of other virtues. Where this *righteousness given by God* is found, *peace* assuredly will be present, and from the union of *righteousness* and *peace* the *joy in the Holy Spirit* inevitably will arise. Here there can be no real doubt that the Holy Spirit is directly related to the *joy* and only indirectly related to the other members of this triad. Thus the keynote of the whole verse is Christian *love,* and Verse 18 adds that to serve Christ by such *love* is to win the approval of

God and of men. One may ask whether the men whose approval is sought are Christians or non-Christians. Without wishing to eliminate possible consideration of the outside world, it must be acknowledged that the apostle is speaking of Christians. One cannot believe that the church in Rome was divided into two portions and only two. A minority in good conscience believed in their rules of abstinence and special observance. A larger group believed with equal conviction that freedom in such matters was of the essence of Christianity. But it is probable that the mass of the disciples merely accepted the principle of freedom without making an issue of it in any way. Paul, therefore, in making an appeal to *the strong* is asking them to seek the approval of other Christians as well as the approval of God; in other words he is asking them to avoid the suspicion of bigotry.

In Verse 19 the D manuscript reads the main verb as a subjunctive and adds a second verb, and several modern editors have accepted the first of these readings. Yet there is no good reason to regard this as exhortation. The word ARA with which the verse begins shows that some sort of summary is to follow, and there is little new material in the remaining verses of the chapter. Christians, if they are truly disciples of Jesus, will assuredly follow the things that make for *peace* and for mutual *edification*. With Paul *building up* normally refers to the building of the Church or of its members. Paul is not satisfied merely with *peace* as a goal. He looks for a positive good in the strengthening of the spiritual welfare of the disciples. Verse 20 then repeats the stringent prohibition that had already been pronounced in Verse 15, and it is probable that *the work of God* that is not to be destroyed embraces both the spiritual life of the individual *weak* brother and the unity of the Church. Misuse of Christian freedom by *the strong* can be a threat to God's work no matter in what way it is defined. Yet while this is true, Paul will not abandon his principle. As in Verse 14, he affirms that all things are clean. Mark 7:19 asserts that Jesus made the same point, and it seems entirely probable that the apostle here is quoting a tradition of the Lord's teaching as it had been received in Gentile churches. There is no sufficient support in the ancient texts for the addition found in the corrector of Aleph, *to the pure all things are pure*. This is a proverb illustrating the point, and not a part of the apostle's statement, although there is no reason to believe that Paul would have repudiated it. Yet when one says that nothing is essentially *unclean,* there remains the possibility that clean things may be a cause of injury. This will occur if a person who has scruples of conscience about partaking of a particular food is led to eat of it. This again is a repetition of what was said in Verse 14. Verse 21 adds to this summary another Pauline concept that had previously been set forth in I Corinthians 8:13. Any sort of self-denial that may be essential to the spiritual welfare of another Christian ought to be undertaken gladly. Once more Barrett is deserving of quotation in his statement that it is necessary to preserve and protect the conscience of your fellow Christian and the unity of the Church, even if to do so you must forego your undoubted right as an instructed Christian to eat meat and drink wine, although this does not mean that all Christians should take permanent vows of abstinence. This is the only place in the chapter where Paul makes direct mention of wine as an abstinence, but it is a strong indication that the practices of *the weak* were not of Jewish origin, for this was not included among the prohibitions of the Torah. There is considerable manuscript authority here for omitting the clause *or which causes offense to the weak* at the end of Verse 21, but the support for it is equally strong and it is in no way at variance with Paul's teaching; perhaps it should be inserted in the translation above.

Verse 22 applies the warning even more directly to *the strong.* Their position is an expression of true Christian faith, and they have the advantage of agreement between their convictions and their conduct. On the other hand, those who eat meat when they are doubtful of their right to do so are acting sinfully because of that doubt. But the faith of *the strong* can be a danger. Real faith is such absolute confidence in God that the man who has it knows that no restraints or observances can give him greater security in his relationship with God. But when such faith is selfishly displayed by indulgence in actions that cause offense to others, it is converted into sin. Thus the person who has such faith is to keep it as a matter between God and himself, and is not to impose it upon others. *Blessed is the man who does not bring judgment upon himself by means of that which he approves.* This is a paraphrase rather than a translation of the statement, but it does emphasize its meaning. Unfortunately, Paul has been unduly economical in his use of words throughout this verse. Verse 23 adds a further warning for *the weak.* The man who has scruples brings judgment upon himself if he eats, because what he is doing does not originate in faith. To eat meat for personal convenience or to escape the disapproval of others, when one is not satisfied in his own conscience that it is proper to do so, is to make self rather than God the center of life. This inevitably is sin, a sin in which *the strong* may involve his brother by irresponsible behavior, but at the same time a sin for which *the weak* must also bear guilt. Luther has confused the issue by adding that the lack of faith shown by *the weak* in such a matter is itself sin; the apostle himself made no such statement. It is the *act* that does not originate in faith that is a sin, not the *scruple*; Paul had begun the chapter with a statement that *the weak* brother should be accepted.

The later manuscripts and some of the Fathers have added the doxology of 16:25–27 at this point, but it is evident that the words have no proper place here. No epistle could end on the note sounded in Chapter 14, especially not an epistle written to a church with which Paul had no personal connection. Those texts that have placed the doxology here, either as the end of the epistle or as an insertion, have been misled directly or indirectly by the expurgated version of Romans prepared by Marcion. Further explanation on this point will be given at the end of Chapter 16.

CHAPTER 15

Christian Unity in Paul's Plans

15:1–13 So we who are strong are obliged to bear with the weaknesses of those who are lacking in strength, and not to indulge (or, please) ourselves. Let each of us indulge (or, please) his neighbor in the matter (last three words supplied) for his good and for upbuilding. For Christ did not indulge (or, please) Himself; but as it is written, "The reproaches of those who reproached thee fell upon me." For whatever things were written formerly were written for our instruction, in order that we might hold to our hope on the basis of the perseverance and on the basis of the consolation of the Scriptures. Now may the God of perseverance and consolation grant you to be in agreement with one another in accord with Christ Jesus, in order that with one heart and with one mouth you may glorify the God and Father of our Lord Jesus Christ. Wherefore accept one another, just as Christ also accepted us that God might be glorified (or, to the glory of God). For I claim that Christ became a servant of circumcision on behalf of God's truth, with the intention that the promises of the fathers might be confirmed, and that the Gentiles might glorify God because of His mercy, just as it is written, "For this reason I shall acknowledge thee among the Gentiles and shall sing unto thy Name." And again it says, "Rejoice ye Gentiles together with His People." And again, "Praise the Lord, all ye Gentiles, and let all the peoples give praise to Him." And again Isaiah says, "There shall be the root of Jesse, and He who arises to rule over the Gentiles; in Him shall the Gentiles hope." Now may the God of hope (or, God the source of hope) fill you with all joy and peace in your faith, with the intention that you may increase (or, abound) in your hope by the power of the Holy Spirit.

* * *

No scholar who has treated this paragraph is so helpful as Lagrange. While he admits that verses 1–6 set forth an abnegation comparable to that shown by Christ Himself in His incarnate ministry as an indispensable condition for true unity in the Community, and that 7–12 are an appeal to the dominantly Gentile church of Rome to manifest consideration for the Jewish Christian minority because Gentiles have received God's mercy even more obviously than have Jews, he also demonstrates the close connection between these sections of the paragraph. In both, God's glory is the goal to which all else must lead. In the former the accomplishment of God's glory requires the unity of the believers; in the latter it rests upon that unity. In the former Christ is the pattern of humility; in the latter He is the instrument of that divine mercy which should prompt humility. The chief point of debate about the paragraph as a whole stems from the fact that Verse 1 continues the discussion of relations between *the weak* and *the strong*, while Verse 8 makes a comparison between Jewish Christians whose conversion has demonstrated the reliability of God and Gentile Christians who have been won by mercy alone. From this some writers have concluded that the Gentile Christians are *the strong* and the Jewish Christians *the weak,* and that the whole paragraph is an appeal to the Gentiles to show to the Jews the same indulgence they have themselves received from God.

Yet this conclusion is not inevitable. The vast majority of modern scholars have seen a close connection between this material and that of Philippians 2:1–11. Therefore it is possible and indeed natural to argue that Paul's thought advances here from the limited issue of scrupulosity as a hindrance to unity and that it passes on to the divine mercy on which all Christian unity is founded, and to the humble gratitude for that mercy which makes such unity easy to attain. Yet when Paul gives thought to the theme of God's mercy, he feels forced to touch on the contrast between Gentiles as recipients of the mercy and Jews as beneficiaries of the promise, which he had already treated theologically in Chapter 9. So the issue between *the strong* and *the weak* is not to be thought of as identical with that between Gentiles and Jews. Rather, from Christ's example, Paul makes a careful appeal to the Gentile Christians to show consideration for their Jewish Christian brethren. Since the point of departure for this subject, as set forth in Verse 1, is a reference to the problems of Chapter 14, it is easy to understand how those who read all of Paul's teaching in the light of Galatians have reached the opinion that *the weak* are simply Jewish Christians. Such an identification, however, will not help in the interpretation of the paragraph as a whole.

When one understands this, one will agree with Lietzmann that Verse 1 is a stronger statement of 14:1, and Verse 2 an intensification of 14:6 that states its point almost as emphatically as does I Corinthians 10:33. The picture of the helpfulness *the strong,* with whom the apostle numbers himself, are to give to *the weak* resembles that of Galatians 6:2. *The strong* are to carry the load that is assigned to someone else, to consider the needs of others rather than their own satisfaction. In a footnote in his commentary Michel explains that the phrase *pleasing oneself* is a more emphatic form of *living for oneself* that appears in 14:7; both expressions refer to the attempt to live in independence of God. This paragraph shows the practical operation of Christian love. What is demanded is not merely the charity that tolerates differences of opinion, but the outgoing love that will aid others in the fulfillment of their objectives; it is required by the example of Christ's earthly life. Following his custom, Paul does not mention any particular incidents of the Lord's life that have been preserved by tradition. Instead he sets forth the meaning of that life in language drawn from the pre-Pauline hymn found in Philippians 2:6–11. Thus Christ's life is presented as more than example; it dominates the whole scheme of God's saving action, and is the revelation of the divine Nature to which human nature is to be conformed. The aim of goodness shown by consideration for others is the upbuilding of the Church Jesus Himself had founded.

Verse 3 quotes the Septuagint of Psalm 69:9. Few texts were as popular among the earliest Christians. Verses from this psalm are reflected in Romans 11:9–10, Acts 1:20, John 15:25, and Mark 15:36, and John 2:17 includes a citation from this particular verse. Although several scholars hold that Paul has changed the sense of the words and has interpreted the reproaches of others as what is meant by bearing their burdens, there is every reason to believe that the apostle is following the traditional exegesis here. The reproaches of those who reproach God have fallen upon God's Servant, and for Paul, Jesus is God's Servant. When Christians are united with their Lord, the reproaches fall upon them likewise. Then in Verse 4, as in I Corinthians 9:10, Paul declares the primitive Christian conviction that the Old Testament was written for the benefit of the present generation of believers, that Scripture exhorts *us* to have hope on the basis of the perseverance and the consolation of which it is the record.

Verses 5–6 then introduce the content of the hymn that is quoted directly in Philippians 2:6–11, and Verse 6 even repeats some of the language of that hymn. The key phrase here is *in accord with Christ*, and the two verses are a prayer that Roman Christians may live in accord with the purpose or pattern of Christ. God is identified in Verse 5 not by His eternal attributes but by the gifts He bestows upon Christians. The particular gifts chosen, perseverance and consolation, were referred to God as their source in the Old Testament. The prayer asks that Christians may be in agreement, literally that they may think the same thing among themselves. Again the apostle is stressing the need for concord within the Community. Verse 6 is liturgical in form, and the adverb that stands for *with one heart* is balanced with the phrase *with one mouth* for which Greek did not possess a comparable adverb. This second phrase is also found in I Clement. The communal task of the Church is to glorify God, and those who receive His gifts assuredly will do so. The expression *the God and Father of our Lord Jesus Christ* was an early Christian liturgical form that Paul had used twice in II Corinthians, that Paul's truest disciple used in Ephesians, and that appears in I Peter. At a later date it was abandoned, possibly because it could imply that Jesus Christ Himself was not God, but the people who used it in the New Testament had no such thought in their own minds.

There is a problem of text in Verse 7 and one of theology in Verse 8, and practically all scholars have erred in their treatment of one or other of these. Most manuscripts read *Christ accepted you,* which might indicate that Paul was thinking only of the Gentile Christians of Rome. On the other hand, B and the original hand in D read *Christ accepted us,* which would imply that Jewish as well as Gentile Christians are included and that Paul is referring to himself as well as to others in the statement. The context favors this second reading. In Romans 14:1 and also in Philemon Paul used the verb PROSLAMBANO in the sense of *accept with favor,* in the second case referring to Onesimus. This verse is an exhortation to all Christians to love one another with the same love that Christ has shown to them. This may be compared with the New Commandment of John 13:34. The theological issue of Verse 8 has been treated in various ways. If one holds that in Verse 7 Paul has said *Christ accepted you* and that the apostle was treating the Roman church as almost entirely Gentile, the meaning would be that Christ's coming as Messiah of Israel had made possible the inclusion of Gentiles in the People of God, so that Jews were enabled to glorify God for His faithfulness while Gentiles could do so for His mercy. Yet this cannot be satisfactory, because Chapter 11 has shown that the Roman church was not exclusively Gentile. If one understands Paul's statement as *Christ accepted us,* and admits the presence of Jewish Christians in Rome, it may seem proper to say that Christ became a servant of the Jews whose system of Torah makes them representatives of the most extreme form of religious scrupulosity; then one would have an appeal for concord between the two groups. This surely must be rejected, because Chapter 14 did not in any way identify *the weak* as Jews or *the strong* as Gentiles, and the citations of Scripture that follow this verse cannot be regarded as appeals for concord between the two groups. Lietzmann has it that the sense in which Paul regarded Christ as a *servant of the circumcision* remains a mystery, but that it must be related to the position within Judaism which Jesus held in virtue of His title of Messiah. The mystery is real, but in some degree it may be elucidated. Paul actually means that in the coming of the Messiah God's promises to the patriarchs have found fulfillment, that since they have been fulfilled God's gift of salvation can now be extended beyond the Chosen People, and that by means of this extension God shall be glorified. This explanation may not answer every question, but it does not do violence either to its context or to the rest of the epistle.

The four texts that follow, Psalms 18:49, Deuteronomy 32:43, Psalm 117:1, and Isaiah 11:10, all support this interpretation of Christ as servant of the circumcision, and serve as illustrations of the principle already set forth in Verse 4. All four texts deal with the relations between God and the Gentiles. In all of them the Scripture is seen as the word of God Himself, and therefore a few deletions are made from the Septuagint translation, such as that of the address *Lord* from Psalm 18:49. Once more one may note that the apostle has taken his texts from all three divisions of the Old Testament in order to show how well established is his point that Gentiles are called upon to glorify the God of Israel who is indeed the God of all humanity. The *root of Jesse* in the fourth quotation is, of course, Jesus the Messiah, and its use bears witness to Paul's belief in the Davidic ancestry of Jesus. Verse 13 concludes the paragraph with a prayer for blessing upon those to whom Paul writes. The words here are liturgical rather than rhetorical. As is common in the apostle's prayers, *joy* and *peace* are seen as fruits of the indwelling of the Holy Spirit, and *faith* as the human response to God that makes possible the action of the Spirit within the believer, while *hope* is the means of perseverance. Lagrange holds that *hope* is the central theme here, and he relates it to the perseverance and consolation of verses 4–5. This conclusion on the note of *hope* is a further indication that Paul's thought has passed beyond the matter of concord within the Church to the first principles of the Christian religion. The *joy* and *peace* become a pledge of future blessing, and therefore a ground for the *hope* that will grow in all the believers through the operation of God's Holy Spirit. As is proper for a prayer, the main verb is in the optative, and the prayer itself has for its object that those to whom Paul is writing may abound in all the rich gifts of God. With this blessing the moral teaching of the epistle is brought to its conclusion, as the dogmatic portion had been concluded with a liturgical thanksgiving. What now remains is an epilogue, divided between a statement of the apostle's own plans and a list of greetings to those with whom he is acquainted in this church that he had not himself founded. He seeks aid from Rome in those plans, and he believes that the teaching of the epistle proper proves that he deserves to receive it in the interest of Christian missionary work.

* * *

15:14–33 Now for my own part, my brethren, I am convinced with regard to you that you yourselves are filled with good will, endowed with all knowledge, competent to advise one another. But I have written to you rather freely (or, boldly) in some places (or, matters) to refresh your memories because of the favor (or, commission) which was given to me from God that I should be a minister (or, public servant) of Christ Jesus for the Gentiles, to serve the Gospel of God in the capacity of priest, in order that the offering of the Gentiles may be accepted as consecrated by the Holy Spirit. So in Christ Jesus I make my boast in affairs relating to God. For I shall not venture to make any mention (literally, to say anything) of matters other than those which Christ accomplished through me for the obedience of the Gentiles, by word and by action, by a power of signs and of wonders and by spiritual power (or, a power of spirit), so that in a circuit from Jerusalem all the way round to Illyricum I have brought the Gospel of Christ to fulfillment. Now in this way I have been ambitious to proclaim the Gospel only where Christ was not known (literally, named), in order that I might not be building upon someone else's foundation, but just as it is written, "They to whom it was not announced concerning Him shall see, and those who did not hear shall understand." And it is for this reason that I have often been hindered from coming to you. But now I no longer have a task (literally, place) in these regions, and I have had a longing to come to you for a number of years past (literally, a good number of years), as I should in going to Spain. For I hope to see you in the course of my journey and by you to be sent forward there, if I may be somewhat (literally, in part) refreshed among you (alternatively, if I may enjoy your company) first, but at present I am on my way to Jerusalem in my service to the saints. For Macedonia and Achaea agreed (or, consented) to make a certain contribution (literally, sharing) for the poor among the saints who are in Jerusalem. For they agreed to it, and they are indebted to them. For if the Gentiles were partakers in their spiritual things they are obligated also to minister to them (or, to do them public service) in material (literally, physical) things. So when I have completed this, and have signed over this benefaction (literally, fruit) to them, I shall depart for Spain by way of your city (or, of you). Now I know that in coming to you I shall come with the fullness of Christ's blessing. So I entreat you, my brethren, through our Lord Jesus Christ and through the love of the Spirit, to strive together with me in prayers to God on my behalf, that I may be delivered from the unbelievers in Judea, and that my service which is in the interest of (literally, for) Jerusalem may be acceptable to the saints, in order that by God's will I may come to you with joy and may receive comfort with you. The peace of God be with you all. Amen.

* * *

There is a close parallel between this paragraph and Romans 1:8–17. In a letter as long as this there was good reason to repeat at the end the ideas by which the apostle had sought to gain the good will of the Roman Christians at its beginning. Thus 15:14 is a reprise of 1:8, 15:15 of 1:11, 15:16 of 1:9 and 14, 15:18 of 1:16, 15:22 of 1:10, 15:23 of 1:13, 15:28 of 1:15, 15:32 of 1:10. Other matters are also treated in this paragraph, for the apostle is now eager to explain his plans in detail and to entreat the prayers of the Roman church for their accomplishment, but the parallel between the two sections is obviously intentional. After completing his teaching, both in its dogmatic and in its moral aspects, Paul turns naturally to practical problems and their solutions. Yet Rome is not one of his own churches, and he feels that he must confine his discussion of practical matters to general terms or to plans of his own. Moreover, in writing to a community over which he held no defined authority, he did not feel the same freedom in setting forth his advice as he showed in writing to Corinth or to Galatia. So he relates his own plans to God's over-all plan, and he begins his paragraph with an appeal that the teaching he has given may be received with good will. Thus in Verse 14 he tells the readers that he is convinced of their ability to manage their own affairs, and in a sense he apologizes for the amount of advice he has offered. Any Christian who has truly received the Gospel knows the essence of revelation, and knows its consequences as well, but yet he may receive further benefit from being reminded of that which he already knows.

Authors whose views on the Christian ministry are beyond possibility of reconciliation have found in Verse 16 a basis for their diverse views of what that ministry implies. In some cases these exegetical treatments show surprising fairness and perception. In the Septuagint the combination of the words LEITOURGON and HIEROURGEIN normally describes a performance of spiritual service, a sort of priesthood. Paul insists that his Apostolate to the Gentiles may properly be described in this way. But if this is a priesthood in a technical sense, one might expect a sacrifice to be connected with it. In grammatical construction this sacrifice should be the noun in the accusative case which follows HIEROURGOUNTA, but that noun is *Gospel* which must be thought of as a revelation or gift from God rather than as an offering to Him. Thus Paul's special vocation as Apostle to the Gentiles is not to be interpreted as a sacrificing priesthood but as an administrative one. The agreement on this point between Dodd and Lagrange is truly remarkable in view of the differing attitudes they show toward sacerdotalism. Thus the PROSPHORA or *offering* (the Greek word later became the regular term for the individual's offering of bread for the Eucharist) is made by the Gentile Christians themselves, and it is in fact an offering of themselves. Paul's administrative priesthood must then be seen as that of the minister who brings men to Christ, who instructs and trains them in Christian living, and so makes possible their sacrifice of themselves. In this way one may preserve both the priestly function of the Christian ministry and the equally important principle of the priesthood of all believers. The offering of themselves that the Gentiles make is rendered acceptable to God in being sanctified by the action of the Holy Spirit. This action of the Spirit is related to the fact of Baptism, and it is only as baptized Christians that the Gentiles are able to make an offering of themselves that is acceptable to God. So in 12:1 Paul had called upon the Romans to present their bodies as a sacrifice to God. In connection with this self-offering of the Gentiles, the action of the apostle may be compared with that of a priest who presents before God the acceptable sacrifices of the worshipers.

Verses 17–19 have a close connection. First Paul maintains that *in Christ* he has a cause for pride. In varying ways he makes the same claim in the other epistles. Yet it is only *in Christ* that he can have a cause for pride. He has a cause for pride only as he is mystically united with his Lord and as Christ works in him. Paul would not dare to claim credit for the things he had accomplished as if they had resulted from his own efforts apart from the operation of Christ in him. Through Paul's labor Christ has brought about the conversion of the Gentiles. To Paul Christ has given the power to work signs such as those ascribed to him in Acts. In order that all of this may be achieved through the service of His apostle, Christ has strengthened Paul's *human spirit*. On this last point, however, disagreement among the manuscripts has prompted the exegetes to divergent conclusions. Papyrus 46, Aleph, and the late manuscripts read *by the power of the Spirit of God*. The A, C, D, and G manuscripts have it *by the power of the Holy Spirit*. With this much textual support it is natural to conclude that the signs which it has been given to Paul to perform are manifestations of the action of the Holy Spirit. The text here followed, which omits both the adjective *holy* and the possessive *of God* with *spirit*, is based simply upon the B manuscript. Normally this would not constitute sufficient evidence. Yet on the assumption that *of God* or *holy* could be added to *spirit* more readily than either could be substituted for the other, the B reading must be accepted. The strengthening of Paul's *human spirit* expresses all that is needed here for us to understand the apostle's pride. Paul need demand nothing beyond this to make good his claim that he holds a special place or vocation in the unfolding of God's plan as that plan leads on to the end of history.

The second half of Verse 19 sets out the scope of Paul's work, which ranges from Jerusalem through Syria and what is now called Asia Minor and Greece into the Province of Illyricum which is the modern Yugoslavia. Clearly Paul does not intend to tell the Romans that all the Gentiles in that vast area have been converted or that he has done more than bring the Gospel to individual cities. There is some doubt whether Paul actually worked in Illyricum itself. Acts makes no mention of a ministry there. Some scholars point out that since it is obvious that Paul had not been preaching to Gentiles in Jerusalem the other terminus in this list should likewise be excluded from the field of operations. In Harrison's treatment of the Pastoral Epistles, however, it is said that the genuine Pauline fragments contained in II Timothy and Titus do imply a ministry in the Province of Illyricum, and this argument does seem to be satisfactory. Once the scope of the apostle's past work has been given, verses 20–21 serve as a natural introduction to Paul's further plans. In I Corinthians 3:10 and II Corinthians 10:15–16, as in Verse 20 here, Paul had stated that his efforts were devoted to the establishment of new Christian work rather than to the carrying forward of work begun by others. An exception to this is Paul's activity in the church of Syrian Antioch of which he had not been the founder. Indeed, Paul seems to have thought that bringing the Gospel to areas where it was previously unknown was a particularly appropriate way of fulfilling his own vocation as Apostle to the Gentiles. In Verse 21 he justified the Gentile mission in general and his own special phase of it in particular by the quotation of Isaiah 52:15.

Several scholars hold that Verse 22 begins a new section, but it is closely related to what has just been said. Paul declares that his labors have made it impossible for him to fulfill his long-standing desire to visit Rome. Now that his work in these areas is nearly complete, he should be free to accomplish this purpose. But in view of his program of building the Church in new areas only, he is not planning to serve the Roman church in any official capacity, or to spend a protracted visit there. His real objective is to begin new missionary work in the west, specifically in Spain, which is still untouched and in which he believes conditions will be favorable for him. For such work, however, he will need a base of operations, so he appeals for support and encouragement from the Roman Christians. Rome is to take the place of Ephesus as Ephesus has supplanted Antioch in serving as Paul's headquarters, and Verse 24 might imply that this scheme was already understood by those for whom the apostle was writing.

Yet before he undertakes this program Paul has other duties to discharge, namely, the bringing of poor relief raised in Macedonia and Achaea to the needy Jewish Christians of Jerusalem. So in Verse 25 Paul interrupts the explanation of his design by the mention of this preliminary task. The poor relief is a free-will offering of the Gentile churches, and it is mentioned in I Corinthians 16:1 and in II Corinthians 8:1–4 and 9:2 and 12. Yet it is more than a free-will offering; it is a small effort to repay a debt, and it can never be an adequate return for the spiritual blessings received by these Gentiles from the Jewish Christians. Dodd's treatment of the relief fund is excellent. It was without doubt patterned after the contributions of Jewish communities of the Dispersion to the support of the religious establishment in Jerusalem. The Jewish Christians of Jerusalem had no complex establishment to maintain, but they had a continuing need for aid to their poor brethren, and so they used the funds they obtained for that purpose. The reference to the recipients of this relief in Verse 27 as *the poor among the saints* is the subject of a special note by Lietzmann. The use of *saints* simply as a term for members of the Church is common in Paul, and it appears also in Hebrews, I Peter, Acts, Revelation, and Jude. Of these five books only three can be said to have been influenced by Paul directly, and the other two are representative of Jewish Christianity. This usage of *saints* simply as Christians, however, is absent from the Johannine Gospel and Epistles. In the Septuagint, Aaron, the prophets, and the Nazirites had been described as *saints*, and the People as a whole was called *the Holy Nation*. Among the postcanonical works I Maccabees takes *saints* simply as Jews. Lietzmann's reasonable conclusion is that the early Jewish Christians simply took the name from Jewish usage as their own, and that Paul extended it to his Gentile converts. Verse 28 then explains that when Paul has completed this task and has signed over the contributions of his churches to the Jerusalem Christians, he will begin his journey to Spain by way of Rome. The word SPHRAGISAMENOS has puzzled some scholars, but it makes perfectly good sense as indicating the final seal affixed to official business. The appearance of the word does not mean that official transactions within the primitive Church were carried on with the same formality as those of the Roman Empire. Even today we may say that a debt has been *discharged* when we mean only that it has been paid. The contribution is called *fruit* because it represents a return for spiritual blessings. Verse 29 can be understood in two ways. Paul's coming to Rome will bring to the Christians there blessings from the Lord. But greater stress is given here to the apostle's conviction that he will himself receive a blessing in coming because the Roman Christians will set forward his work in the new field that he has chosen.

Verse 30 takes up this idea by appealing to the Romans to pray for the success of the apostle's plans. The words are carefully composed, with something of the tone of liturgical formula. In commenting on this, Origen declared that all prayer is a struggle and that it is appropriate for the apostle to ask others to join with him in *the striving of prayer*. This time the *Spirit* unmistakably is the Holy Spirit, and the *love* is God's love that the Spirit has poured forth into the hearts of Christians, as in Romans 5:5. Yet there is more than liturgical formula here. The apostle hints of his foreboding, which is also mentioned in Acts, that all may not go well in Jerusalem. There was personal danger at the hands of the unbelievers in the Jewish capital, a possibility that martyrdom in the Holy City might prevent him from coming to Rome and going on to Spain as he desired to do. The attitude of the Jews can be understood. Paul had done tremendous damage to the religious establishment of Jerusalem by diverting the contributions of many Gentile *God-fearers* from the Temple hierarchy to the Christian Church. Since he was a former leader among the Jews, this defection had caused him to be hated much more intensely than he would have been if he had not once been a prominent Pharisee. Yet this was not the only danger, nor even the greatest one. Many of the Jewish Christians were convinced that Paul had subverted the Gospel. There was the ever-present danger that such people might denounce him to the Jewish authorities, as apparently they did. Dodd also notes that there might have been a fear in Paul's mind, indicated by the last words of Verse 31, that the Jerusalem church might refuse the offering he brought in order to foster unity between his converts and the Jewish believers. These doubts need not cause surprise. In matters of conscience there are many people today, who are otherwise honest and decent, who show no moral sense whatever. While Paul could hope to conceal his presence in Jerusalem from the Temple leaders, he could not hide it from the Jewish Christians. Therefore he expresses the wish that the poor relief may be well received by the *saints* of Jerusalem, so that their hostility will be disarmed. With the majority there this desire seems to have been fulfilled, although Dodd holds that James was no more than guardedly friendly and that he caused Paul to take an unnecessary risk. But there were extremists who were unmoved by the bounty the Apostle to the Gentiles had brought. Verse 32 then sketches what will happen if the prayer the Romans are to offer has the intended effect. If God wills it and he escapes harm in Jerusalem, Paul will come to Rome with joy and will spend some time there. This visit should mean refreshment to the apostle, for he will be encouraged in this strong and united church. While he understands the dangers and prays to be delivered from them, Paul does expect that all will turn out well and that his visit to Jerusalem will strengthen unity between Jewish and Gentile Christians. But in any case he is resolved to go, even if it should end in his own death. So Paul went, and his hope of good was accomplished, even though many of his own fears were brought to realization in the course of it. The epistle proper closes with a benediction in Verse 33. In most of the epistles, including this one, Paul had set forth a wish for peace for his readers along with the initial greetings. But in a letter as long as this it was certainly appropriate to repeat that wish as part of the conclusion. The reference to *the God of peace* may be included because of threats to the unity between Jewish and Gentile Christians, but it is not an indication of any real dissension at Rome itself.

CHAPTER 16

The Exchange of Greetings

16:1–23 (24) Now I introduce to you our sister Phoebe, who is a worker of the church which is in Cenchreae, in order that you may welcome her in the Lord in a manner worthy of the saints, and that you may assist her in any matter in which she may need help from you. For she herself has been a patron to many, and to me personally. Greet Prisca and Aquila, my fellow workers in Christ Jesus, who put their own necks on the block to save my life, to whom it is not I alone that render thanks but all the churches of the Gentiles do so as well, and greet the church that meets in their house. Greet Epaenetus my beloved, who is the first fruits of Asia for Christ. Greet Mary who has done much work for you. Greet Andronicus and Junias my compatriots and fellow prisoners, who are men of note with the apostles who were in Christ before I was. Greet Ampliatus my beloved in the Lord. Greet Urban my fellow worker in Christ and Stachys my beloved. Greet Apelles who is eminent in Christ. Greet the people from the household of Aristobulus. Greet Herodion my compatriot. Greet the people from the household of Narcissus who are in the Lord. Greet Tryphaena and Tryphosa who labored in the Lord.

Greet Persis my beloved who did great work in the Lord. Greet Rufus the chosen in the Lord, and his mother who has also been a mother to me. Greet Asyncritus, Phlegon, Hermes, Patrobas, Hermas, and the brethren who meet with them. Greet Philologus and Julia, Nereus and his sister, and Olympas, and all the saints who meet with them. Greet one another with a kiss of peace (literally, a holy kiss). All the churches of Christ greet you.

Now I call upon you, my brethren, be on guard against (or, watch for) those who create dissensions and obstacles in relation to the teaching which you learned, and avoid (literally, turn away from) them. For such people are not doing service to Christ our Lord but to their own belly, and by means of plausible and fine-sounding arguments are deceiving the hearts of the innocent. For your orthodoxy (literally, obedience) is known to (literally, has come to) everyone. Therefore I rejoice about you, but I wish you to be wise in regard to what is good, and without knowledge in regard to what is evil. Now the God of peace will quickly crush down Satan under your feet.

The grace of our Lord Jesus be with you.

Timothy my fellow worker greets you, and Lucius and Jason and Sosipater my compatriots. I, Tertius, who wrote this letter greet you in the Lord. Gaius greets you, who is host to me and to the whole church. Erastus greets you, who is Treasurer of the City, and Quartus, the brother.

(The grace of our Lord Jesus Christ be with you all. Amen.)

* * *

In ancient as in modern times greetings were placed at the end of letters. Among the undoubted Pauline epistles only Galatians lacks this expression of politeness. In Romans greetings are sent to more people than in any of the other epistles for the very good reason that Paul was not well known at Rome and that he desired to enlist the support of as many Christians in that city as he had met, so that they may give help in the ambitious plans he has outlined in the previous chapter. But even before he begins the greetings themselves, he seeks to commend to Rome a new arrival, a woman named Phoebe. She comes from Cenchreae, which is the eastern harbor of Corinth where Paul is writing the epistle. Many scholars have said that she was bringing the letter from Paul herself, and as there is no suggestion that her arrival is an event in the future this seems likely. There is no other reference to her in the New Testament. An inscription of the sixth century from Jerusalem describes a deaconess named Sophia as *a second Phoebe*, but this obviously depends upon the text here. The name itself is a feminine form of Phoebus, which was the alternative name for the pagan god Apollo. Thus it is certain that she did not come of a loyal Jewish family, for Jews avoided the names of pagan deities. It is almost certain that she was a Gentile. In the ancient world the only women who traveled much were wealthy. Moreover, since Phoebe had served as a patron (the man's world of Greece had no feminine for this word) of many Christians, including Paul himself, it is evident that she had given much for the Lord's work in her home territory. She is referred to as DIAKONOS of the church in Cenchreae. The form of the word here is masculine, and Paul often uses the term without meaning a technical order of ministry. Thus it is wrong to call Phoebe a deaconess. Paul's statement cannot mean more than that she had served the church faithfully and effectively. As yet no order of deaconesses had been established. Elsewhere Paul and the Deutero-Pauline writings mention *widows* as performing those duties which at a later date were entrusted to deaconesses.

Prisca and Aquila in verses 3–4 head the list of people to whom Paul sends greetings. The apostle indicates their Jewish background by calling them his *kinsmen*. Acts informs us that they first became Christians in Rome, but were forced to leave by the edict of Claudius. Paul met them in Corinth, and later they accompanied him to Ephesus. It seems that they operated a business, tentmaking or leatherwork, and that Paul had supported himself once at Corinth by working in their enterprise. Both here and in I Corinthians 16:19 the wife Prisca is mentioned before her husband; one may assume that it was her inherited capital that had started the family business and that she was a more forceful person than her husband. It is said that they were wealthy enough to rent or buy a house in Ephesus that could serve as a place of worship. On their return to Rome after Nero had allowed the edict of Claudius to lapse, they set themselves up in a house of similar size. So Paul adds greetings to the church that meets in their house. We have no knowledge of the occasion on which they had risked their lives for Paul; the most probable occasion would have been the apostle's peril in Ephesus. In Verse 5 Epaenetus is described as the first fruits of the Province of Asia, which means that he was the first convert from the area. As Acts 19:1 tells that Paul found disciples in Ephesus whom he had not himself converted, this man must have been among them and so would not have been Paul's spiritual child. The Jewish form of the name Mary was Miriam, and it was a popular feminine name in Israel since its original exemplar was the sister of Moses. The alternative form, Maria, could be a Latin feminine of Marius, but the inscriptions of the period do not give support to this as a name used for Gentile women; in any case Papyrus 46 and the Aleph and D manuscripts give ample textual support for the Jewish form of the name. From the words here one would gather that Mary's Christian service had been performed principally in Rome. It is a fair inference that she had been driven from the capital by Claudius, along with other Jews, and had taken refuge in Corinth or Ephesus where Paul had made her acquaintance through Prisca and Aquila. Like them she had returned to Rome when it became possible for her to do so.

Many of the names in the following verses were commonly used among slaves, but some appear to have been reserved for free citizens. Christianity, in Rome as elsewhere, had cut across class barriers. Some of the names are Greek in form, and some Latin; the majority of people whom Paul would have known were from the Greek-speaking provinces of the empire, and in Rome one would expect to find Latin names. The large percentage of Jewish names bears witness to the Jewish origin of Christianity. Verse 7 is devoted to Andronicus and Junias. There is uncertainty about the latter name, because the W manuscript has it Junia, which would be a feminine name, and Papyrus 46 and some ancient versions read Julia. Most of the reliable texts, however, favor Junias, and the rest of the verse will be understood more readily if two men are in question. They are Paul's *kinsmen* simply in the sense of being Jews, and when they are called his *fellow prisoners* this may mean that they were currently held as prisoners in Rome or that they had shared a previous imprisonment with the apostle elsewhere or simply that they were bondmen of Christ as Paul was. Actually, when he wrote Romans it seems that Paul was not imprisoned. The translation of the next clause as given in the Revised Standard Version, *men of note among the apostles,* is misleading. We have no reason to affirm that Paul means anything more than that they are *highly regarded by the apostles who were in Christ before me.* While the title of Apostle was not strictly limited to the Twelve and the Lord's Brethren and Paul and Barnabas, to translate it as *missionary* with Goodspeed is a doubtful expedient. Thus it is not clear whether Andronicus and Junias were Christians of longer standing than Paul himself, but their acceptance by the older apostles would indicate that they were Jewish rather than Gentile disciples.

The next five names are either Latin, such as Urban, or Greek, such as Stachys. When these two are called *fellow workers* it need not mean that they are associates of Paul; it indicates that they were active Christians and probably missionaries. Ampliatus was a common name among slaves. All that is said about Apelles is that he is a worthy man, but there is every reason to believe that he was also a Christian. The fifth of these names, Aristobulus, is Greek in form, but it was widely used among Jews and was common in the Herod family. Here the greeting is addressed only to the household of Aristobulus, which would indicate either that the man had recently died or that he was not himself a Christian. It is possible that Aristobulus was one of the three contemporary Herods who bore this name, and that the greeting was for those of his slaves who had become Christians. The next name, Herodian, sounds as if its bearer had been a slave of the Herod family; he is described as Paul's *kinsman* and is thus a Jew, but nothing is known about him. Verse 11 gives a greeting to those who are Christians in the household of Narcissus, again implying that the master of the house is not a believer. The former Emperor Claudius had employed a secretary by that name, but there is nothing in favor of identifying him with the Narcissus mentioned here. Verse 12 mentions two women who are otherwise unknown, but whose similar names have been held by some to indicate that they were sisters. A third woman who is to receive a greeting is named Persis; with such a name she may well have been a slave of Iranian origin.

Verse 13 speaks of Rufus and his mother. Since Mark's Gospel, written in Rome, identifies Simon of Cyrene as "the father of Alexander and Rufus," it would appear that the sons were well known in Rome and that this *Rufus* is one of them. If so, Rufus would be a Jewish Christian with whose family Paul might have had some contact before they moved to Rome. The apostle does not specify in what way the mother of Rufus had been a mother to himself. Nine more names appear in verses 14–15, and relatives are mentioned in connection with some of them. The one woman whose name is given here, Julia, may be the wife or sister of Philologus. All these people are unknown, unless Hermas is the author of the late first century work *Pastor* which originated in Rome. Evidently Paul does not know these people very well, but he is attempting to mention everyone in Rome whose acquaintance he has ever made. The greeting with the *holy kiss* of Verse 16 is the scriptural origin for the liturgical *kiss of peace*; the same term is found in I Corinthians 16:20. This verse also says that all the churches of Christ, presumably meaning all those with which Paul has contact, send greetings to the Christians of Rome.

The list of greetings to be sent to Rome is now complete, and normally one would expect the greetings of Paul's companions in Corinth to follow at this point. Instead four verses that warn against false teachers are inserted. In many respects this resembles the harsher warning of Galatians 6:11–16. There are examples in the epistles in which Paul evidently took the pen from his scribe at the end of the letter to add a few words of particular significance in his own hand, and both Dodd and Lietzmann have suggested that this is the procedure followed here. Those who read all of Paul in the light of Galatians assume that the issue here is the demand of the Jewish Christian extremists for complete observance of Torah. Yet it is not Galatians dealing with Jewish practices that refers to the apostle's opponents as people whose god is their belly; it is Philippians 3:18–19 that does so, and if we may believe Acts Philippi had no Jewish population of any consequence and not even a synagogue. Here it is said that the false teachers are doing service to their own belly rather than to our Lord Christ, and it seems likely that Paul is discussing the non-Jewish ascetic practices of Romans Chapter 14, or is even directing a warning against some form of Gnostic libertinism. Whatever the false teaching is, Verse 19 shows that it has not yet made serious headway in Rome, for Paul compliments the Christians of that city for their obedience or reliability, even their orthodoxy. This suggests that the same qualities for which the Roman church was celebrated in the fourth century were already present in the first. The nature of the false teaching cannot be determined in detail, but it is scarcely a warning directed against *the weak* whom Paul had been prepared to tolerate in Chapter 14. For all the apostle's inconsistencies, there are limits to the reversals found in his teaching. While many scholars consider that Jewish observances are in view here, the Jewish controversy is not to be taken as the key to all that Paul has written, and Gnostic libertinism is certainly a more obvious way of serving one's belly than is the attempt to keep the Torah. Thus the controversy here probably is related to Gnosticism.

Obviously Paul is saying that no divisive ideas are to be added to the sound teachings the Romans have already received, or any concepts that cannot be reconciled with those teachings. Moreover, those who introduce such divisions and offenses are to be avoided. Verse 17 is an appeal for formal orthodoxy. The word CHRESTOLOGIA, which Moffatt translates *plausible arguments*, is fairly common in the Greek of the first century, and is usually derogatory in meaning. On the other hand EULOGIA is rare, although there can be no doubt that it stands for *beguiling speech*, something that sounds well but is destructive in its effects. In Verse 19 when Paul says that he wishes the Romans to be *wise in regard to what is good*, he is probably using the word *wise* as a deliberate contrast to the EULOGIA of the false teachers. Verse 20 consists in two sentences that are not related to each other. The first of them declares that the God of peace will soon beat down Satan under the feet of the Christians. Similar expressions appear in the Testaments of the Twelve Patriarchs. Here, however, the promise of Satan's overthrow looks forward to an early return of Christ in glory and a fulfillment of eschatological hopes, to the reality Paul had described earlier by the term *adoption*. It seems appropriate that in a context dealing with divisive tendencies God should be described by the attribute of *peace*. The other sentence in this verse is a liturgical formula of blessing, *the grace of our Lord Jesus be with you*. With minor variations this formula appears near the conclusion of every genuine Pauline epistle, even in the vehemently partisan Galatians. It occurs also in every surviving imitation of the Pauline writings. It sets forth the apostle's wish that those to whom he has written may possess the totality of blessing that is available to them because of their union with Christ.

The appearance of greetings from those who are with Paul at Corinth seems strange at this point. One would rather have expected that the final word of blessing in Verse 20 would follow these salutations, and the D manuscript and those that depend on it have made this transposition and so have created Verse 24. No Alexandrian or Caesarean text, however, follows this reasonable arrangement, and since it is an obvious correction it must be rejected. First place among the salutations is given to Timothy, Paul's closest and most trusted associate who is too well known to the Church for any comment to be needed. Next stands the name of Lucius. It would be tempting to identify him with Luke, but the form is not right and he is said to be Paul's compatriot and therefore not a Gentile; most scholars identify him with Lucius of Cyrene who is mentioned in Acts 13:1. Although Lucius was a Latin name, it was often used by Jews as a substitute for Joshua. Jason and Sosipater are Greek names, but they also are Paul's compatriots and therefore Jewish Christians. In Acts, Jason is connected with Corinth in Achaea, and Sosipater (or the shorter form Sopater) with nearby Beroea in Macedonia. It seems likely that Sosipater was serving as delegate from the church in Beroea for the relief fund to Jerusalem and that Jason was serving in a similar capacity for Corinth. Tertius, acting as Paul's scribe, then adds his own greeting. This name is Latin, and so are those that follow it, but this need not cause surprise, for Corinth had been destroyed by the Romans two centuries before and had been rebuilt as a Roman colony. By this time it had once more become dominantly Greek, but there were still many people of Roman origin living there. Among the bearers of Latin names, Gaius is evidently a man of wealth if he can serve as host not only for the apostle himself but for the whole church. Even if this last phrase means no more than that he provided hospitality to any traveling Christian who might seek it, he must have been more than solvent. There is a good chance that Gaius was the person whom Paul claimed to have baptized in I Corinthians 1:14. Erastus as city treasurer or comptroller must also have been a person of some importance, at least a civil servant of high rank. Evidently the church in Corinth had made some gains among the civic leaders. Nothing is known of Quartus; the name is Latin. Some writers suggest that he might have been the brother of Tertius, but one hesitates to believe that a Roman father would name his sons One, Two, Three, Four. Verse 24 is a repetition and a slight expansion of the blessing from Verse 20, and, as was said above, this Western interpolation cannot be accepted.

Many scholars contend that the greetings of Chapter 16 were intended for Ephesus, where Paul knew more people than in Rome, and that they were attached to the Roman epistle by mistake. This issue has already been discussed at some length in the introduction; as

Lietzmann has said, a letter that consists of little beside greetings raises more difficulties than it solves. Paul's desire to rally personal support in Rome is the only explanation needed for the number of individuals mentioned here.

* * *

16:25–27 To Him who is able to make you firm (or, strong) in accord with my Gospel and the proclamation of Jesus Christ, in terms of a revelation of a mystery (or, secret purpose) which was kept secret (literally, passed over) in times eternal, but now has been made plain by means of the Prophetic Writings (or, Scriptures) in accord with the command of the eternal God for the purpose of an obedience that comes from faith which might be made known to all the Gentiles, to the only wise God be the glory through Jesus Christ unto the ages of the ages. Amen.

* * *

It is not usual for Paul's epistles to end with a full doxology. Indeed, there is no other genuine epistle in which such a conclusion is found. The doxology seems to be the regular form for the conclusions of such later writings as II Peter and Jude. Therefore some thought must be given to the origin of these verses and their inclusion in this epistle. First, however, we should analyze the text itself. The address to God as *He who is able* is imitated in Ephesians 3:20 among the Deutero-Pauline writings and in Jude 24, among others. The idea that God can confirm the faithful in their possession of the blessings pertaining to their new life in Christ appears frequently with Paul, as in Romans 1:11. The phrase *according to my Gospel* is joined with *the kerygma of Jesus Christ*, so it cannot be a specifically Pauline Gospel that is under discussion but rather the established proclamation of Christianity that Paul maintains in the same terms as do other Christian teachers. Jesus Christ is the content of the proclamation, whether as declared by Paul or by some other Christian. Goodspeed's translation of the preposition KATA here as *by means of* is not satisfactory, for its purpose is to show that the Gospel or kerygma is the revelation of a mystery and not that it is made known by revelation. The *mystery* itself is God's plan of salvation, which has existed from eternity with the Creator and has now been declared in the revelation received by the Church. This is a fundamental concept of Paul's thinking, and it is found in I Corinthians and Colossians as well as here, and is imitated in Ephesians and in the Pastoral Epistles.

In Verse 26 the word *now* implies a realized eschatology. In one sense the New Age has begun with the Incarnation of Jesus Christ. In the present time the mystery of God's plan of salvation, which had been hidden from eternity, has been made plain. While future expectation, which he calls *adoption*, dominates Paul's scheme of eschatology, he never forgets that the blessings of salvation are already available to Christians; in later generations the blessings already available came to seem more important than expectation for the future. God's plan is said to be revealed by *the prophetic writings*, and at first glance this would seem to stand for the canonical Scriptures. Yet if the Old Testament prophets reveal this mystery, it is not only in the present time that they have done so; but for the purpose of the argument here *the prophetic writings* must make their revelation only for the present. So it has been proposed that these writings are Christian documents contemporary with Paul. Lagrange, however, preserves the reference of this text to the Old Testament by a convincing argument. Between the preposition DIA and the noun *writings* there appears the particle TE, and the only possible reason for its presence is to join *writings* closely with the participle *made known* at the end of this verse. Thus what is being said here is that the testimony of the prophetic writings concerning the Son of God is being made plain now by those who are charged with the proclamation of the Gospel. This testimony makes possible the teaching of *justification by faith* that has proved so advantageous to the Gentiles as compared with Jews. The present revelation of God's plan of salvation is made within the Church in accord with the express appointment of the eternal God Himself, and its object is that all nations may come to the obedience of faith.

With Verse 27 there comes a repetition of the address to God, who is now described by the adjectives *only* and *wise*, both of which appear as divine attributes in some of the apocryphal writings included in the Septuagint and also in non-Pauline portions of the New Testament. The ascription of praise is offered through the mediation of Jesus Christ because it is through His Incarnation that it has become possible for men truly to praise God. The pronoun *to whom*, however, refers to God to whom the doxology is addressed rather than to Christ through whom it is addressed, and the B manuscript does not include the pronoun at all. The translation above has omitted it, without any sense of loss in the text. Paul usually expressed the idea of eternity in a less complex manner, but the sonorous liturgical phrase found here is common in late Jewish writing and also appears in Galatians, II Timothy, and Hebrews. The common Jewish use of AMEN to conclude a doxology seems perfectly natural here, whether the verses are to be understood as Pauline or not.

After this analysis of the meaning and background of the words, we must now take up the question of whether they properly belong to this epistle. The first argument against it is the fact that every other undoubted Pauline writing ends simply with some variation of the formula *grace be with you* which appears in Verse 20 and again in the spurious Verse 24. While Paul might have composed a more formal conclusion for the most systematic of his writings, the doubt is serious. The doxology itself is merely a compilation of pious phrases drawn from the Old Testament and from early Christian prayers, and the verses that compose it add nothing to their context. In tone the words resemble the Pastoral Epistles rather than Paul himself. In the second place, the manuscripts show confusion about the proper place for these words. Papyrus 46 has them at the end of Chapter 15, the majority of manuscripts at the end of Chapter 14, A and P use the doxology twice, Aleph and B and D have it here. Origen was acquainted with manuscripts that had the doxology at the end of Chapter 14. The sum of this evidence indicates that the three verses are not part of the letter as Paul wrote it.

Yet we can scarcely be satisfied with the way in which the epistle breaks off at 16:23. Clearly the greetings from Paul's companions ought not to have been separated from those of the apostle himself by the warnings of verses 17–20. Yet we must accept the text as it comes to us in the most reliable of the manuscripts, and must use the best judgment we can in regard to it. There can be no question that at the end of a systematic epistle Paul allowed a careless conclusion to stand. Naturally the feeling that something more was needed would prompt the composition of a supplement, just as the inadequacy of Mark 16:8 prompted the composition of a supplement to the Second Gospel. This supplement would reflect the Christianity of its time of writing, and since the doxology here is akin to the Pastoral Epistles and to Jude it may be dated in the early second century. Thus it is too early to be the composition of Marcion, and its stress on the value of the Old Testament contradicts Marcion's teaching. We may accept Michel's judgment that it is based upon an early Christian hymn, although it lacks the greatness of those primitive hymns that Paul himself had used in Romans 11:33–36 and elsewhere. Yet Marcion did contribute to the confusion of text here, for in his expurgated edition of Paul he found the content of chapters 15–16 unsatisfactory, and so he suppressed them. Romans 14:23, however, is even less satisfactory than 16:23 as the conclusion of a great epistle, and the orthodox Christians whose copies of Romans had been derived from Marcion's edition pressed into service a portion of a Christian hymn of the early second century to supply the deficiency. Thus Marcion probably was responsible for the addition of the doxology, although it was not his own work. Later the full text of the epistle came to be known in areas where the abbreviated version had been in circulation, and chapters 15–16 were united with it. But when this happened the non-Pauline doxology usually was left at the end of Chapter 14 and the last clause of 16:20 was repeated as Verse 24 to end the whole work. Yet when this happened in the late second century, it had come to be felt that a full doxology was appropriate as the ending for such a work, and so some copyists transferred verses 25–27 to their present position, and others left them at the end of Chapter 14 and merely repeated them. In some instances 16:24 was removed from the text as was proper. Thus we can account for the textual confusion, along the lines laid down by Lietzmann. Obviously the Scripture could have been preserved with greater accuracy if it had not been for the efforts of Marcion to improve upon Paul.

APPENDIX

1 *Sin, the Human Predicament*

The Pauline understanding of sin treats its reality from two points of view. The first of these is simple. Sin is any act or word or thought to which a person may give his assent that is objectively displeasing to God. A sin may be a matter of omission as well as of commission, and the duty neglected may be quite as serious in relation to God or one's neighbors or oneself as the misdeed performed. Moreover, the heinous character of a particular sin depends not upon the seriousness of its consequences but upon the intention of the sinner. It may be defined by objective law or by the way in which it affects the relationship of the sinner to God or to his neighbors, but its quality as sin is determined by the purpose or attitude that prompts it.

From this standpoint sin is a matter of will. The person who fails to do right because he does not understand what is right is not culpable; sin is not taken into account where there is no law. The honest mistake is no more than a mistake. Yet error in itself is not necessarily an excuse for sin, because man has a responsibility for trying to learn his duty by whatever means are available to him, and God has provided all the help man requires. Paul recognizes that there is a natural revelation in God's governance of the universe, and a natural affinity in man for the perceiving of that revelation by means of conscience. If it were not so, it would not be possible to declare that the Gentiles are without excuse for their failure to perform God's will. Whenever a person does wrong because he has failed to seek God's purpose for him, he is as much a sinner as when he deliberately defies God.

In essence Paul sees man's will as good, but he also finds that it is often misled. Most commonly the apostle finds the source of this perversion in what he calls "the flesh." Physical nature makes demands that are often irrational and disordered. Indeed, it may be regarded as the base of operations from which sin makes its inroads upon the human personality. Not only are lust and sloth and gluttony, which the moral theologians define specifically as "sins of the flesh," seen by Paul as manifestations of this disorder in man's physical nature; the same force likewise prompts man to greed and quarreling and arrogance. Thus it becomes possible to speak of a conflict within man in which *flesh* and *spirit* oppose each other. This conflict must not be described as dualistic, for every element in man has been created by God and therefore must be good. Yet Paul followed his rabbinic teachers in believing that the *flesh* was weak and especially susceptible to evil.

It is the experience of internal conflict, however, that leads Paul to his other and more profound account of sin. Often man does evil when his real desire is to do good. The apostle himself speaks of sin dwelling in him and compelling him to do the evil he hates, and so he gives the picture of sin as an external power or principle that takes control of the person even against his own will. Paul regards this power as conscious and purposeful, and thus he personifies it as a demon. To yield once to the promptings of this *demon-sin* is to make oneself its slave and so to give it a claim upon oneself. The sinner is no longer in control of his will, and the struggle he himself may make against sin is bound to be a losing struggle. Man goes from evil to greater evil until he is so completely subjugated that it is no longer a matter of sin dwelling in his *flesh* but of his entire personality dwelling in *sin*.

Furthermore, the individual does not begin with a clean slate. He is born into a world where *sin* is already in control, where it impinges upon every life through outward circumstance and through the actions of others, through the examples one encounters and through the irrationality of physical nature. Thus no set of rules, however good they may be in themselves, can protect anyone from this *demon-sin*. Human strength is totally unequal to the task. Only the power of God can deliver man from this power with which he is unable to contend.

From the time of his conversion Paul was convinced that God had acted. In Christ God had entered the world order. In Christ a human life had been lived that did not yield to sin, and therefore upon Christ sin had no claim. This act of God in Christ was a saving act, because it was now possible for other human beings to find union with Christ and so to share in His freedom from the claims of sin. As Paul saw his own situation, *demon-sin* was still present in the world, and still in control of most of it, but this power was broken so far as the Christians were concerned. The believers were one with Christ, and shared His victory over evil.

This did not mean that struggle was over for the Christian. Paul had no illusions on this point. Sin was not only purposeful, but remarkably tenacious. Even for those who had been set free in Christ temptation was still a reality ever present, and a man could always give himself back to that slavery from which the Saviour had delivered him. What no man can do is to live to himself. He must belong to some power greater than himself, either to Christ who has won the victory and who offers him life or to *demon-sin* from which the only reward is death. For this reason the union with Christ must be preserved at all times, for in the moment in which that union is lost a man returns to the dominion of sin and is once more unable to help himself.

2 Original Sin

The evident power of sin in a world that God created to be good is an intellectual problem for everyone who believes in divine omnipotence. This is a development that God could not have intended without doing violence to His own moral nature. The existence of evil in itself is an affront to Him. The fact that man, as the climax of physical creation, is prone to evil implies a limitation on God's power. There must be an explanation of how defiance of God's will began.

Pagan philosophers of the ancient world suggested that the world order was the imposition of *form* by the Absolute Intelligence upon uncreated *matter* and that disorder had arisen because the uncreated *matter* was intractable. For those who began with the Old Testament this could not be accepted. Jews and Christians alike insisted that God had created the universe from nothing and that the *matter* belonged to Him as much as did the *form*. Therefore some other explanation had to be advanced.

The Genesis story of creation depicted a world that had once been free from sin, and told of how the first man had been tempted and had sinned and had been punished. The temptation had been to become as God; the crime had been self-assertion; the punishment had been the denial of immortality and the necessity to labor for sustenance, and it had affected the entire created order. The first man's progeny, therefore, were not born into Paradise but into a fallen world, where they were obliged to labor as he labored, and they failed to inherit from him the immortality he had lost.

Moreover, the first man by his failure had given sin a claim upon the world in which his descendants were to live. All men were cut off, at least in part, from communication with God and from receiving divine grace. All, likewise, were endowed with those qualities the first man had found it so easy to misuse. Thus each in his turn gave way to sin, grasping at an independence of God that could be had only at the price of servitude to evil. Various rabbinic teachers embellished this account in diverse ways, but the features outlined above remained constant in the Jewish teaching. Only the most overwhelming evidence to the contrary could justify the claim that Paul's teaching was cast in a different mold from that of others who made use of Genesis.

Thus the apostle never says that man's heredity is itself tainted, or that the first man's unborn posterity were rendered sinful in their ancestor's misdeed. Such ideas, as shown in comment upon Romans 5:12, depend upon inaccurate Latin translations rather than upon the apostle's Greek. The man who has squandered his estate has less to leave to his heirs than he would have had by preserving it, but the character of the heirs themselves is not directly affected by his improvidence. In the same way, the person born into a fallen world must live an existence more limited than that which God had originally designed for him, but limitation is not sin, and hardship does not create sinners. Indeed, the greater one's privilege, the greater is one's temptation to grasp at equality with God, because for those who are exalted equality with God seems more likely of attainment.

Thus Paul cannot be held responsible for the hymns and the sermons that have spoken about "our tainted nature," or for the assertion that all of us became sinners in the moment of Adam's rebellion. Probably this is fortunate in view of the number of modern Christians who do not understand Genesis as literal history. Paul contends that all men have sinned, each in his own person, and that while the first man set a bad example others were not obliged to follow him. Adam's priority in sin is simply a temporal one, and must not be regarded as a cause of sin in others.

Yet the fact remains that sin is universal in mankind, and if this prevalence of evil is not to be ascribed to a tainted heritage some other explanation must be found for it. As the assent of man's will is essential before thought or word or deed may be defined as sinful, the universality of sin must be related to man's will. One may so relate it, in complete consistency with the Genesis narrative, by acknowledging that the freedom God has conferred upon man is real. Many times in the Scripture it appears that in God's sight creation was a calculated risk and that it was not only possible in theory for man to do evil but entirely likely in practice.

It is well known today that walls and fetters are not the only means of exercising constraint upon a person. A code a man accepts for himself, a pattern of training he has never questioned, even a prolonged treatment of brainwashing may prove to be far more effective in the control of human behavior than any material barriers. No one is truly free to do that which he feels no desire to do.

Thus sin would not truly have been possible for mankind unless it had exercised real attraction upon him. But if there had been no real freedom to sin, all human action would have been determined externally, and so would have been deprived of moral value. Therefore, by God's own creation man was subjected to the temptation to evil, specifically to the type of self-assertion that is described in the Genesis story. This does not mean that God is the cause of evil, for with the temptation there was also given the possibility of resistance. Divine grace was available to man until he turned from it, and is available to each particular man until he turns from it for himself. Freedom of will, and with it the attraction of sin, belongs to the constitution of truly human nature quite apart from any question of a *Fall.* So the Bible indicates that with creation God set forth the plan of redemption because He foresaw that the need for redemption would arise. This preserves the values of what is described by others as *original sin* without bringing in the questionable morality of a transfer of guilt from the first man to his descendants.

3 *The Inclination to Evil* (Yetzer Ha-Ra)

Rabbinic Judaism in the time of Paul had its own account of the attraction of sin for man, and the apostle's teaching on the subject should be considered in the context of this account. Here the internal conflict that man experiences was defined in terms of a strife between two inclinations (*yetzers*), the evil (*ha-ra*) and the good (*ha-tob*). Of these the former was believed to be present from birth, or even in a prenatal state, while the latter was held to be implanted when one reached the age of reason that was normally defined as one's thirteenth birthday. Since the *evil inclination* was the older, it could also be thought of as the stronger, and thus one might account for the power of sin upon the individual. This theory also served to explain the all too evident self-assertion and other forms of misbehavior found in children long before they reach the age of reason.

Yet as the Jewish teachers defined the *evil inclination,* it was not entirely bad even though some rabbis said that God repented of having created it. Indeed, it was an essential element of human nature without which no man would build a house or beget children. It comprehended both sexual instinct and personal ambition, and therefore it was the source of every misuse of sex and of all contention between individuals and societies and of all personal arrogance and greed. These are precisely the types of sin against which Paul gave the most frequent warnings in his epistles. At the same time both Jewish rabbis and Christian teachers recognized that there could be a right use of sex manifested in the development of stable family life, and likewise a right use of ambition manifested in the effort to excel in virtuous and useful tasks.

This is directly related to the teaching that Paul shared with the Jewish rabbis of his time regarding the *flesh* as the element in man that is weak and susceptible to sin. When the *evil inclination* manifests itself in the misuse of sex, it inevitably operates through *flesh,* and its dependence upon the physical element in man is scarcely less evident when it manifests itself in contention and arrogance and greed. Paul, however, went beyond his Jewish contemporaries in representing the *evil inclination* as the instrument of an external *demon-sin* that is within man's *flesh* and that strives against the will (which may be regarded as the dwelling place of the *good inclination*) to bring disorder to the personality.

The *evil inclination* may also stand for what Augustine and the Latin Fathers described as *original sin.* It is innate in all mankind, and it provides the impulse for every sort of evil. But unlike the *original sin* of which Augustine and his successors spoke, its existence is not evidence of a *Fall.* Instead it is a part of the endowment God intended every man to possess, and it can be directed to good uses. So when Paul's teaching regarding sin and man's state is defined in terms of this element of the apostle's Jewish heritage, instead of in the language of Gentile thinkers of later times, it becomes possible to offer a more consistent account of the Pauline doctrine of Baptism. For Paul, Baptism does not cancel any part of the endowment God intended man to have; it marks the breaking of the control *demon-sin* has established over an element of human nature. Even in the baptized Christian the inclination to evil is still an inclination to evil, although it has its proper uses, and so sin after Baptism is not an inexplicable defeat for God but merely a failure of man to hold fast to the divine grace that has been made available to him. Thus sin after Baptism can be repented, providing that it has not reached the point of total apostasy. This is another way of expressing the definition of *original sin* that was given in Appendix 2. Christian history would have been spared many unhappy episodes if the understanding of this Jewish concept had not been lost in the second century of the Christian era.

4 The Wrath of God

Moral theologians have taught that anger is a sin. For human beings this teaching is valid because anger manifests self-assertion, and wrath is most commonly provoked by the thwarting of one's purposes or desires. Moreover, human wrath is passionate and unreasoning and it strives to bring harm to those against whom it is directed. Since none of these qualities may properly be ascribed to God, Pauline teaching about *the wrath* has been misunderstood, and the phrase *God's wrath* has seemed to many incomprehensible.

Accordingly, the concept of *the wrath* in Romans and the other epistles is in need of precise definition. In the first place it cannot be emphasized too strongly that God's attitude to His entire creation is invariably that of love. God's desire is always for good and never for harm. Like the human love of parents for their children, God's love will sometimes need to be expressed in severity and punishment, but whether it is shown in mercy or in judgment it is always directed to the welfare of God's creatures.

Therefore *God's wrath* must be defined as the execution of His judgment. It is the divine response to sin in which disapproval of the evil is always conjoined with love for the evildoer. As such it is a rational judgment that stands apart from all passion and self-assertion. Its object is never retaliation but always redemption. While Paul sometimes cites texts of the Old Testament that refer to divine vengeance, these are never used as explanations of *the wrath*, and the apostle gives no suggestion that *God's wrath* bears any analogy to human anger.

Indeed *the wrath* may be represented as operating quite apart from God's particular intention for specific cases. In this it may be compared to the physical laws of God's universe, laws that are of divine appointment and exact their appropriate penalties whenever they are disregarded without requiring any specific intervention by God to bring them into operation. For Paul the moral order is no less firmly established than the physical, and the *wrath of God* designates the inexorable judgment upon every form of wrongdoing.

5 *Justification*

The Greek words in which Paul sets forth the idea of *justification* are capable of being translated in several ways, and it is usually possible to deduce the theological convictions a writer holds from the shade of meaning his translation reflects. The simplest Greek word for *right* was DIKE, and originally it had implied what was right because it was in accord with custom; because it had come to be the name of the pagan goddess of retributive justice, Paul avoided it in theological argument. He did, however, make use of the adjective related to this which was DIKAIOS. In classical Greek this meant *honest, fair,* or *lawful,* and Paul's Jewish contemporaries added the meanings of *righteous* (performing what is right) and *justified* (acquitted by God's judgment). The apostle likewise employed the verb DIKAIOO, which could mean *to make something right* or to *adjudge* either as condemned or as acquitted; this could be extended to signify *to do what is right,* but in strict use it would not mean *to be in the right.* Even more significant in Pauline thought is the abstract noun DIKAIOSUNE. In Latin this was rendered as *justicia* or *abstract justice,* but it must be remembered that the Judaism of Paul's time did not think in abstract terms, and a person with rabbinic training would be much more likely to interpret it as *the state of being righteous* or as *a right relationship.* In addition to these terms the apostle sometimes had recourse to the concrete nouns DIKAIOMA and DIKAIOSIS which were roughly synonymous; these could stand for *an act of justice, a just claim, an acquittal,* or the *justification* or *ground of acquittal.*

The chief difficulty in understanding Paul's use of these words arises from the assumption by the Greek and Latin thinkers of antiquity, and by their successors, that Paul followed European patterns of thought. The apostle can be understood correctly only when his thinking is related to the Old Testament and to Judaism. But the Old Testament is not cast in abstract terms. When the Jews spoke of God as *righteous* they thought of His *doing right* rather than *being right,* and when they spoke of *righteousness* they thought of *right action* rather than *good character.* This fact contributed in large degree to the importance the rabbis of Paul's day placed upon the Law of Moses. If God was righteous because of doing right, then man was righteous because he did what was commanded in that Law, and human righteousness was determined by performance.

This was the system in which Paul had been trained and to which he had given the best efforts of his youth. By his own account his performance of the commandments had surpassed that of others, and in Philippians 3:6 he even declared that he had been blameless in terms of the righteousness that belongs to the Law. Yet he had been unable to find satisfaction in this attainment because it had never brought release from that internal conflict with the power of sin that he had experienced in common with all other people of sensitive conscience. His evil inclination (*yetzer ha-ra*) did not cease to be evil as a result of his striving, and while he might control his external actions he found that he was unable to determine his own motives and desires. Thus even while he performed the commandments, he felt that he was in the wrong in relation to God.

In his conversion all was changed. He was a sinner, the chief of sinners, because he was persecuting the Church of God, and no acts of righteousness could be weighed in the balance against the crime of that persecution. But God accepted him as he was and called him to service. In responding to the call, simply in trusting himself to God's forgiveness, he discovered that for the first time in his life he stood in the right relation to God. This was DIKAIOSUNE. His *evil inclination* might still be evil, his motives and desires might still be unworthy, all the objective righteousness in terms of the Law from his past life might count for nothing. He was in the right without having earned it, and he was conscious of a new freedom because he no longer had to earn it. This new relationship to God he could not keep to himself, but must share it as widely as God would allow.

He could share it only in terms of his own experience. As he had not earned the privilege of *being in the right in relation to God*, but had accepted it as a free gift, so all must recognize that it could never be earned but is always to be accepted as a gift of which the recipient is completely unworthy. For the establishing of this relationship one's past performance or nonperformance of specific duties is irrelevant; no one can be worthy of God's mercy, and it is fruitless to discuss varying degrees of unworthiness. The effort to set forth conditions necessary to God's gracious act to which man must submit, whether circumcision or some standard of accomplishment, is itself the negation of all that is meant by *favor*, and this explains the vehemence of Paul's handling of the issue in Galatians.

Thus theological controversy regarding what is meant by *justification* can be resolved as far as it concerns the person who has not yet been brought into a right relationship with God. One comes to be *in the right* in the moment of making a trusting surrender of himself to God's forgiveness. The significant debate arises over what happens in the moment of *justification* and over what must follow from it.

In the moment itself God forgives and accepts a person who does not deserve to be accepted or forgiven. Why does God do this? Some have said that it is an anticipation of foreseen merits, in other words that God discerns in the person He accepts a goodness which is as yet only potential and not actual. In one sense this may be true, but it means little because there is a potential goodness in every man whether he receives forgiveness or refuses it. At the opposite extreme there are those who declare that God *imputes* to the sinner whom He accepts a goodness that he does not have and that this imputed righteousness is the basis of acceptance. Yet this appears to many to be a fictitious goodness that is not an adequate basis for forgiveness, and since some of the sinners are chosen while others are not it may be represented as a dual predestination based upon caprice. God is not capricious.

Many efforts have been made to achieve a reconciliation of these views with one another, or with human experience. The theories have been refined and modified by criticism through the ages, but none of them has yet won universal acceptance among Christians. Beginning with the certainty that no one can earn salvation, that the right relation with God is always a gift conferred upon the unworthy, a suggestion can be set forward. A gift must involve both the giver and the recipient. If a beggar finds a coin in the street, he may take it for his own but he has not received a gift because it was not willingly offered to him. If someone drops a coin beside a beggar and he refuses to take it, the transaction is a waste and not a gift. Only that which is willingly offered and graciously received can be called a gift. So it is with God's forgiveness. It is offered to all, and all are unworthy of it. Many refuse it, and because God will not deny human freedom those who refuse are not forgiven. But those who make a trusting surrender of themselves to God's forgiveness receive it and are accepted even though they are unworthy. This does not mean that faith is an accomplishment of man that earns his salvation; it is merely the response that must be made before God's offer can become a gift that man receives.

If this may be accepted as an account of how man comes to be *in the right in relation to God,* it is necessary to ask what is to follow from this right relationship. The sinner is accepted without actual goodness. Can he go on without actual goodness? Can he be satisfied to remain in his unworthiness, trusting only in his faith? Here the key to the answer is *love*. He who truly accepts God's gift knows that he can never repay it, but at the same time he can never be satisfied until he has given himself as fully as he can to God in service, in worship, and in sacrifice. No effort can be too great and no discipline too severe when it is undertaken to express love to God who has redeemed us. This is not to begin in the spirit and then seek completion in the flesh; it is the gracious response to God's gift that was manifested by Paul himself.

6 *Predestination and Free Will*

No question of Biblical teaching is more difficult to solve than that of predestination. Philosophically it is related to the omniscience of God, to whom the limitations of created time cannot apply. God sees the whole of history so that nothing shall happen without his foreknowledge of it. Yet if God knows in advance what a man will do in a given situation, the question must arise whether the man is free to make a choice when God is already aware of what that choice will be, and so whether the man can be held responsible for what he does. This issue becomes more pressing when one reads the words in Exodus, which Paul repeats in Romans, that God will harden Pharaoh's heart so that the Egyptian ruler will refuse God's command given by Moses.

For the early Christians, however, the problem of why some people accepted God's message as proclaimed by the Church while others rejected it was practical rather than philosophical. The mission to Israel enjoyed very limited success, while that to the Gentiles was more fruitful. Yet Israel was far better prepared by its history and its worship and its standard of behavior to receive the message than was the Gentile world. Thus it was almost inevitable that Jewish Christians such as Paul would suggest that response must depend upon God's choice, that in His wisdom God made an effectual call to some while passing over the rest. This might serve as an apology for the fact that most of Israel had failed to respond to the Christian proclamation.

For the Jewish Christian, however, this raised other problems, because he could not bring himself to believe that God had cast off His Chosen People forever. This is especially clear in the Epistle to the Romans. Accordingly, with the aid of Deuteronomy 32:21, "I will provoke them to jealousy with that which is not a people," and some words from Hosea, the concept of predestination was set within God's plan of redemption rather than outside it. Paul declared that the disobedience of Israel was providential because it made possible the proclamation of the Gospel to the Gentiles, and he held to a hope that God's evident acceptance of the Gentiles in its turn would prompt Israel to the response of faith. This would mean that when God elects what Paul calls "a vessel of wrath," such a divine choice is made to serve the ruling purpose of mercy.

When consideration is given only to final results, such an explanation may be accepted readily enough; God overrules evil so that it may contribute to the accomplishment of good. But in the moment when predestination is applied to specific situations and particular individuals, and when personal factors are involved, the matter assumes a different aspect. God chooses one man who is undeserving to be a "vessel of mercy." Another, who is also undeserving, is left to his own devices or perhaps is prompted by God to set himself against the divine purpose, and so he becomes a "vessel of wrath." Can such a choice be moral? Can either the person who is chosen or the one who is not chosen be called to account for the part that is assigned to him? God called Isaiah, but it must be remembered that Isaiah answered, "Here am I, send me." God called Paul, but when he received the call he waited obediently to be told what he should do. One may say that the subsequent accomplishments of the prophet and of the apostle were the Lord's doing rather than their own, but it remains true that God was able to act through them only because they made the response of faith and of obedience.

In actuality, predestination is significant only for those who are conscious of a divine intervention that has changed the course of their lives. Paul, Augustine, and a number of the most influential Christians of history have felt that they were brought to their vocation against their own wills. It was not for them to choose what they would do; Paul himself declared that constraint was laid upon him. Such people readily give God the glory for all that they do in His service. At the same time they assume that those who oppose their understanding of God's purpose, or who stand aside from it, do so because they have not received God's call. Yet there is no need to assume that one's own experience should be shared by everyone else, and few people ever understand their own experiences completely. Perhaps Paul could have refused the ministrations of Ananias in Damascus, just as the rich man who came to Jesus in the Gospel did refuse his call.

The reality of evil demands that one accept the freedom of man's will. That which distinguishes man from the rest of creation, and which must be understood as the divine image man bears, is the power of reason by which he is able to make a choice. Without free will we would not be truly human. But when God created beings who possessed freedom of choice, by that action He placed a limitation upon Himself. For the fulfillment of His over-all purpose God can overrule the consequences of any human action, but for the particular purpose of an individual's salvation God will allow His power to be frustrated; if it were not so, salvation would mean nothing. Yet this is a limitation upon divine omnipotence. In the same way, God is aware of all the potentialities in any individual, and of all the possible actions a person may take, but divine omniscience is limited by the freedom that has been given to man to choose which of his potentialities he will develop. Thus Judas was called to be an apostle, but he became the traitor. The moral nature of God, His universal love, is the element in the divine being upon which no limitation may be placed, and universal love means that God's call is issued to all. The consequences of God's call depend upon human response, and for that reason any feeling that one may have of being predestinated against his own will must rest upon a lack of understanding of the reality of his response.

7 *Grace (Favor)*

In classical usage the Greek word CHARIS denoted *favor, kindness, good will, gratitude,* or *charm.* One encounters it frequently in literature. Paul could use it in some of these ways, but generally in his epistles it refers to God's dealing with those whom He accepts, and acquires the meaning of *grace* as a word of technical theology. Yet one must not stress this special meaning to the exclusion of other nuances. Paul also used the word to describe his own reaction to God's mercy, and in such texts it may be translated as *gratitude*. Moreover, as has been indicated in the translation of Romans in this work, one cannot always be sure whether Paul is discussing *grace* in a technical sense or whether the word could be rendered more accurately by the general term *favor*.

Grace may be defined as God's free gift to man. It is the expression of uncaused love. It cannot be earned, and no one can ever be worthy of it. It is the first prerequisite for human salvation, because God's grace or favor must precede man's faith, and without grace the response of faith could not be evoked. It comprehends the call of Abraham and the promise made to him, the guidance Moses received, the inspiration of Scripture, the conversion of Paul and his commission as an apostle of Jesus Christ, and the spiritual strength God confers upon those who obey Him. It is most perfectly exemplified in the self-offering of Christ at Calvary and in the vindication of the Lord's Resurrection.

When looked upon as external to man, grace is the saving purpose or saving action of God. When considered as an experience of man, grace is the operation or possession of God's Holy Spirit. The Church, or fellowship of believers, is the primary sphere of grace, but since the Holy Spirit is not bound by any human limitations a sufficient degree of grace would be available to all mankind if the human race had not fallen under the dominion of sin. Thus Paul believed that grace had been available for Adam before he sinned.

For the individual Christian, grace is first manifested in the fact that Christ died for the ungodly. When this calls forth the response of faith, grace is applied to him as an individual and God accepts him as a member of the Church or community of the redeemed; he is made one with Christ. In his life as a believer, grace is strength to persevere and to resist temptation, guidance to avoid error and to come to greater knowledge of God's truth, protection from evil powers and the conferring of a capacity to give service to God. In his particular vocation within the Church it is his commission for the task to which God assigns him and the particular talent of preaching or administration or healing or whatever else may be necessary to perform that task.

8 The Torah (Law)

In the translation and text of this work the Hebrew word Torah has been used of all references to the Law of Moses. Paul used the Greek word NOMOS in various ways; sometimes he quoted from Scripture as what was written in "the Law," and sometimes he employed the word to describe natural revelation or a principle of reason, but in his most important texts it refers to the Torah. The Law of Moses itself had been codified by the rabbis into 613 specific commands and prohibitions. Paul distinguished these from Torah in general by using the Greek word ENTOLE, or commandment, but for him this could also apply to particular requirements of God apart from the Torah, such as those given to Abraham before the time of Moses.

The Judaism of Paul's time was a religion of practice rather than of creed. Great latitude was allowed in what one might affirm or deny, but no one was accepted as a valid representative of Israel's religion unless he carried out the requirements of the Torah in his daily life. Some rabbis declared that if all Israel would keep the Torah in its entirety from one Sabbath until the next the Kingdom of God would come. Moreover, it was believed that the Torah was the eternal purpose of God. Thus when Genesis declared that God had rested on the seventh day, this was construed as meaning that God Himself had kept the Torah, although it was not delivered to men until the time of Moses. It was also held that Moses had ascended to Heaven to receive the Torah from the hands of the angels; certain Pauline texts refer to this belief.

The Torah was also looked upon as spelling out the terms of a contract between God and His People. Deuteronomy 30:15–19 promised that God would bless the People if they kept His commandments, and would curse them if they turned away from the Law. Likewise the individual who performed God's Law would be accepted while the one who failed to do so would be rejected. From the time of Ezra a tradition of casuistry had grown up which applied the Torah to changing conditions and to new areas of life. The system of casuistry was referred to as the *tradition of the elders,* and it was preserved by the scribes. Its acknowledged aim was to give a predetermined answer to every moral question that could arise. The faithful Jew was expected to abide by these traditions as well as by the obvious written requirements, although it was recognized that the peasants and artisans and small shopkeepers had neither the education nor the leisure to acquire a complete knowledge of the teachings the scribes had developed. Yet the system was administered with mercy rather than with severity, and while all were obliged to learn as much of the Torah as they could and to perform all the commandments they had learned, for those who did not possess special training repentance was expected to secure forgiveness for such failures as did occur.

Thus, despite the complaints which appear in the Gospels and in Paul's epistles, the Torah did not appear to the practicing Jew to be a burden. It was, on the contrary, a support that set him free from the necessity of working out decisions by his own fallible judgment and limited wisdom. To the weak and the ignorant it set a minimum standard that could be understood and attained. To the strong and the intelligent it gave an assurance of the right answer in hard cases. Its restraints were embraced with love and joy even by many who could make no claim to understand them. In a world dominated by Gentiles, it would have been a simple matter for anyone who chose to abandon such a religion; the survival and continuing strength of Judaism is sufficient proof of the vitality of Torah and the willingness with which it was accepted.

Paul's own reaction to the principle of legalism was almost unique. Certainly it went far beyond anything that Jesus had taught, for it was not a prophetic classification of primary as distinct from secondary duties but a calling in question of the concept that man's relationship to God could be interpreted in terms of *law* at all. This was the fruit of Paul's individual struggle to observe the Torah in its completeness. As a trained rabbi of great abilities, and at the same time a man of sensitive conscience, he had not been able to find satisfaction in the Torah. He could plead no lack of knowledge of its provisions as an excuse for his failures, and a repentance that was followed by repeated sins appeared to him unreal. If he could exercise control over word and action, he found that he was not able to do so over desire and intention. Yet the Torah itself, as he understood it, applied to desire and intention. In the Decalogue itself there appeared the injunction "Thou shalt not covet." Nevertheless, Paul was aware of every sort of covetousness within his own being. Had the Torah not made an issue of such matters, he felt that he could have been happy in his innocence and that if he had not known the sinfulness of such desires he would have been free from guilt in regard to them.

The weakness of *law* as a principle, in Paul's mind, was that it brought to man a knowledge of sin without providing any help for the overcoming of such sin. To do what the Torah directed was good. Its particular commandments were right and just. But when it was given to a human race that was already under the domination of the power of sin, that evil power perverted the Torah into an instrument to serve its own purposes. Awareness of what was wrong added impetus to one's desire to do what was wrong, and at the same time increased the guilt of doing it. A wrong action that was not recognized as such might have been passed over, but a known sin became a barrier between oneself and God and made further sin more likely.

So Torah was a force directed against man, although God had not intended it to be so. As misused by the power of sin, it was the source of guilt and the cause of separation from God. Man needed not only to be delivered from *demon-sin,* and from *death* that was the punishment for sin, but also from *law* that had proved to be the occasion of sin. In Christ this deliverance took place. Because Christ had fulfilled the Torah in its completeness, it had not become an occasion of sin for Him. Because His life was sinless, Christ as the Representative Man had destroyed the claim of *demon-sin* upon mankind, or at least upon those who were brought into union with Him. Thus He had also set man free from *law* as a force directed against him and separating him from God, and from death as the punishment for sin. In the moment of *justification,* when a person realized that he no longer had to earn salvation, *law* ceased to be a perverse instrument of sin. When one trusted entirely to God's forgiveness, then the score keeping that legalism induces in one's personal life becomes irrelevant.

This did not mean for Paul that performance was a matter of indifference. Any suggestion that it was always encountered vehement reaction from the apostle, and likewise has encountered vehement reaction from his truest interpreters. Paul was no advocate of cheap grace. The only grace he knew had cost the sacrifice of Christ at Calvary and must cost the complete self-offering of every person who was to be united with Christ. The apostle's point was that whenever performance is made a matter of *law*, relationship to God becomes a contract. In reality acceptance with God is always a gift and never a contract, and performance when one lives under grace must be more heroic than when one lives under law, for in filial devotion to God no one can ever say that he has done his duty, for his obligation is limited only by the power God has conferred upon him to render service.

9 *The End of the Torah*

In Romans 10:4 Paul declares that Christ is the end (TELOS) of the Torah in righteousness for everyone who believes. This statement may be explained in a variety of ways, because the Greek word TELOS like its English equivalent may stand for *termination, completion, conclusion, result, purpose, goal,* or *fulfillment*. Patristic writers took the words to mean that Christ is the *goal* of the Torah, that His life is the achievement to which it was directed. Thus the Lord's sinless life has fulfilled the Law completely and given the example of what it was intended to produce.

In this interpretation there is much philosophical truth, but it is not supported by the other Pauline texts on the subject. As was noted in the commentary on Chapter 10, Paul means that Christ's ministry is the *termination* of Torah. Yet even if this is accepted, there can be uncertainty about the sense in which this is true. In I Corinthians it appears that Paul did not intend Jewish Christians to abandon the performance of Torah, for he declared that each man should continue in the vocation in which he was called. Moreover, it is apparent that he did not abandon the practice of Torah for himself excepting in those commandments that would have been destructive of fellowship between Jewish and Gentile Christians. It is also clear that he was horrified by the suggestion that anyone might be permitted to cease from keeping the Ten Commandments.

From these facts some scholars have been led to suggest that Paul considered the ceremonial requirements of the Torah to have been abrogated in Christ while believing that the moral requirements were still in force. Yet this would not really be a termination of the Torah at all, but merely a revision of the manner in which it was to be applied. Paul did not mean to say that the Torah had been revised. In the apostle's mind it had been abolished because man's relationship to God was no longer to be conceived in terms of law at all. Therefore Latin scholars such as Lagrange are entirely right in saying that within the Church the Law of Moses is abolished *in toto*, except as it may still apply to those who have accepted its authority before their incorporation into the Church as the Body of Christ. Moral requirements belonging to the Torah as such are no more binding than ceremonial requirements. An example of this may be seen in the general Christian change of the day of worship from the seventh to the first day of the week. But when one declares that the moral regulations of the Torah have been abrogated, this does not mean that morality itself has been abandoned. Paul recognized that Gentiles might do the will of God even though they had not received the Torah, and if they did they could be considered as a law to themselves. In other words natural revelation that Paul recognized included a *natural law* of conduct. This *natural law* was a part of the nature of man as God had created it and of the constitution of God's universe. It had been expressed in essence in the Law of Moses, and was itself the basis of all true morality. Thus for Christianity Torah is abolished except as it conforms to *natural law*, while *natural law* is binding upon all mankind and preeminently upon the Christian.

It is only through Christ's ministry, however, that the Torah comes to be abolished. This is so because only in Christ has the Torah been accomplished. The Old Testament bears witness to the failures of Moses and David and other heroes of Judaism. Christ did not fail. At last Torah had been discharged as if it were a sort of debt laid upon mankind. Now that it was fulfilled, the debt was paid, and the force of Torah was ended. Everyone who believed was united with Christ, and hence set free from the claims of the former dispensation.

10 Substitutionary Atonement

The New Testament writers are unanimous in seeing the work of Christ as an act of Atonement by which man, who had been estranged from God, became reconciled. In the work of Atonement Christ's Death was the central feature, and the Lord's Crucifixion was spoken of as *ransom* and as *sacrifice*. From this many of the Church Fathers deduced that Christ gave Himself as a *substitute* for man, and a number of modern scholars have accepted such a line of reasoning. In popular devotion the concept has long been firmly established, and it is reflected in Christian hymnody. A familiar example is the verse which begins, "There was no other good enough to pay the price of sin." Here the teaching clearly is that Christ discharged a debt that man himself could not discharge, that He suffered in our stead.

Yet before one can accept this account of Christ's suffering, it is necessary to give careful attention to the words used in the New Testament and in particular to the words of Paul. Actually, the apostle never says anywhere that Christ died *instead of us* (ANTI HEMON). Only Mark 10:45 with its parallel in Matthew and the Deutero-Pauline I Timothy 2:6 have made use of the expression *instead of* to define the purpose of the Lord's offering. Paul regularly says HYPER HEMON, which has the sense *on our behalf*. This phrase appears four times each in the two Corinthian epistles and in Galatians, and five times in Romans. The Romans texts are 5:6, 5:8 (twice), 8:32, 14:15. In addition PERI HEMON, which has much the same meaning, is found once each in I Thessalonians and in I Corinthians. Thus it has been possible for some scholars to reject the thought of substitution in connection with Christ's Death and to say that the essential New Testament understanding of the subject does not move in the realm of penalty or satisfaction to be paid to God's righteousness at all.

In terms of philosophy there are difficulties in the way of believing that an abstract justice could credit the penalty that Christ paid willingly when He did not owe it to those who owed it and did not pay it, and yet more difficulties in believing that the act of Atonement could change the attitude of God to His creatures. To speak in this way is to assume that there can be a change in God's relationship to mankind that does not originate within the divine Being. It is also to postulate an infinite store of *merit* established in Christ upon which the believer can draw at need. For these reasons the *Moral Influence* theory of the Atonement has become increasingly popular in modern times and the whole concept of substitution is now denied in many quarters.

No matter how much one may discount patristic teaching, however, it is not easy to eliminate the thought of substitution completely from the Pauline epistles. Two texts in particular must be mentioned. These are Galatians 3:13, "Christ redeemed us from the curse of the Torah, becoming a curse on our behalf," and II Corinthians 5:21, "God made Him who did not know sin to be sin on our behalf." In both texts Christ as the Representative Man enters into the experience of penalty for sin, although without sin Himself, in order to share that experience with us. But as Paul sees it the penalty is not one exacted by divine justice but is the domination of *demon-sin* made effective in death. Since Christ is free from actual sin, *demon-sin* exceeds its rights in causing His Death, and so the claim of sin is made void. Thus Christ is a substitute, not in the sense of paying a penalty to God but as making a skillful foray which overcomes those spiritual powers that are hostile to man. What Paul is saying is not that Christ's Atonement has altered the attitude of God to us, and not merely that the Atonement has changed our attitude to God, but that it has affected the external circumstances in which we must live so that we may once more stand against sin by God's grace. This is a substitution relatively free from philosophical difficulty, and one that gives to the Atonement itself an objective value as well as a subjective one.

11 *Christ as a Sacrifice*

In the ancient world, in Jewish culture as much as in that of the pagans, priesthood was defined as the offering of *sacrifice*. Both in the Jerusalem Temple and in pagan shrines the oblations offered might be of various kinds, but no one could be thought of as a priest unless he presented offerings to his god. When the Epistle to the Hebrews was written, the Jerusalem Temple had been destroyed, and the sacrifices of Israel had ceased to be offered. This fact suggested to the author of that epistle that the repeated sacrifices of the former dispensation had been superseded by the *sacrifice* that Christ as the Great High Priest had presented once for all. That *sacrifice* was the offering of Himself upon the Cross. Through subsequent Christian history this concept has been preached and expounded, with a variety of developments, and it has also been read back into the earlier portions of the New Testament. It is important, for the purposes of the present study, to consider whether the thought of Christ as a *sacrifice* may legitimately be discerned in the work of Paul, and if it is present the sense in which the apostle understood it.

Three texts may be cited that make it clear that the concept was not absent from Paul's mind. These are I Corinthians 5:7, Colossians 1:20, and Romans 3:25. The phrases are, "Our passover has been sacrificed, namely Christ"; "having made peace through the Blood of His Cross"; "whom God set forth as a reconciliation (HILASTERION) by means of faith in His Blood." None of them, however, carries the thought of sacrifice as far as does the Epistle to the Hebrews. In the first of them the emphasis is upon the idea that Christ's act of Atonement has secured for the believers a release from the power or penalty of sin, just as the first Passover secured for the Chosen People freedom from the plagues visited upon Egypt. In the second the stress is upon the violent death Christ endured in His work of restoring man to a relation of peace with God, rather than upon the technical meaning of an offering presented to God. The text from Romans, however, does indicate expiatory sacrifice, although this is not limited in its reference to the violent death of Calvary but embraces the life and ministry and Exaltation of Christ as well as His Death, and so refers to the Lord's total Obedience.

So it may be seen that for the apostle Christ is not a *sacrifice* in the sense of cult practice, and it has been shown in the previous appendix that the Atonement was not intended to placate an angry God but to set man free from the domination of sin. Christ is the Representative of the new humanity, and He stands before God on man's behalf. For man He presents to God not only His Death but

His whole self, all that He does upon earth, and because of the reality of His Obedience it is all acceptable. Thus Christ is the exemplar of the offering that each of His followers is likewise to present. Paul does not hesitate to call the offering of *obedience*, whether by the Lord or by His followers, a *sacrifice*. But whether as offered by Christ or by the Christians it is not intended to alter the divine attitude toward mankind, for that attitude is invariably love. As offered by the believers it is the response of gratitude to the mercy of God. As offered by Christ who did not stand in need of mercy, it is the pattern of that grateful response. Therefore one ought not to say that Paul described Christ as a sacrifice of propitiation in the conventional sense. This does not mean that the author of Hebrews, and subsequent Christian teachers, have been in error in the interpretation of Christ as High Priest and Victim. Theologically this picture is valid. But it is not truly an element of Pauline Christianity. It must be acknowledged as a clarification of a concept that Paul held only in germ and not in full development.

12 *The New Creation in Christ*

In Romans *newness of life* is seen as dying to the old world order and its demands and being raised to the possibilities of a new order that Christ has inaugurated. Only those who are brought to union with Christ are able to enter upon this *new life*. This teaching is set forth in Chapter 6 where it is related to the experience of Christian Baptism. In Chapter 8 of Romans the same *newness of life* is explained as the possession of the Holy Spirit whose operation within the believer accounts for the new capacities enjoyed by members of the Church. What comes closest to a formula describing the *new life* in Paul's epistles, however, is the phrase *in Christ*, and this phrase finds its clearest expression in II Corinthians 5:17–21.

There the formula itself is built upon the results of Christ's act of Atonement. The apostle sees man's *flesh* not merely as the instrument of sin but as a substance in which the cosmic *demon-sin* has possession. In causing Christ to enter into flesh which has proved itself sinful (to become incarnate), God has caused Christ *to be sin*. But the incarnate Lord, without performing actual sin in this *flesh* He has entered, has taken His *flesh* to the Cross. When He was slain the effect of His Death was transferred to all *flesh* because *demon-sin* had exceeded its claims or rights. When Christians appropriate the effect of the Lord's Death by a union with Christ ratified in Baptism, the claim of *demon-sin* upon their *flesh* is slain or destroyed. So life *in Christ* is the antithesis of life in the old world order. When one is incorporated into the Body of Christ, *flesh* and all the guilt that belongs to it become changed, and the guilt and sinfulness no longer exist. Thus salvation cannot be defined either as faith or as the forgiveness of sin; in reality it is being *in Christ*.

13 A Glossary of Terms

Adoption (HUIOTHESIA): The practice of legal adoption was common among the Romans of Paul's time, but not among the Jews. The idea did have precedents in the Old Testament, such as the call of Abraham and the position ascribed to the king in some of the coronation psalms, while in the Synoptic picture of John Baptist's preaching it is asserted that God can raise up children to Abraham from the stones. For Paul, Christ is Son of God by nature, although the apostle makes no reference to the Virgin Birth. Christians become children of God by virtue of their union with Christ. This adoption demands a likeness to God on the part of those who receive it, and its fullness cannot be achieved until the end of history when the believers shall reign with Christ and enjoy all the powers of the *New Age*. In the present time, however, it is real though incomplete, because Christians already possess the Holy Spirit and thereby do exercise some of the powers for which they are destined.

Apostle (APOSTOLOS): The Greek word is derived from a verb that means *to send away on an errand*. In classical usage it meant the commander of a naval expedition. Greek-speaking Jews had adopted it as the title for a delegate from the sanhedrin of one congregation to that of another, and the most important of such Jewish *apostles* were those who served the Great Sanhedrin of Jerusalem. Christian *apostles* received their commissions directly from Christ, Paul on the road to Damascus and the Twelve during the earthly ministry, James the Lord's Brother apparently in the Resurrection Appearance of which he was a witness; the appointment of Matthias to replace Judas was directed by the Holy Spirit, and there is no record of the manner in which Barnabas came to be included. In order to receive this title it was essential that one should have witnessed the Lord's Resurrection. Thus Christian *apostles* were the delegates of Christ to His People, and they were responsible to the Lord rather than to the congregation. They formed the primary ministry of the Church, and Paul did not hesitate to exercise authority in virtue of this position which he held.

Authority (EXOUSIA): This term is used of state officials in Romans 13:1. Elsewhere it describes authority within the Church, such as that of the *apostles*. Most commonly for Paul, however, it is used of spiritual powers, especially of those hostile to man, such as *demon-sin*. It is from the control of such *authorities* that Christ's act of Atonement has set the believers free. Yet until history reaches its final goal these *authorities* continue to exist and to be a threat to man's spiritual welfare, and they still have general control of the unredeemed world order and of those persons who have not been delivered by their union with Christ.

Body (SOMA): Man is composed of three elements, body and soul and spirit, or in more modern terms body and mind and will. As the creation of God, the body is good, and Paul never uses this Greek word to describe the element in man that is morally weak or sinful. Indeed, it is as much an object of God's redeeming act in Christ as is any other element in man. As Paul believed that Christ's Body was raised from the grave and exalted to Heaven, so in I Corinthians 15 he affirmed that the bodies of the faithful would be raised and exalted and that those who were alive when the world came to its end would be exalted without first having to die. The exalted body would have powers the present body does not possess. Moreover, between Christ's own Exaltation and the end of the world, Christians are incorporated into the Lord so that the Church is the Body of Christ upon earth. A third use of the term is in connection with the Lord's Supper, where the bread and wine objectively convey to those who partake of them Christ's Body and Blood, either as spiritual strength to those who partake as the Lord intends or to damnation for those who receive in an unworthy manner.

Called (KLETOS): With some of the early Christians the thought of being called by God was applied only to the question of vocation. One accepted the task God assigned to him rather than choosing for himself. With others, among whom Paul must be included, the idea of being called applied to salvation as well as to vocation. In part this served as an apologetic for the relative failure of the Christian mission to Israel, but at the same time it expressed the truth that the work of salvation is begun by God and not by man. Paul's own conversion, in which he was brought to Christ against his own will, caused the apostle to lay great stress upon the concept of being called, and to affirm that God's calling is always effectual. So he taught that only those who were called could make the response of faith.

Commandment (ENTOLE): This word may be used for any particular injunction, but most commonly it applies to the individual commands and prohibitions of the Torah in distinction from the legal system as a whole. In Romans 7:12 Paul uses *commandment* to stand for the Law as a whole, but elsewhere in his writings he distinguishes between them, and one may press the distinction even in this text.

Creation (KTISIS): In most Pauline texts this stands for the whole created order, inanimate as well as animate, and the apostle insists that creation as a whole is to be redeemed along with the people who come to faith in Christ. It may also apply to individual created beings, angels or men or objects, as when Paul speaks of the heathen as worshiping the creature in preference to the Creator.

Death (THANATOS): As a general rule death is simply the termination of life, whether from natural or from external cause. In connection with Christ, for Paul and for the New Testament writers generally, it is the central part of the act of Atonement without which man's release from the power of sin would not have been possible. In pre-Christian Jewish teaching death was also the penalty for sin, and this led Paul to his own specialized use of the term. Death is sometimes represented as a cosmic demon, to whom the cosmic *demon-sin* has given power over man. By submitting to death Himself, Christ has freed His followers from the dominion of death, but the deliverance will not be complete until the consummation of history. So in I Corinthians 15:26, "the last enemy that shall be destroyed is death."

End (TELOS): Commonly the word applies to the conclusion of history when God's final victory shall restore all things to the glory the Creator intended for them. Thus it is the goal of all Christian striving, although it is to be brought by divine rather than by human power. It refers also to the termination of the power of Torah, as discussed in Appendix 9.

Faith (PISTIS): The fullness of this concept cannot be understood if it is defined as objective assent to the truth of a particular proposition. Nor can it be comprehended if faith is regarded as a defined body of dogma. These elements are present to Paul, but the apostle's primary approach to faith is subjective. It is trust in which one surrenders oneself to God without reserve. It is a commitment to God of one's whole life which goes beyond any material evidence in favor of making such a commitment. The faith that is trust can be a valid ground of justification, as the faith that is merely assent cannot.

Flesh (SARX): When Paul speaks of the physical element in man as prone to sin and unresponsive to the guidance of God, the word he employs is "flesh." Flesh may be set in opposition to spirit, while body is not so treated. Yet the terms are not sharply distinguished, and the Hebrew *basar* would stand both for *body* and for *flesh*. One may understand the matter by saying that a fist is a hand as used to deliver a blow, and that flesh is the body as serving physical interests. From earlier Jewish rabbis Paul had learned to think of flesh as the seat of man's *evil inclination*, and he extended this to speak of flesh as possessed by *demon-sin*. Yet because flesh is body it is to be included in God's redemption, although when that redemption is complete there will no longer be any occasion to refer to it as *flesh*.

Foreordain (PROORIZO): The idea of *calling* or *election* is common in the New Testament; *foreordain* is not widely used, and its chief advocate is Paul. The Old Testament spoke of the foreordaining of prophets, and of the prenatal choice of Jacob over Esau. From the latter incident Paul adduces support for his own teaching. The concept of predestination is discussed in Appendix 6 and in the treatment of Romans 9. Paul considered it essential to his teaching that salvation depends entirely on God's grace without regard for human deserving. The teaching itself is true, but the philosophical problems involved in foreordaining a person to salvation indicate that the teaching ought to have been developed in some other way.

Free gift (DOREMA): In denying that man can earn anything from God, Paul is obliged to say that one receives everything from God as a free gift. The term applies particularly to the realities of justification and salvation, and to the act of Atonement performed by Christ, but it also embraces the further aids which the believer receives from God. These are the guidance and the powers made present by the indwelling of the Holy Spirit.

Glory (DOXA): First of all, glory is an attribute of God. In rabbinic teaching it had also belonged to the first man Adam before his sin. It is an attribute of Christ as the Representative of the new and redeemed humanity. By reason of the union with Christ that the believers possess, it is also to be conferred upon them at the consummation of history, as the resurrection body of those who have died before that event and as the changed body of those who are alive when it occurs. So for the Christian it is equivalent to the fullness of *adoption.*

Gospel (EVANGELION): The term means the Christian message, the story of God's saving act as revealed in the Life, Death, Resurrection, and Exaltation of the incarnate Lord. Thus it is the content of Christian preaching. Paul wrote before our present accounts of the earthly ministry of Jesus had been compiled, and therefore he did not consider the Gospel to consist in biographical details. It is indeed *the good news* (the primary meaning of the Greek word), but there is no reason to substitute *good news,* as some modern translators have done.

Grace (CHARIS): This concept is treated in Appendix 7. Often for Paul it is synonymous with *free gift,* but in some texts it has a special meaning as a divine commission, and in others grace is not to be distinguished from the indwelling of the Holy Spirit. It may also stand for divine favor in general, as distinguished from particular manifestations of that favor that may be expressed by the term *free gift.*

Hope (ELPIS): Despite the thirteenth chapter of I Corinthians, it is not easy to distinguish between *hope* and *faith* in Paul's epistles. Both essentially must be regarded as trust in God. Yet there is a difference of emphasis. Faith is trust in God's forgiveness, by which the believer may begin his pilgrimage, while hope is trust in God's reward at its end. Faith is trust in God's dispensation in general, while hope applies to particular realities, of which the primary one is eternal life.

Justification or ***Righteousness*** (DIKAIOSUNE): This reality is treated in detail in Appendix 5. It is a relationship to God, not an achievement of man. Thus one may translate the word *being in the right in relation to God.* Such a right relationship is a gift from God to man. It cannot be conveyed by any mechanical or judicial process, but must be received by faith. In logic it is the first term of a series, and it leads on to reconciliation, forgiveness, redemption, adoption, and sanctification.

Law (NOMOS): This has already been discussed in Appendix 8, which deals with the *Torah*, or Law of Moses. It stands for Israel's legal system, and may also refer to the *natural law* which is recognized by conscience and is the basis of morality in general, or to the principle of reason, or to the claim by which *demon-sin* exercises control over man. These special uses have been treated in the text above.

Life (ZOE): As death is the reward *demon-sin* provides for those who yield themselves to sin, so life is the free gift God confers upon those who obey Him. In the present world order it is manifested in the new capacities the indwelling of the Holy Spirit creates among the Christians, but its fullness belongs to eternity, and so it may be described as *life eternal*. It is the life that those who share in the general resurrection of the righteous will possess, and its quality has been revealed in the exalted Life of Christ Himself. Thus it may be regarded as another term for *adoption*.

Love (AGAPE): The same word may be used for the love that proceeds from God to man and to the whole creation, or for that which responds from man to God, or for that which exists between persons either corporately (love of the brethren) or individually (love of one's neighbor). The love that moves from God to man is always uncaused and self-giving, because there can be nothing in creation worthy to evoke God's love and no return that creation can make by which God will benefit. The love that moves from man to God is not uncaused, because God is supremely worthy of it, but it is self-giving because one serves God in gratitude, asking to be used by Him and not for the sake of reward. Corporate love between persons is caused by the fact that the members of the brotherhood have value in God's sight; they are the brethren for whom Christ died, however unlovable they may be in themselves. It is also self-giving; the Christian wishes to build up the brotherhood. Ideally, individual love between persons has the same cause; the neighbor has potential if not actual value in God's sight, and one must show him goodness because of that value rather than for any individual interest in him. Likewise in such special relationships as friendship and conjugal or parental or filial love, these factors should hold first place, although there one may allow greater scope to the expectation that love should be returned. In every relationship the self-giving of God's love is the pattern for the love man can show, and at its best human love is really the reflection of the divine love.

Mind (NOUS and PHRONEMA): The Old Testament spoke of thinking as taking place in the heart rather than in the head, and for Paul the whole intellectual process was much more closely related to emotions and to will than it is for modern man. Mind was soul as organized for the task of reasoning. Like body, it was morally neutral; there could be a fleshly mind or a spiritual mind. The term PHRONEMA is used in preference to NOUS for one's estimate of himself, especially when that estimate is lacking in humility.

Ministry (DIAKONIA): In the Pauline epistles this is not related to the professional ministry of the Church, and when Paul speaks of his own *ministry* he is not referring to his commission as an apostle but to the task that God has laid upon him. The word means simply *service*, any service or duty or vocation one may perform. Because the Christian ministry was first conceived as service to God's People, this term was adopted to describe it.

Mystery (MYSTERION): The Greek word applies to that which has been unknown because it was kept secret rather than to that which is unknowable because it is beyond human comprehension. Thus within the Christian dispensation the *mysteries* may now be revealed, and Paul undertakes to reveal many of them. The act of Atonement in Christ has been unknown to angels and to men, but now that it has taken place it stands revealed. The acceptance of the Gentiles has been unknown in Israel, but as God receives them Paul is free to declare it. Moffatt's translation as *secret purpose* is truly inspired. There is in this nothing of the thought that some divine realities cannot be understood, although for some teachings such a thought also has validity.

Obedience (HYPAKOE): Christ's total work may be represented as an act of obedience to God His Father, an obedience in which the Lord kept back nothing for Himself. This not only preserved His sinlessness and made possible the transfer of the fruits of His victory over sin to others, but it is now the pattern of behavior for those who are accepted by God. When Paul is read attentively, it is seen that justification is nothing without the obedience that is to follow from it, for only the person who obeys can be said to have faith. Yet it is not a matter of obeying the provisions of a law, but of letting one's own will become conformed to that of God.

Promise (EPANGELIA): The entire Old Testament is dominated by the thought of promise by God to man; often it is expressed by the term *covenant*. There is a distinction between these terms. Covenant is a conditional promise. God will bless Noah and his heirs if they observe the simple rules He gives to them, or He will protect Israel's possession of the Promised Land if the Nation abides by the Torah. Promise is unconditioned. God will never again destroy the world by water, and the rainbow is a sign of this assurance; God will cause Abraham to be the father of many nations; God will restore His People to their Land. In Christ the promise is for salvation, the inheritance of eternal life. It does not depend upon what man may do, but upon the divine favor. As a gift it is to be appropriated by faith, and can be received in no other way.

Propitiation or ***Atonement*** (HILASMOS and HILASTERION): The Greek word normally means that which placates a man or a god, or that which removes guilt, while the cognate verb refers to the action of a god in forgiving an offense. In Christian usage, however, the thought of placating an angry God is not to be admitted. One must avoid both the extreme of saying that Christ is a *propitiation* in such a way as to imply that His Death has changed the attitude of God to man, and the defect of denying all sacrificial meaning to the word when it is applied to Christ. This is best done by holding to the term *Atonement*. Christ's Death is sacrificial and removes an external barrier between God and man, but that barrier consists in the power of sin and not in the resentment of God toward sin, and the change in attitude applies to man rather than to God.

Sin (HAMARTIA and HAMARTANO): The primary sense of the word is to miss the mark, to make a mistake, but in the New Testament it is used of errors where the will is misdirected and from which guilt results. Appendix 1 offers a detailed account of the distinction between particular acts of sin and the Pauline concept of sin as a cosmic demon which has gained control over the world and its inhabitants as a result of the universal human indulgence in sinful acts.

Spirit (PNEUMA): Like Hebrew *ruach*, this word may be used for *wind, breath, animating principle, inspiration*, or for a *spiritual being*. In Christian usage it may be said that God *is* spirit or that He sends His *Spirit*. The personal experience of God operating within one is the indwelling of the Holy Spirit. At the same time Paul holds that man has PNEUMA as distinct from PSYCHE (life, soul) and SOMA (body). The human spirit is the element in man most open to divine influence, but it is not to be redeemed apart from the rest of the person. It may be regarded as an aspect of man's will.

Spiritual gift (CHARISMA): This type of gift is not to be confused with the *free gift* of salvation. It is a particular talent conferred for the accomplishment of a given vocation. Such CHARISMATA may consist in speaking with tongues or healing the sick; they may be ability to preach or to administer; they may be commissions to some office within the Christian ministry. The apostle expects that each man or woman will have a personal gift or talent from God, and that in the union of all the gifts Christ's work on earth will be made effective.

Transgression (PARAPTOMA and PARABASIS): This stands for a particular sin or trespass. It is any intentional defiance of God's will. Where the intention is lacking, transgression does not take place. In the words of the apostle in Romans 4:15, where there is no law to reveal the wrong to man, there is no transgression. Sin is a term of far wider scope.

Wisdom (SOPHIA): In the Pauline epistles this term applies in essence to God's plan of redemption. The *wisdom of God* is revealed in the preaching of the Cross. As a quality in man, wisdom is the capacity to comprehend the divine intention, and it is absolutely distinct from what the world regards as wisdom. It is a divine gift rather than an achievement.

14 *Bibliography*

English Language Commentaries

Barrett, C. K. The Epistle to the Romans (New York, 1958)

Barth, Karl. The Epistle to the Romans (English Translation, Oxford, 1933)

Brunner, Emil. The Letter to the Romans (E.T., Philadelphia, 1959)

Dodd, C. H. The Epistle to the Romans (New York, 1949)

Hunter, A. M. The Epistle to the Romans (New York, 1955)

Kirk, K. E. The Epistle to the Romans (Oxford, 1937)

Luther, Martin. Commentary on the Epistle to the Romans (E.T., Grand Rapids, 1954)

Nygren, Anders. Commentary on the Epistle to the Romans (E.T., Philadelphia, 1949)

Sanday, W., and Headlam, A. C. A Critical and Exegetical Commentary on St. Paul's Epistle to the Romans (Edinburgh, 1902)

Foreign Language Commentaries

Bardenhewer, O. Der Römerbrief des heilege Paulus (1926)
Lagrange, M. J. Epitre aux Romains (1950)
Leitzmann, H. An die Römer (1933)
Michel, Otto. Der Brief an die Römer (1955)
Zahn, Th. Der Brief des Paulus an die Römer (1925)

Reference Works in English

Angus, S. The Environment of Early Christianity (New York, 1915)
——— The Mystery Religions and Christianity (London, 1925)
——— The Religious Quest of the Graeco-Roman World (New York, 1929)
Aulén, G. Christus Victor (E.T., New York, 1931)
Baillie, D. M. The Theology of the Sacraments (New York, 1957)
Barclay, W. The Mind of St. Paul (New York, 1958)
Barth, Karl. The Resurrection of the Dead (E.T., London, 1933)
Bell, G. K. A., and Diessmann, A. (ed.) Mysterium Christi (London, 1930)
Branscomb, B. H. Jesus and the Law of Moses (New York, 1930)
Bultmann, R. Primitive Christianity (E.T., New York, 1957)
——— The Theology of the New Testament (E.T., New York, 1955).
Carrington, P. The Early Christian Church (Cambridge, 1957)
Case, S. J. The Evolution of Early Christianity (Chicago, 1914)
Cullmann, O. The State in the New Testament (E.T., New York, 1955)
Daube, D. The New Testament and Rabbinic Judaism (London, 1956)
Davies, J. G. Social Life of the Early Christians (London, 1954)
Davies, W. D. Paul and Rabbinic Judaism (New York, 1948)
Davies, W. D., and Daube, D. (ed.) The Background of the New Testament and Its Eschatology (Cambridge, 1956)
Dibelius, M. From Tradition to Gospel (E.T., London, 1934)
Dibelius, M., and Kümmel, W. G. Paul (E.T., New York, 1953)
Dix, Dom G. Jew and Greek (New York, 1953)
Dodd, C. H. The Gospel and Law (New York, 1951)

——— History and the Gospel (London, 1943)
Enslin, M. S. Christian Beginnings (New York, 1938)
Foakes-Jackson, F. J. The Rise of Gentile Christianity (New York, 1927)
Gavin, F. The Jewish Antecedents of the Christian Sacraments (London, 1928)
Gilbert, G. H. Greek Thought in the New Testament (New York, 1928)
Grant, F. C. An Introduction to New Testament Thought (New York, 1950)
——— (ed.) Early Christianity (Greenwich, Conn., 1954)
Hatch, E. The Organization of the Early Christian Church (New York, 1909)
Herford, R. T. Aboth (New York, 1945)
——— Pharisaism (London, 1912)
Hunter, A. M. Paul and His Predecessors (London, 1940)
Jones, G. V. Christology and Myth in the New Testament (New York, 1956)
Klausner, J. From Jesus to Paul (E.T., New York, 1943)
Knox, W. L. St. Paul and the Church of the Gentiles (Cambridge, 1939)
——— St. Paul and the Church of Jerusalem (Cambridge, 1925)
——— Some Hellenistic Elements in Primitive Christianity (London, 1941)
Levison, N. The Jewish Background of Christianity (Edinburgh, 1932)
Macgregor, G. H. C., and Purdy, A. C. Jew and Greek, Tutors unto Christ (London, 1936)
Manson, T. W. The Teaching of Jesus (Cambridge, 1931)
Morrison, C. The Powers That Be (Naperville, Ill., 1960)
Nock, A. D. St. Paul (London, 1938)
Parker, P. Inherit the Promise (Greenwich, Conn., 1957)
Ramsay, A. M. The Gospel and the Catholic Church (New York, 1936)
Rawlinson, A. E. J. The New Testament Doctrine of the Christ (London, 1926)
Robinson, J. A. T. The Body (London, 1952)

Robinson, H. W. The Christian Experience of the Holy Spirit (London, 1928)

——— Redemption and Revelation (London, 1942)

Schürer, E. The Jewish People in the Time of Jesus Christ (Edinburgh, 1885)

Schweitzer, A. The Mysticism of Paul the Apostle (E.T., New York, 1931)

Scott, E. F. Varieties of New Testament Religion (New York, 1943)

Stevens, G. B. The Pauline Theology (London, 1892)

Taylor, V. The Atonement in New Testament Teaching (London, 1940)

——— Jesus and His Sacrifice (London, 1937)

——— Forgiveness and Reconciliation (London, 1941)

Weiss, J. The History of Primitive Christianity (E.T., New York, 1937)

Williams, N. P. The Ideas of the Fall and of Original Sin (London, 1927)

Reference Works in Foreign Languages

Bornkamm, G. Das Ende des Gesetzes (1952)

Bousset, W. Die Religion des Judentums in späthellenistischen Zeitalter (1903)

——— Kyrios Christos (1921)

Cullmann, O. Die Christologie des Neuen Testaments (1957)

Cumont, F. Les Religions Orientales dans le Paganisme Romain (1929)

Norden, E. Agnostos Theos (1913)

Reitzenstein, R. Die Hellenistische Mysterienreligionen (1927)

Windisch, H. Paulus und das Judentum (1935)

Some Patristic Works

Augustine, St. On Grace and Free Will (Nicene and Post-Nicene Fathers, First Series, vol. 5, New York, 1887)

——— On the Grace of Christ or Original Sin (*ibid.*)

——— On Nature and Grace (*ibid.*)

Chrysostom, St. John. Homilies on the Epistle of St. Paul the Apostle to the Romans (*ibid.*, vol. 11, New York, 1889)

INDEX OF SUBJECTS

INDEX OF OLD TESTAMENT CITATIONS

INDEX OF PROPER NAMES